CW01371790

THE STUNTWOMAN

THE STUNTWOMAN

❖

The True Story
of a Hollywood Heroine

David L. Robb / Julie Ann Johnson

Copyright © 2013 by David L. Robb / Julie Ann Johnson.

ISBN: 1-4923-4910-0

ISBN-13: 978-1-4923-4910-5

All rights reserved. No part of this book may be reproduced or transmitted in any form or by any means, electronic or mechanical, including photocopying, recording, or by any information storage and retrieval system, without permission in writing from the copyright owner.

This book was printed in the United States of America.

Contents

Foreword 11
Introduction 15

Chapter 1	Julie Johnson versus *Charlie's Angels* 17
Chapter 2	*Charlie's Angels* on Coke 21
Chapter 3	"I Object, Your Honor!" 27
Chapter 4	A Stuntwoman Is Born 29
Chapter 5	Taking Care of the Problem 43
Chapter 6	The Toughest Little Girl in Fullerton 47
Chapter 7	Sexism Is Not Sexy 53
Chapter 8	The Blacklisting Begins 60
Chapter 9	Granddaughter of Greatness 63
Chapter 10	Julie and Eddie 68
Chapter 11	The Phone Call to Monty 79
Chapter 12	Julie and the Shrink 83
Chapter 13	A Settlement Offer 86
Chapter 14	The Bombshell 89
Chapter 15	Three-Card Monty 94
Chapter 16	"Some Thoughts about Loss" 99
Chapter 17	Norma Connolly Testifies 102
Chapter 18	"A Piece of Cake" 106
Chapter 19	A Sad Good-bye 118
Chapter 20	Kathleen Nolan 126
Chapter 21	The Jungle Years 132
Chapter 22	Home at Last 138
Chapter 23	A New Beginning 146
Chapter 24	Leslie Hoffman Takes a Stand 154
Chapter 25	A Career Is Launched 160
Chapter 26	Ronnie Rondell Takes the Stand 168
Chapter 27	The Cattle Call 174
Chapter 28	Aaron Spelling Takes the Stand 186
Chapter 29	Good-bye, Sam 192
Chapter 30	Jeannie Coulter Takes the Stand 197
Chapter 31	Life Goes On 213

Chapter 32	Bobby Bass Takes the Stand	219
Chapter 33	The Comfort of Angels	228
Chapter 34	The Return of Bobby Bass	235
Chapter 35	Snuffy	240
Chapter 36	Monty Mason Goes to Jail	245
Chapter 37	The Last Days of Bobby Bass	247
Chapter 38	Betrayal	251
Chapter 39	Julie Johnson Takes the Stand	253
Chapter 40	Damages	270
Chapter 41	We, the Jury	277
Chapter 42	A Reversal of Fortune	282
Chapter 43	Lily	285

Julie Johnson: In Her Own Words 309
Postscript 313

This book is dedicated to Lilyan Chauvin, without whose unique ability to care, this book would not have been possible.

A Note to the Reader

THIS IS A TRUE STORY. ALL COURTROOM SCENES ARE TAKEN FROM THE ACTUAL COURT TRANSCRIPTS.

Foreword

By Kathleen Nolan

Hollywood does not like troublemakers. I should know. As the first female president of the Screen Actors Guild, I made plenty of trouble for the powers that be. I championed equal opportunities for women and minority actors. I led a strike for better pay and working conditions for commercial actors, and after Julie Johnson and two other stuntwomen came to see me, I established and chaired SAG's first Stunt and Safety Committee to help protect the lives and livelihoods of Hollywood stuntmen and women.

As an actor, it has been my pleasure to work with many of the top stunt performers in the business. Hollywood is a tough place for actors, but it is a tough and dangerous place for stunt performers. And it is even tougher for stuntwomen, who face the added burden of sexual harassment and gender discrimination in a male-dominated profession.

Stuntwomen are some of the bravest women in America. They risk their lives every day to make films and television shows more exciting and entertaining. But Julie Johnson was the bravest of the brave. Julie was not only a pioneering stunt coordinator on *Charlie's Angels* in the days when very few women held that position, but she was also an outspoken advocate for a safe and drug-free workplace for all stunt performers—men and women alike.

For speaking out, she was branded a troublemaker, blackballed and run out of the business.

In the 1970s there was a drug culture in Hollywood, and it was particularly pernicious in the stunt community, and it was becoming a serious problem. Stuntmen and women were being pushed beyond their limits. They were being asked to jump higher and farther, to drive faster and faster, to blow it up bigger and bigger. Unfortunately, some turned to cocaine to give themselves an edge. But it only provided a false sense of invincibility. Drug use was endangering not only their lives but also the lives of their coworkers. Something had to be done about it. Julie had been quietly battling drug abuse in the stunt community for years, but now, with the backing of the Stunt and Safety Committee, we were able to tackle the problem together.

I had known Julie for years. She doubled for me a dozen times, and I always asked for her whenever a scene I was performing required a stunt double. She was one of the best in the business. But even she was subject to gender discrimination, which I witnessed firsthand while filming an episode of *Charlie's Angels* when the producers insisted that a stunt*man* double for me instead of Julie.

During my term as SAG president, Julie and I worked together frequently on the many issues facing stuntwomen; and when she sued Aaron Spelling for sex discrimination, it was my honor to testify on her behalf.

All these years later, she is still one of the bravest women I have ever known, and there is no doubt that her courage and determination have helped make Hollywood a better and safer place to live and work. Today's stuntwomen, and future generations to come, owe her a debt of gratitude.

Kathleen Nolan

Introduction

She was one of Hollywood's first whistle-blowers, a fearless stuntwoman who put her career on the line in 1980 to speak out about sex discrimination—and against the rampant abuse of cocaine by Hollywood's stunt community.

"Someone's gonna get hurt," she thought. "Someone's gonna get killed. Someone has to tell the studio execs what's going on."

For her troubles, she was ridiculed, blacklisted, and threatened by the Mafia. When she sued, her attorney swore under oath that he was so afraid of being murdered that he intentionally sabotaged her case on orders from the mob.

Her name is Julie Ann Johnson, and in her day, she was one of Hollywood's highest-paid stuntwomen and one of the first women to work as a stunt coordinator on a major television series. The show was *Charlie's Angels*.

The year 1980 was an eventful one: John Lennon was assassinated in New York City, strikes across Poland heralded the coming fall of the Soviet Union, fifty-two Americans were being held hostage in Iran, Ronald Reagan was elected president of the United States, and cocaine abuse was sweeping America. In Los Angeles that year, comedian Richard Pryor nearly burned himself to death while freebasing cocaine.

And in 1980, Julie Johnson began her descent into Hollywood hell.

Chapter 1

Julie Johnson versus *Charlie's Angels*

Julie Johnson sat with her hands folded before her on the plaintiff's table in Department 23 of Los Angeles Superior Court, her eyes darting nervously between the blank faces of the jurors and the clock ticking silently above their heads. It was 1:38 p.m., August 11, 1987, and the trial she'd waited so long for was finally about to begin.

"All rise!" the bailiff bellowed, and Julie, startled from her thoughts, fairly jumped out of her seat. "The court is now in session!"

Judge Leon Savitch, wearing black robes and a scowl, entered the courtroom from his chambers and took the bench. Banging his gavel to bring the court to order, he asked, "Are all the attorneys present?"

"Yes, Your Honor," they all said in unison.

"Counselor," he said, nodding to Julie's lawyer, "you may begin."

Richard Grey, short in stature and professorial, approached the jurors.

"Ladies and gentlemen of the jury," he explained, "the opening statement is a preview of coming attractions—an opportunity for the jury to preview the evidence that may be presented by each side to make it easier for you to closely follow the testimony from the witness stand."

He'd said those exact same words to jurors many, many times before. It's what he always said at the beginning of a trial. But what came next was different. This was going to be a trial about Hollywood—something new for him—so he crafted his next words carefully to evoke an image familiar to them all.

"This case," he said, "will resemble an evening television action series or a soap opera—if you will—such as *The Fall Guy* or *Charlie's Angels*, *Dynasty* or *Hotel*. The difference is, here we are involved with a true-life drama, not a fictional story."

"This case," he continued, "is about a woman who worked for nearly twenty years in the stunt field of the entertainment industry and who worked hard and earned a very high reputation in her field."

Indeed, Julie had been one of the most respected stuntwoman in Hollywood for many years and one of the few female stunt coordinators in a business dominated by men.

"Hearing the testimony to be offered," he explained, "you as jurors will learn something about the stunt field beyond common knowledge and learn about the risks and hazards that are built into that line of work.

"The jury will also become acquainted with the plaintiff, Julie Ann Johnson, and you will have an opportunity to observe her closely every day and to get to know her quite well as a person.

"In this matter, after twenty years of excellent work and after building an outstanding reputation and at the peak of her career, Ms. Johnson became employed by the defendant, Spelling-Goldberg Productions, and went to work on *Charlie's Angels* in the late 1970s.

"There, she had two assignments: First to be a stunt player and to work on a regular basis doubling for the female leading stars of that series—not coming and going when the need arose for her services, but to be there on a full-time basis. After that, she was able to gain recognition and support and became a stunt coordinator—first as co-coordinator with one of her colleagues, and then doing the work entirely on her own and coordinating all of the stunts for *Charlie's Angels*."

Grey paused for a moment to study the jurors' faces. Several of them, he could tell, were impressed already. This was not going to be a boring case about some arcane legal dispute between the manufacturer and buyer of men's pants. This was going to be about a top-rated hit TV show that they'd all seen. This was going to be about Hollywood and movie stars and *Charlie's Angels*! And who in America didn't know that Farrah Fawcett had risen to fame on the show? Who in America hadn't seen Farrah's famous poster, with the bathing suit and the big smile and the big hair?

Familiarity may breed contempt, but in the courtroom, it breeds victory. It gives jurors something they can relate to, something they can sink their teeth into. It makes things personal, and for a good lawyer, that's a head start from the first bang of the judge's gavel. And Richard Grey was a very good lawyer.

"The stunt player," he continued, pacing back and forth in front of the jury box, "appears in front of the camera and does the physical work—the actual stunt work—and the stunt coordinator supervises those stunt players and has responsibility for finding them, making recommendations about their compensation, and planning the stunts."

The planning of a successful stunt, he explained, begins with a budget and then goes to the creation of a stunt script. After that, the coordinator must ensure that the stunt looks good on screen. But first and foremost, he said, it must be safe.

"Ladies and gentlemen," he told the jurors in his sternest voice, "safety on the job is a fundamental requirement, and in my opinion, it is the most important responsibility of the stunt coordinator. Basically, it is the very reason for having that position."

Safety—or the lack of it—in Hollywood was something that all of the jurors knew a little something about already; there'd been a rash of high-profile stunt accidents and deaths on Hollywood films and TV shows in the years preceding the trial.

The most famous accident in Hollywood's history happened five years earlier, when actor Vic Morrow and two children were killed when a special effects explosion brought a low-flying helicopter crashing down on top of them during the filming of *Twilight Zone: The Movie*. A sensational manslaughter trial had ended just the previous May—in this same courthouse—with the acquittal of the film's director, helicopter pilot, associate producer, and unit production manager. The case grabbed national headlines for months.

Since then, there had been many other tragic accidents. Just a few months before Julie's trial began, stuntman Victor Magnotta drowned when the stunt car he was driving plunged off a bridge during filming of the movie *Skip Tracer*, and a few months before that, stuntman Dar Robinson—one of the greatest stuntmen of all time—was killed in a motorcycle accident on the movie *Million Dollar Mystery*. And just a year before Julie's trial, Hal Needham—Hollywood's most famous stuntman—went on trial for contributing to a horrific accident on the set of *Cannonball Run* that left stuntwoman Heidi von Beltz paralyzed from the neck down for life.

The year before that, stunt pilot Art Scholl was killed when the jet fighter he was flying crashed into the Pacific Ocean during filming of *Top Gun*. And a few months before that, stuntman Reid Rondell was killed when the helicopter he was flying in for a dogfight sequence on *Airwolf* crashed into a mountainside. An autopsy found cocaine in his blood.

A few months before that, actor Jon-Erik Hexum accidentally killed himself on the set of the TV series *Cover Up* while horsing around with a gun he didn't think was loaded.

And there had been many more deaths as well. Between June of 1980 and August of 1981, camera assistant Rodney L. Mitchell was killed during a stunt on *The Dukes of Hazzard*; camera assistant Robert Van Der Ker was killed when his helicopter crashed into the ocean off Hawaii during filming of a scene for *Magnum, P.I.*; camera assistant Jack Tanenberg was killed when a stunt car hit him during filming of a TV movie called *The Five of Me*; director Boris Segal was killed when he accidentally walked into the tail rotor blade of a helicopter during filming of the miniseries *World War III*; and stuntman Jack Tyree was killed when he missed an airbag during an eighty-foot-high fall during filming of *The Sword and the Sorcerer*.

All of these accidents and deaths grabbed headlines and then faded to the back pages. But they had a cumulative effect; anybody who was paying any attention at all had to know that something was horribly haywire in Hollywood.

"The true-life drama of this case," Grey continued, "involves a person who was wrongfully terminated from her employment as the stunt coordinator for *Charlie's Angels*, and the evidence will establish that she was terminated for a very simple reason: she became too vocal, too visible on matters involving safety."

Grey paused again and then spoke to the jury in a voice like that of a doctor giving a patient bad news. "In addition . . . and this is a touchy subject . . . she became painfully and personally aware that lives were being placed at risk because of someone else's use of illegal drugs on the job."

He paused again to let the weight of his words sink in.

"This is a very difficult subject for anyone to confront, to control, to deal with," he said, almost apologizing to the jury for having to tell them the awful truth. "And here we're talking about one of the most dangerous and life-threatening of all illegal drugs—cocaine."

Some of the seven men and five women on the jury, he knew, had probably tried the drug, which had swept the nation in the early '80s and was still sweeping lives away every day. Nearly all of them, he figured, knew someone whose life had been touched by drug abuse.

"So this real-life drama," he said, "is primarily about a highly successful stuntwoman and stunt coordinator who, after she complained about safety and drug-related incidents, found herself unceremoniously dropped, terminated from her employment after twenty years of being held in the highest regard, and without ever receiving any serious criticism about her performance. She was dropped, we submit, because she would not, and could not, ignore serious safety problems, including drug-related problems that confronted her every day she went to work. She saw fit to protest these problems, to take issue with them, to the point where she was labeled a troublemaker, a person to be avoided, a person to be gotten rid of, a person who could no longer be trusted in the very visible and highly responsible position of stunt coordinator."

"That," he said, "is the case in a nutshell."

CHAPTER 2

Charlie's Angels on Coke

Julie first became aware that *Charlie's Angels* had a coke problem on January 3, 1979. The show was filming on location at Indian Dunes that day at a dirt airfield out by Magic Mountain, some thirty miles north of Los Angeles.

"I was sitting in the backseat of the stunt car—an old Ford station wagon—waiting for the driver to return," she recalls. "I had the window down when a member of the crew in jeans and a white T-shirt walked by and yelled out to someone up ahead, 'Bobby got the last of the coke this morning! God damn it!'"

Bobby, she knew, was Bobby Bass, her stunt driver that day. They'd just finished four practice runs of the stunt they were going to do that day. During a brief break before shooting the scene, Bobby had gone into the honeywagon—a restroom on wheels—and that's when Julie heard someone say that he'd gotten the last of the coke.

What she didn't know, at first, was that the crewmember was talking about cocaine.

"My first reaction was, 'Who drinks Coca-Cola at nine thirty in the morning? And why are they out of it?'" she laughs. "That's how naive I was."

That day's stunt called for Julie and veteran stuntwoman Jeannie Coulter to bail out of the backseat of the speeding station wagon and hit the ground rolling. After a quick summersault, they'd both spring to their feet and charge a small plane about to take off with the bad guys. The entire "gag"—as stunts are known in the business—would depend on the driver slowing the car down just before they jumped so it wouldn't be going too fast when they hit the ground.

But Bobby had gotten the last of the coke that morning, and Bobby was in no mood for slowing down.

"Before coke, Bobby was a great guy," Julie says. "He was our protector. He was like a teddy bear. But coke changed him."

And not for the better.

After the first rehearsal, Julie could tell that the camera placements were all wrong.

"Why am I even in this scene?" she asked Blair Gilbert, the show's assistant director. "The way the cameras are set up, you'll never see me exit the car."

"Sure we will," Gilbert told her. "We have a high camera and a low camera. We'll see you from the high camera."

"No, you won't," Julie insisted. "You've got both cameras on Jeannie Coulter's side of the car. You'll never see me."

"Don't worry, Julie," Gilbert said, growing impatient. "We've got it covered."

"Okay," she said skeptically. "We'll see."

When Bobby returned from the honeywagon, they drove to their mark, waiting for the assistant director to call for action. Julie, doubling for Farrah Fawcett, wore a blond wig with huge curls—the same as Farrah's, who was said to have "the most famous hair in the world." Jeannie, sitting to her right in the backseat, was still fussing with the blond wig she was wearing to make her look like Cheryl Ladd. Stuntman Howard Curtis, sitting in the front passenger's seat, was on the walkie-talkie to the assistant director, the AD.

"We're ready to roll," Curtis yelled into the walkie-talkie as Bobby revved the engine nervously, waiting for the go from the AD.

"Bobby," Julie yelled above the engine noise, "are you sure of your speed and when to slow down? Should we rehearse it one more time?"

Bobby let off the gas. "No," he said, the car suddenly quieter. "I've got it."

"Let's go! Curtis yelled into the walkie-talkie.

"Okay," the AD squawked back. "Come ahead."

The stunt car began rolling and was soon speeding down the dirt runway. In the backseat, Jeannie started fidgeting with her wig again.

"Jeannie," Julie whispered, "if you don't feel right . . ."

Jeannie stopped fussing with the wig and gave Julie the thumbs-up.

Julie, however, could tell that something was wrong: the car was going too fast. Up ahead, she could see the flag that had been planted in the runway to serve as the mark for their bailout, and it was coming up too quick.

"Slow down, Bobby!" she yelled from the backseat. "Slow down! Slow down!"

As they approached the mark, Julie and Jeannie opened their doors and prepared to jump. At that moment, Bobby was supposed to slow down hard; but as the girls were halfway out of the car, he suddenly hit the gas, sending both back doors slamming into them. They were too far out now to climb back in, and with the doors continuing to pound them, there was no way to jump and gracefully tuck and roll as they'd planned.

"The last thing I remember," Julie says, "was my legs starting to fall, and I saw the back wheel—and I thought, 'If my legs go, I'm going under the wheel.' I knew that if my legs went down another inch, I'd have been dragged under the car and the wheel would have run right over my legs. So I kicked off as hard as I could. My head and neck hit the ground first."

They both hit the ground hard, tumbling like rag dolls thrown from a speeding car on a dusty back road.

When the dust cleared, Julie lay flat on her face, her body convulsing violently.

Jeannie, meanwhile, was having a near-death experience.

"After I hit the ground," Jeannie recalls, "I heard a big bell in my head and I went up into a bright light, and it was dead quiet and very bright. I looked down, and I could see everyone on the ground, and I could see Julie flailing on the ground in convulsions."

After a few moments, Jeannie, still delirious, got up and started running toward the stunt car that had been chasing them, not knowing where she was or what she was doing.

Farrah and Cheryl Ladd, who had been watching the scene from the sidelines, were horrified as the accident played out before them. Cheryl, seeing Jeannie staggering to her feet, rushed over to her to stop her from running headlong into the oncoming chase car.

"She had to come and stop me," Jeannie says. "I didn't know what I was doing. I was out of my mind, trying to complete the scene. She ran up and held me."

Ronnie Rondell, the show's second unit director, ran to help Julie, followed closely by Farrah.

"Julie! Jesus, stop shaking!" he yelled at her, throwing himself on her convulsing body to keep her still and to prevent further injury. "Julie! Stay still! Stay still! Don't move!"

Suddenly, Julie stopped shaking and lay still on the ground. She was unconscious, but she was alive. Ronnie's quick thinking may have saved her life—or from a life in a wheelchair. Julie came to a few seconds later. "I think I broke my back," she moaned. "I can't feel my legs."

"You're going to be okay," he assured her.

"Then why can't I move my legs?" she asked, each word tinged with fear.

"Because I'm lying on them to keep you still," Ronnie told her with a nervous laugh, hoping that Julie really would be okay.

"I want to get up," she said.

Carefully, Ronnie eased his weight off her. "Okay," he said, "but slowly."

Julie slowly stood, but her knees buckled, and she started to fall. Ronnie and Farrah held her up, and somebody brought over a director's chair for her to sit in. Ronnie and Farrah then started peppering her with questions to see if she was okay—to see if she had a concussion.

"What day is it?" Ronnie asked.

"Tuesday," she answered.

"No," he told her. "It's Wednesday. When's your birthday?"

She struggled to remember.

"What's your name?" Farrah asked, not waiting for the answer.

Struggling, and then smiling, she said, "Farrah Fawcett."

Everyone laughed, and all around her, stuntmen and crewmembers reassured one another that she was going to be okay. Someone went back and picked up their wigs, which lay on the dirt road like two dead blond birds.

Julie and Jeannie had survived—but just barely. The car they'd jumped out of was supposed to be going less than fifteen miles an hour, but it was going much faster.

"When Bobby floored it just as we were getting ready to jump," Jeannie said, "we were probably going thirty-five miles an hour."

The near-fatal accident was filmed and used in the "Angels in a Box" episode of the third season.

Julie and Jeannie were put into the backseat of a station wagon and sent to a nearby hospital. On the way, Julie told Jeannie what she'd heard about Bobby getting the last of the coke; and later, while sitting in the hospital's waiting room, both women knew what had gone wrong with the stunt.

"He sped up," Julie said, holding her Farrah wig on her lap.

"He was supposed to slow down, but he sped up," Jeannie agreed, holding her dusty Cheryl Ladd wig on her lap.

And they both knew it wasn't Coca-Cola that Bobby had gotten the last of.

Both women had sustained concussions, and x-rays revealed that Julie had suffered a hairline fracture in her neck. They were both lucky to be alive.

Afterward, they went back to the location; but when they arrived, the crew had broken for lunch.

"Jeannie, we have to eat a little something," Julie said. "Then we gotta finish the shot."

They got in the chow line and noticed Bobby Bass standing up ahead of them. Julie started to walk over to him, but when he turned, Jeannie caught his eye. It was a menacing look, cold and cruel.

Jeannie grabbed Julie's arm and pulled her back into line. "No, no," she whispered. "He's not good."

Jeannie didn't know anything about drugs—she was married to a cop—and never tried them herself. But she knew something was wrong with Bobby. The look in his eyes was one of pure hatred. Then Julie saw it too.

"He just glared at us," Julie recalls. "That wasn't the Bobby we knew. Bobby was fun and helpful, but this was a different Bobby. This wasn't anyone we knew—or wanted to know."

So they got something to eat, put on their wigs, and went out to finish the scene they'd started when they got hurt—a pickup shot of the girls getting up off the ground and chasing after the bad guys.

But that scene didn't go well either. Bobby was supposed to spin the car he'd been driving and slide it under the wing of a waiting airplane. It was an easy job for any good stuntman, but he couldn't do it; he just couldn't get the car to spin.

Finally, on the fourth try, one of the wheels came off, and Ronnie Rondell had to step in and do the stunt.

When it was done, Ronnie told Julie and Jeannie to go home and to get checked out by their own doctors.

Julie woke up the next morning, stiff and sore. Her head hurt and her neck was killing her. They'd be screening the footage from the day of the accident—called dailies—over on the Fox lot on Pico later that day, and Julie wanted to be there.

"I went in to see the film whether I was hurt or not," she recalls.

When she got to the lot, she showed the guard her pass and then went over to Aaron Spelling's production office to ask where the dailies were being shown. One of the secretaries told her.

The lights were on in the screening room when she got there. Julie took a seat and looked around. Kim Manners, the unit production manager, was there, as were several others from the company. Then Spelling himself came in and took a seat in the front row.

The accident scene was shown, and sure enough, the cameras didn't capture Julie's exit from the car, nor her ragged tumble along the dirt airstrip. All they got was Jeannie falling out on the road and tumbling, tumbling, tumbling.

When the scene was over, the lights came up, and everybody stood up to leave. Julie approached Spelling.

"We can correct that if you like," she told him. "We can shoot it again, with cameras on both sides of the car."

Spelling looked at her glumly. She could tell what he was thinking—that that would cost more money.

"Who was driving the car?" he asked.

"Bobby Bass," she said.

"Ah, jeez," he said with a disgusted look and turned and walked straight out of the screening room.

Julie left too. She walked across the lot to her car and headed back to the Valley, stopping at her chiropractor's office to have her neck x-rayed again before going home.

"Well, you've got a hairline fracture there on your third vertebrae," the chiropractor told her, showing her the x-ray photos. "Just take it easy," he said, handing her a neck brace, "and wear this collar."

The next day, and still recuperating at home, Julie called Ronnie Rondell at his office in Studio City and asked him if he could stop by her house after work. He was her supervisor after all—the supervising stunt coordinator on all of Aaron Spelling's shows—and she thought he should know what was going on.

Julie was still wearing the neck brace when Ronnie arrived at her little frame house on Van Noord Avenue in Van Nuys.

"How you feelin'?" he asked when she greeted him at the door.

"Oh, not too bad," she said, her hand going instinctively up to the brace.

Ronnie came in, and they sat down.

"I wanted to tell you something, Ronnie," she said.

He looked at her without saying anything.

"I was in the car," she said, "and saw Bobby go to the honeywagon, and we heard a guy walking by and say, 'Bobby got the last of the coke this morning.' Bobby wasn't right that day. When we were about to bail out of the car, he sped up. We didn't have a chance to get out. He just sped up, and the doors came back and slammed against us. We almost died on that show."

Then miming Jeannie staggering around in a trance, she said, "Jeannie's walking around like this and I'm in convulsions."

Ronnie nodded his head.

"This is serious," she continued, growing angrier with each passing moment. "I put my life on the line on this stunt! I could have been killed! This drug situation has gotten out of hand, and something has to be done about it! I don't want to see that stuff around next season. That stuff better not be around. Period."

"Don't worry," he assured her. "I'll take care of it. I'll take care of it."

Julie looked at him to see if he was telling the truth.

"I gotta go," he said and got up and left.

It's been said that "Hollywood is high school with money." In the early 1980s, it could just as easily have been said that Hollywood is high school with cocaine.

Coke was everywhere in those days—on the sets, on location, in the executive suites, in the dressing rooms, at the wrap parties. People were even snorting coke at the Oscars. In March of 1981, the headline on a *TV Guide* article about the coke epidemic sweeping the town read, "It's Snowing in Hollywood Every Day."

Some of the worst abusers—and many of the dealers—could be found in the stunt community.

Coke got you up; coke gave you confidence; coke made you feel invincible. For a dangerous day of shooting that might begin at 5:00 a.m. and end at three the next morning, it seemed the perfect drug for stunt work.

In 1982, Julie cochaired the Screen Actors Guild's Stuntwomen's Subcommittee when it conducted a survey of stuntwomen to gauge their working conditions. What they found was shocking.

More than half of the forty-one stuntwomen who responded said they'd witnessed "drug dealing on a set or location." More than half said they'd "worked with someone under the influence of drugs." More than half said they'd been "offered drugs on a set or location." One out of six said they'd lost a job because they'd refused drugs that were offered to them on the job. Nearly a quarter said they believed that the use of drugs was the "cause of most accidents" on film and TV shoots.

And there were lots of accidents. SAG records show that in 1982, more than two hundred actors and stunt performers were injured in accidents on the job.

Chapter 3

"I Object, Your Honor!"

William Koska, counsel for the defense, was outraged. After a recess in the court proceedings—and outside the presence of the jury—he asked Judge Savitch to declare a mistrial.

Koska, a dapper dresser who seemed to wear a different fancy suit to court every day, thought they had a deal. He thought the judge had made it clear that allegations of drug use on the set of *Charlie's Angels* would not be allowed into evidence. But during his opening remarks, Julie's attorney had mentioned drug use on the set repeatedly.

"Your Honor," Koska said, "reluctantly I am moving for a mistrial at this time in light of plaintiff's counsel, by my count, making eleven references to drug usage, despite the court's admonition this morning prior to concluding the selection of the jury. That took place at roughly 9:40 a.m. when the court indicated to both counsel that the court was not going to permit drug usage by plaintiff's counsel, who indicated he was going to make—I believe the words he used were 'innocuous references'—and now we have eleven references, by my count, and I would hardly term those 'innocuous.'"

"Any comments?" the judge asked, turning to Richard Grey.

Everything rested on what Grey would say next. If evidence of drug use could not be admitted, the case could be lost. It was a central issue—that Julie had been fired as the show's stunt coordinator because she'd complained that rampant drug use was creating an unsafe workplace.

"Your Honor," he said, "I saw the lines of demarcation drawn insofar as those things that Julie Johnson personally encountered were concerned, and I carefully limited my references to the one incident, and I said nothing about the general problem that might permeate a broader society—only those things that Julie was confronted with in her responsibilities as the stunt coordinator of the series."

Grey held his breath and waited for the judge's ruling.

"The motion is denied," the judge said.

Grey breathed a sigh of relief. He could continue his opening statement.

"The first cause of action in Julie's case is based upon public policy," he told the jurors. "These are the safety and drug-related issues."

The public policy of the State of California, he told them, "is to protect employees against being placed into hazardous conditions at work, and especially to protect those who, once they discover the hazard, speak out and protest and complain about it.

"To terminate somebody's employment in retaliation for their speaking out about safety would be considered a very serious violation of California's public policy. To put it differently, all people must be able to take a stand on the working conditions of their employment and speak out and protest unsafe conditions as they discover them, without the fear of putting their jobs into jeopardy. As the evidence will disclose, when Julie spoke out and protested, she was terminated. It's as simple as that."

The second cause of action, he continued, "has to do with a promise that the law implies in every employment relationship. It's called the covenant of good faith and fair dealing." The evidence, he said, will show that Spelling-Goldberg broke that promise and did it deliberately. In such cases, he told the jury, the law provides that extra weight—and more damages—can be added to a verdict if jurors find intentional and deliberate infliction of emotional distress.

"You will have to ask yourselves: Was Julie Johnson treated in her work in good faith? Did the defendant, Spelling-Goldberg Productions, deal with her fairly?"

They would also have to decide whether or not Julie suffered economic and emotional damage because of Spelling's actions, and what amount of money should be paid to compensate her. In the end, Grey told the jurors, they would be asked to decide how much a career is worth. They would have to decide how much being blacklisted is worth. They would decide how much years of depression are worth, how much being utterly and completely destroyed is worth.

"There will be a good deal of evidence about what came after Julie's termination," he continued, "and how she tried and was frustrated and faced disappointment after disappointment in trying to hold on to her career, and how this caused her tremendous amounts of harm, suffering, emotional harm, and economic injury."

Grey explained that there were several other causes of action in the case, as well, that Spelling-Goldberg had breached her contract and that Spelling had failed to give her the residuals she'd been promised. But he couldn't argue the merits of what had originally been the central issue in Julie's lawsuit: that she had been fired because of sex discrimination and that she had been terminated because she was a woman.

That was off-limits because Julie's previous lawyer had seen fit to drop the sex discrimination cause of action without her knowledge, without her permission, and under the most mysterious circumstances that many legal observers have ever seen. The Mafia, he said, made him do it.

CHAPTER 4

A Stuntwoman Is Born

Julie Johnson was born to be a stuntwoman.

In April of 1941, when she was just seven months old, her mother wrote in her baby book: "Fell out of chair in living room, facedown. Didn't cry."

That was her first stunt.

She performed her second stunt a few years later in her backyard in Fullerton, a small town in Orange County, California, surrounded by vast orange groves.

The stunt involved a baseball, a bat, and a wicker chair.

Spring is easily the nicest season in Fullerton. Winters there are too cold, summers are too hot, and autumn is too hot too. But spring is just right—warm during the day, cool at night, with an occasional rain to turn the hills and orange orchards green and gold.

In the spring of 1944, with World War II raging in Asia and Europe, Julie first learned how to hit a ball with a bat. She was only three years old. The daughter of a coach and the granddaughter of a Hall of Fame baseball player, Julie was a natural at sports.

"When I was three," she recalls, "my dad taught me how to throw the ball up and hit it by myself. He said, 'Keep your eye on the ball, and you'll hit it.'" And he was right.

"I threw the ball up, but I was only three, so of course, I missed it," she laughs. "The second ball I swung too soon. But the third ball—I smacked it! And I couldn't lay the ball and bat down. I was so enthralled at being able to do this by myself."

Julie hit the ball hard a few more times—her dad laughing and encouraging her every swing. Then he had to go—he was late for a meeting at school. As he drove away, she waved bye-bye and then returned to hitting the ball back and forth across the backyard—hittin' it and gettin' it, hittin' it and gettin' it.

It was getting dark when Julie's mom, Virginia, called her in for dinner.

"Just one more!" Julie yelled and whacked the ball across the yard.

"Get in here!" her mom yelled back. "It's getting dark!"

"Just one more!" Julie laughed, chasing after the ball one last time.

As she bent down to pick up the ball, she heard the back door slam. A moment later, the porch light went out. Julie picked up the ball and ran across the lawn to the back door. She reached up and grabbed the doorknob, but it wouldn't turn. It was locked. Her mom had locked it. Her mom had locked her out.

Julie knocked on the door. Nothing. She knocked again then put her ear to the door to see if she could hear anything inside. There wasn't a sound. Now she pounded her little fists on the door. Still nothing. She was getting scared now. She banged again then gave the door a couple of good kicks. Suddenly, the porch light came back on. A moment later, the door swung open so fast little Julie thought it might come off its hinges. Her mother was standing there, towering over her, a look of rage in her eyes. She was drunk.

"She took me by my arm and just yanked me in and slammed the door," Julie recalls. "She yanked me upstairs to my bedroom and then threw me in this little wicker rocking chair so hard that it broke the bottom out of the chair."

That was her second stunt. But this time she cried. Her bottom was stuck in the little chair, and she couldn't get out. Tears rolled down her face. Then her mother stomped out of the room and slammed the door behind her.

Julie stopped crying. She held her breath—too scared to cry or breathe. Then, when she heard her mother stomping back down the stairs, she started to cry again—whimpering, ever so softly.

When Julie was little, her mother, who was kind and attentive when she was sober and angry and abusive when she was drunk, was often drunk.

"She was drunk," Julie says with a sigh. "She'd been drinking, or she wouldn't have done that."

As it turns out, there were a lot of things her mother wouldn't have done if she hadn't been drinking.

Virginia's favorite drink was gin. She preferred gin martinis, but sometimes she'd drink her gin straight out of the bottle.

One day when Julie was five years old—still in kindergarten—she went with her mother to a neighbor's house three doors up the street. The grownups were drinking, and Virginia got drunk. After dark, Virginia decided it was time to go, so she took her little girl out the backdoor and staggered home through the alley. Virginia was so drunk that little Julie had to hold her up.

"She was lurching all over the place," Julie recalls.

The alley was dark, and Virginia stumbled. She fell against a garage door and then slumped to the ground, almost taking little Julie to the ground with her. Virginia muttered something under her breath.

Fighting back tears, Julie gathered all her strength and pulled her mother to her feet and then guided her safely home.

That was her third stunt—a stunt very few little five-year-old girls have ever had to perform.

Julie performed her fourth stunt that same year. It was the day her father taught her how to kick a football like they do in college. There are no records from those days, of course; but when she was in kindergarten, Julie could probably kick a football farther than any other five-year-old girl in the country.

Julie and her dad were out in the front yard tossing a football around one day when he showed her how to kick it off a tee. He dug his heel into the grass to make a little wedge then stuck the football in it so that it stood on its end straight up. He backed away and told Julie to take a run at it and kick it as hard as she could. With a determined look on her face, she ran to the ball, her long pigtails trailing behind her, and kicked the ball as hard as she could. She hit it squarely, and it sailed high over her father's head. If there had been goal posts in their front yard, she would have kicked a perfect twenty-yarder.

Her dad laughed and raised his arms, signaling a field goal, and Julie wanted to do it again and again.

The next day at kindergarten, when the recess bell rang, all the other little girls ran out to play on the swings and the merry-go-round. But Julie headed over to where the boys were playing with a football on the playground grass.

One of the bigger boys tried to punt the ball, but it went off the side of his foot and dribbled a few yards away.

"Let me show you what my daddy taught me," she said, picking up the ball.

"With your heel you dig a small wedge in the ground," she said, demonstrating it for the boys. "Then you rest the ball in it so it won't fall over."

Placing the ball on its end in the wedge, she backed up a few paces and took a run at the ball, kicking it high in the air, end over end, halfway across the playground. The boys stood in wonder as they traced the flight of the ball with their eyes.

The bell rang ending recess. Julie started walking back to her classroom and was halfway there when suddenly a fat little kid ran up from behind her and buried his shoulder into her back. The blow sent her skidding face-first across the asphalt.

"Ow!" she moaned, sprawled on the blacktop playground. She put her hand to her mouth and then looked at it. There was blood on her fingers.

"*My* daddy taught me how to do that!" the fat little boy said triumphantly, to gales of laughter from the other boys who'd gathered round.

"That'll teach you to kick better than us!" the fat kid said, standing over her. "If they wanted a girls' football team, they'd have one. But they don't!"

This cracked the other boys up even more, some of whom were bent over in laughter.

"So go back to your little girlfriends and practice the merry-go-round!" he growled.

The boys all ran away laughing, leaving Julie lying there, her lower lip cut and bleeding, her upper lip swelling to the size of a large grape.

The school nurse patched her up as best she could. She put some Mercurochrome and a Band-Aid on her cut lower lip and gave her a cold, wet washcloth to hold against her swollen upper lip. Her face would be bruised for days, but what she learned that day in kindergarten, at the tender age of five, would last a lifetime: boys don't like it when a girl can kick a ball better than they can. It was a lesson she would never forget. But it only made her want to kick the ball farther.

Six months later, Virginia divorced Julie's dad.

Julie didn't just love her father. She adored him, worshipped him. Art Johnson—better known as Coach Johnson—was the coach at Wilshire Junior High School in Fullerton, where he coached seventh and eighth grade boys—a job he'd hold for thirty-three years.

Movie star handsome with high cheekbones, a great shock of wavy brown hair, and a Tom Cruise smile long before anybody'd ever even heard of Tom Cruise—Art Johnson coached his boys as if they were his own sons. Calm and patient, he always tried to get the best out of them no matter what that was: athleticism, leadership, or just plain old good sportsmanship and love of the game—no matter what the game was. He coached just about everything: baseball, football, basketball, track, and tennis, depending on the season. (In those days, of course, nobody played soccer.)

He had plenty of offers to coach high school and college, but he always turned them down. "Too much pressure," he'd say. He liked developing young talent and getting his boys ready for high school.

But he was not a rich man, and although he was almost universally loved, he was not loved by the one person he wanted to be loved by the most—his wife.

Virginia liked to have fun. The daughter of a famous old-time baseball player, she liked to go places and buy fancy things. But most of all, she liked to drink. But her husband was a teetotaler. He had ulcers and couldn't drink alcohol. So when Julie was six years old, her mother left her father for a man who drank. And that was about the only thing they had in common. They were both very thirsty.

Julie vividly remembers the day her mother left her father.

Her mom's 1939 Oldsmobile was parked in the driveway, its trunk open and stuffed with clothes. Boxes filled with their belongings were jammed haphazardly into the front and backseats. When the car was loaded, Virginia grabbed Julie by the arm and dragged her out of the house and pushed her into the backseat of the car, next to a cardboard box filled with half-empty booze bottles.

Julie was scared. "Where are we going?" she cried.

"To a new house," her mother replied dully.

"Why?" Julie asked, still crying. "Where is Daddy?"

"Never mind that now."

Virginia slammed Julie's door then went around back and slammed the trunk. The sound each made was the sound of finality—the sound of leaving for good and not coming back. Julie was really crying now. "Where's Daddy!"

Looking around at the boxes piled to the roof inside the car, Julie wondered if her mom had remembered to pack any of *her* stuff. Then looking out the side window, she saw the only two things she couldn't leave behind or live without—her ball and bat, lying in the grass.

Wiping away her tears, Julie pushed the heavy car door open, climbed down off the seat, and ran straight to them. Then just as she picked them up, her mother grabbed her by the arm and dragged her back to the car, pushed her in and slammed the door.

As they drove away, Julie turned around and saw her house recede into the distance then disappear to the sound of booze bottles rattling in the box beside her.

Twelve miles later, Virginia pulled the car into the driveway of an old two-story house on Florence Avenue in La Habra and turned the engine off.

"We're home," she said, unconvincingly.

Yes, if home is where the car is parked, they were home.

Virginia took Julie inside, where Stan was waiting to greet them.

"Welcome home," he said, smiling broadly at Julie.

"Who's he?" Julie asked.

"My name is Stan," he said.

Stan Lawrence: 5'10", pitch-black hair, forty years old, and a nice-enough guy—when he was sober.

"You must be Julie," he said, extending his hand.

"Yes, I am," she said, refusing to shake it. "Where's my daddy?"

"Let me show you your room," he said coldly, miffed at her rebuff.

Picking up Julie's bags, Stan led her upstairs to her room. It was a nice room, a comfortable room with a window that looked out over a park.

Setting her bags by the bed, Stan left so that Virginia could talk to her daughter.

"We are living here now," she told Julie, "but you will spend every weekend with Daddy."

"You and Daddy are not going to live together anymore?" Julie asked in disbelief.

"No."

"Not ever?"

"No."

Julie started crying, and Virginia comforted her.

"It will be all right," she told Julie. "You'll see. Give it a chance. Stan is a very nice man."

Virginia opened one of Julie's bags and took a framed photograph out and hung it on the wall. It was a picture of Julie, brown as a copper penny and smiling proudly in her one-piece bathing suit, after she'd won a race at the Fullerton High swimming pool. In the years to come, many others would be hung beside it: Julie golfing, running, bowling, shooting baskets, and playing tennis. The girl was crazy about sports.

Julie would stay at her father's house in Fullerton on the weekends, but this would be her room until she started high school. This would be her refuge. This would be her prison.

Julie performed her fifth stunt in 1951 when, at the age of eleven, she ran away from home. Or rather, *bicycled* away from home.

Virginia had divorced Art and married Stan, and Julie's life with her mother and stepfather became a nightmare. They drank every night, and when they were drunk, they were cruel and sarcastic. It may not have been the childhood from hell, but it was certainly the childhood from limbo—the edge of hell.

They thought up nicknames for her: they called her Splinter Butt because she had a small rear end; they called her the Little Beaver because she had buckteeth and had to wear braces all through high school; they called her the Titless Wonder because she was small-breasted until she blossomed in her senior year. They'd say, "Hey, where's the Little Beaver?" Or "It's time for dinner, Splinter Butt." Or "Here comes the Titless Wonder.'"

Back then they thought it was funny. Today it would be considered child abuse.

"It was verbal abuse," Julie recalls. "They were mean and sarcastic, especially when they were drunk." Which was pretty much every day.

Julie lived in constant fear that her mother was going to be killed in a drunken car crash. More than thirty-five thousand Americans—nearly one hundred a day—would die in car crashes in 1951, and more than half of those fatalities would be alcohol-related. In those days, there was virtually no stigma attached to drunken driving, and at one time or another, nearly everyone who drank drove drunk. Stan and Virginia drove drunk nearly every day.

One Saturday evening that summer, Virginia was cooking dinner and sipping gin. There was a peach pie in the oven, and its fragrance fairly filled the house.

"Oh, Mommy, it smells so good," Julie said, opening the oven door to get a full blast of the aroma.

"Julie, don't burn yourself," Virginia cautioned. "Why don't you set the table? Stan should be home shortly."

As if on cue, a car horn honked in the driveway. Julie looked out the kitchen window and saw Stan and his friend, Bill, pouring out of Stan's car. They'd just come from the golf course, and they were both drunk.

Stan, still wearing his golf clothes, entered through the kitchen door.

"Come on, Virginia," he slurred. "We're going to have a drink at the club."

Julie instinctively backed into a corner of the kitchen, watching the adults intently.

"Stan, it's late," Virginia replied. "I have a nice dinner prepared. Why don't you just sit down?"

"I can't," he huffed. "Bill is with me. I have to take him home."

Julie could almost smell the booze on his breath above the aroma of the peach pie.

"Hey, Bill!" he yelled out the window. "Get in here!"

Bill staggered in through the kitchen door.

"Hi, Virginia," Bill said, greeting her and ignoring Julie.

"Would you like to have dinner with us?" Virginia asked.

"Helene is waiting for us at the club, Virginia," Bill said, his voice high and whiny. "We just came to pick you up."

He didn't even look at Julie in the corner.

"Well, okay," Virginia said, giving in easily. Removing her apron and turning off the oven, she went over to Julie in the corner.

"Julie, dinner is ready," she said. "If you get hungry before we come back, just help yourself."

"Oh, hi, Julie," Bill said, finally realizing she was standing only a few feet away from him.

"Hi, Splinter Butt." Stan waved, smiling broadly as if he'd just said something funny.

"Splinter Butt?" Bill laughed, as if he'd just heard something hilarious.

"Mommy, when will you be back?" Julie pleaded, ignoring Stan and Bill. "Mommy, please don't drink."

Virginia kissed her on the forehead, grabbed her purse, and left with the two drunken men. Julie watched through the window as they walked to the car. She had the distinct feeling that this might be the last time she would ever see her mother alive.

Stan backed the car carelessly out of the driveway, knocking over a garbage can, and then took off for the club at high speed. Julie looked at the kitchen clock. It was six o'clock. She was alone, and it would be dark soon.

She didn't eat dinner; she didn't touch the peach pie. She wasn't hungry; she was scared. She lay down on the sofa in the living room and cried herself to sleep. When she awoke four hours later, the house was dark. Somewhere down the street, a dog was barking. She jumped up and ran to the front room window. There was no car in the driveway. She turned on a light and paced the room. After a while, she realized that she couldn't stay there any longer. She would run away from home.

The wind in her face was cool as she pedaled her bike through the dark streets of Fullerton, her two long pigtails tucked safely under a cap. Her mother hadn't let Julie cut her hair since the day she was born, and her pigtails were so long now that she had to be careful every time she sat down not to sit on them, and she had to wear a cap whenever she rode her bike lest they get caught in the spokes of the wheels.

Every morning before school, her mother would brush out Julie's braids and dutifully rebraided each pigtail. It was a process that took twenty minutes, and if Virginia was hung over, which she usually was, it was a painful twenty-minute ordeal. But that was all behind her now.

Up ahead she saw the headlights of an approaching car, so she pulled her bike off the road and hid in the bushes. She watched carefully as the car raced by, a country-western song blaring loudly on its radio. It wasn't her mom and Stan retuning from the club. She got back on her bike and continued pedaling—ten miles south to Fullerton.

She made it to her father's house after midnight. She was very tired. She knocked on the door and rang the bell, but there was no answer. Checking the garage, she saw that his car was gone. He wasn't home.

She thought about bundling up, lying down in the garage, and going to sleep right there until he got home. But she quickly visualized her father's return: he pulls his car into the driveway, gets out—leaving the headlights on—and walks over and raises the garage door. Then, in the bright beams of the car's headlights, he finds his daughter lying in there. The startled look she imagined on his face was not a good picture.

So she went around back and tried the backdoor, but it was locked too. Maybe there was an open window. She walked around the house and tried them all, but they were all shut tight, until she got to the last one—the kitchen window, which was open just a crack. She went back to the front yard where she'd left her bike and brought it around to the side of the house and leaned it up against the wall under the kitchen window. Then she climbed up on the seat—bicycle seats were big in those days—and, balancing carefully, pulled the window open and climbed in over the kitchen sink.

The house was dark. She turned a light on in the living room, lay down on the couch, and fell asleep. She awoke an hour later when she heard her father's house keys jangling to open the front door. When the door opened, Julie sat up and saw that her dad had come home with Margo—his girlfriend at the time, who would later become his second wife.

Art was surprised to find his daughter there on the couch—but not as shocked as he would have been if he'd come home and found her lying on the garage floor.

"What's wrong?" he asked, a worried look replacing the startled one.

"I came over here on my bike," Julie blurted out, "because Stan came home drunk and he and a friend took Mother out drinking and they were all just drunk."

Art looked at his daughter for a moment and then patted her on the head.

"Okay," he said. "You can stay the night, and I'll take you back to your mom's in the morning."

That was good enough for Julie, although she wished she didn't have to go back there at all. The constant worrying about her mother being killed in a drunken car crash was becoming more than she could bear.

The next morning, Art took his daughter back to her mother's house in La Habra.

Virginia was sunning herself on a chaise lounge in the backyard. She got up quickly when she saw them and said something to Art. Then, turning to Julie, she barked, "Go to your room."

To this day, Julie doesn't know if her dad had called her mom and told her what had happened, or if her mom had come home drunk and gone to bed without realizing that her daughter was missing. But it was probably the latter.

Julie went to her room. That day she got no lunch or dinner, but that wouldn't be the worst of her punishment.

Julie's sixth stunt began one night at the dinner table a few weeks later, when Julie's mother and stepfather told her that they were sending her to Mexico to finish out the school year.

"What?" Julie asked, nearly dropping her fork.

"Mexico," her mother replied. "You'll be staying with Terry and Charlie."

"Terry and Charlie?" Julie repeated, barely believing what she was being told.

Charlie, she knew, was her stepfather's brother who worked for some American company down in Mexico City and Terry was his wife. She'd met them a couple of times, but she barely knew them.

"You'll finish out the sixth grade there," her mother said. "They have very good schools there."

"But why?" Julie asked.

Her mother, who'd been drinking martinis all day, wouldn't say. All Julie could figure was that it was punishment for running away from home.

A few weeks later, Virginia packed Julie's bags, and that night, they drove her to Los Angeles International Airport in a pouring rainstorm.

Julie sat sullenly in the backseat of the car all the way there.

"Why do I have to go?" she kept asking. "Why do I have to go?"

They arrived at the airport at 11:00 p.m., well past Julie's bedtime. Stan parked the car, and Virginia took Julie to the Pan Am terminal. Julie carried her suitcase and Virginia held the umbrella, but Julie still got wet in the downpour. Stan joined them inside the terminal as Virginia checked the suitcase. Then they walked Julie out to the plane—a brand-new twin-engine DC-6—with propellers. It would be Julie's first ride on an airplane.

Halfway to the plane, a stewardess approached them with an umbrella.

"Okay," Virginia told her daughter. "She'll take you the rest of the way."

Julie kissed her mom good-bye and walked alongside the stewardess to the stairs leading up to the plane.

Once inside the plane, the stewardess, dressed in a snappy blue Pan Am uniform and cap, took Julie to her seat and buckled her in.

"You'll be there in the morning," the stewardess assured her, smiling and patting her arm. "They'll be waiting for you in the morning in Mexico."

When the stewardess left, Julie started crying quietly. And when the pilot started the engines, she was so startled she would have jumped out of her seat if she hadn't been buckled in. Julie had a window seat, but she didn't look out as the plane taxied down the runway and then lifted gracefully into the air. She fell asleep whimpering, never having once looked out the window.

She awoke just after dawn as the plane noisily lowered its landing gear on its approach to the Benito Juárez International Airport in Mexico City. When the plane landed and taxied toward the terminal, Julie looked out the window for the first time and noticed that all the signs and billboards were written in Spanish.

The only Spanish word she knew was *gracias*.

Charlie and Terry were there to greet her. They gave her a big hug and then drove her to their apartment.

"You're going to love it here," Charlie assured her from behind the steering wheel.

Julie looked out the side window as they passed a donkey pulling a cart piled high with junk and old mattresses.

"You're going to just *love* it here," Terry said, with more conviction.

Julie didn't think so.

Arriving at their apartment building, Julie noticed several kids playing handball on a court next to the parking area.

"At least there's that," she thought.

Taking a rickety old elevator to the eighth floor, Julie was taken inside Charlie and Terry's apartment and shown the room she would share with Charlie's sister, Marie, a nice enough lady in her early fifties. Julie's bed, they told her, was the one closest to the window. Julie went over and looked out. It was a long way down.

Late one night not long after arriving, Julie got out of bed and started looking for her shoes. Maria was still awake and watched curiously to see what her young roommate was up to. She was sleepwalking. She'd been doing it for years. When she was little, her father would often find her late at night wandering around the house, turning the lights on. He'd follow her patiently, turning the lights off behind her, and then put her back to bed.

Julie found one of her shoes and put it on. Then she got down and found the other under the bed and put it on. She was apparently going somewhere in her pajamas and black-and-white Oxfords. Marie watched without saying a word.

Tying the laces, Julie then got up and went to the window. She stared out for a moment and then started cranking it open. Marie sat up in bed.

Once the window was half open, Julie started to climb out, lifting one leg out the window and putting her foot on the thin ledge outside then getting ready to do the same with the other. Marie jumped out of bed and rushed to her.

"Whoa!" she said, grabbing Julie by the waist. "Where you going?"

"I'm going home," Julie replied, still asleep.

"You can do that tomorrow," Marie said, pulling her back in. "Come back to bed now." Marie put her back in bed and tucked her in.

"Had she not been there," Julie recalls, "I might have gone out the window and down eight floors."

It was Julie's first close brush with death, and at the time, she didn't even know it was happening.

On her first day in Mexico, Julie was introduced to Andrés Velázquez, a little Mexican boy about her age, who lived one floor up. Andy spoke English, and he would show her how to get to school. It would require jumping on two moving busses—each way. Sometimes he would be with her, and sometimes she'd have to do it alone—in one of the most congested and traffic-jammed cities in the world.

The Spanish words for "bus stop" are *nombre parada de autobus*, but the busses rarely stopped. Usually, they just slowed down a little and the passengers had to jump on or off from a little step in the back, or hop on and cling to a railing outside. Julie always preferred the railing because it was so noisy and crowded inside. Sometimes they even had live chickens in there.

"Those buses were rickety and old, with people hanging off of them," Julie laughs. "You never sat down. You would jump on and hold on to the railing. Then you'd look for your spot to get off and jump off and wait for the next bus. That's what I learned in Mexico. That's where I became streetwise."

Back then, Julie considered it an adventure; it was one of the most fun parts of having to live in Mexico with steprelatives she barely knew and going to the sixth grade with students and teachers she didn't know at all. But today, sending an eleven-year-old girl alone to Mexico to jump on and off moving busses four times a day, five days a week for six months would be considered child abuse, child neglect, child endangerment.

And there were other dangers for an eleven-year-old American girl alone in Mexico City.

She'd asked Charlie for a handball, and he'd given her one, and one day, she was down in the parking area hitting it against the wall when it got away from her and rolled over near the attendants' shack. She went to get it and looked in the open door. There were two men inside, watching her. They said something to her in Spanish and motioned for her to come closer.

"Okay," she thought. "Maybe they want to play handball."

She took a few steps closer.

"Do you want to play?" she asked, holding up the ball.

They said something in Spanish and motioned for her to come inside.

Slowly, she stepped through the door. It was very hot in there.

"Bonita, bonita," one of the men said and reached out to touch her long blond hair.

Suddenly, Julie realized that the men weren't interested in playing handball.

"I knew instinctively that something wasn't right," she recalls.

So she backed out of the shack, turned, and ran back inside the apartment building.

Over the next six months, she'd still play handball down there whenever she could, but she made sure to steer clear of that shack.

Easily the best thing to happen to Julie in Mexico City was befriending Andrés Velázquez, the little boy who lived on the ninth floor. It turned out that Andy, as she called him, was an actor—something of a movie star in Mexico. He'd just finished work on a Disney film called *The Littlest Outlaw*, in which he played the title character who steals the horse of a cruel Mexican general.

"That was my first introduction to somebody who'd made a movie," Julie recalls with a fond laugh. "Here's this little kid riding horses in a movie for Disney. It was fascinating."

And Julie, being Julie, figured that if he could make a Disney movie, so could she.

And she was right. Twenty-five years later, she'd be the girl dangling from the strut of a helicopter while being transferred to the wing of an old biplane in a Disney film called *The Cat from Outer Space*. It wasn't that different than jumping up and holding on to the outside rail of a moving bus in Mexico City.

"Dad and Mom"

"Oops . . . I'm here"

"Cat From Outer Space" with stuntman Dick Warlock, Disney Studios

Chapter 5

Taking Care of the Problem

Ronnie Rondell said he'd get rid of the *Charlie's Angels* coke problem, but they got rid of Julie instead.

Julie had been hired as a stuntwoman on the sixth episode of the show's first season. Farrah Fawcett, the show's breakout start, had injured a knee during a car stunt scene, and her stuntwoman and the show's stunt coordinator were fired. So they brought in Julie, who by this time had become one of Hollywood's top stuntwomen. She'd already doubled for many of Hollywood's top stars, including Ava Gardner, Jane Fonda, Doris Day, Ida Lupino, Carol Burnett, Vera Miles, Jean Simmons, Juliet Prowse, and Geraldine Paige, just to name a few. She'd already appeared in numerous films, like *Little Big Man, Earthquake, Play Misty for Me, Caprice,* and *Dr. Doolittle* and on lots of TV shows, including *Star Trek, Mission Impossible, The Mod Squad, The Beverly Hillbillies, The Man from UNCLE, Laverne & Shirley,* and many others.

In the beginning, Julie was to be Kate Jackson's main double on *Charlie's Angels*, but she'd frequently double Farrah Fawcett and Cheryl Ladd as well.

Toward the end of the second season, Dick Ziker, who was her mentor and one of the stunt coordinators on the show, began campaigning to give Julie a shot at coordinating. They'd known each other for years, going back to the late '60s when they worked together on *Mannix*. Ziker thought she'd make a great stunt coordinator.

"He would tell Ronnie Rondell and everybody, 'Let Julie coordinate,'" Julie recalls.

So at the beginning of the third season, they started letting her share coordinating responsibilities on a few shows.

"I would co-coordinate with Ronnie," she recalls. "I would be his backup. If he had to go do *Hart to Hart*, he'd leave me alone to finish the stuff on the set. And I'd finish it. So I was the co-coordinator then."

Halfway through the third season, Julie was coordinating shows on her own; and over the next year and a half, she would coordinate the stunts on twenty-eight episodes of *Charlie's Angels*, becoming one of the first female stunt coordinators on a network TV show.

One year after Julie and Jeannie were nearly killed because Bobby Bass was high on coke, Ronnie Rondell called Julie and told her that she wouldn't be coming back as stunt coordinator for the show's fifth season.

"What?" Julie asked, thinking at first that she hadn't heard him right.

"No, you won't be back as coordinator," he said. "They're going to have Gary Epper coordinate."

Gary Epper was one of the top stuntmen on the show. As coordinator, Julie had given him as much work as she could.

"We worked very well together," she recalls. "He was one of my number one men."

And now he was going to be replacing her.

"Why, Ronnie?" she asked. "Why?"

There was a pause on the other end of the line, as if he were trying to find an answer she would believe.

"Well," he said, "they say you overpaid on adjustments."

Julie couldn't believe it. Overpaid on adjustments? It was ridiculous. Absurd. In the stunt business, adjustments were the pay increases you got for doing difficult stunts. The going rate was $50. That's what she paid. That's what everyone paid. There were no overpayments.

"Ronnie," she said, "how can I overpay?"

"Well," he said, not having a better explanation, "I don't know."

"Is there any other reason I won't be back?" she asked, growing more and more suspicious by his answers.

"Well," he said, trying to come up with one, "they say that some of the work was substandard."

Julie was floored. No one had ever complained about the quality of her work.

"Ronnie, how could the work be substandard?" she asked in amazement. "Some of the top stunt people work that show. You know very well that if anything was substandard, it was because it was a nickel shot and they didn't have time to do anything decent."

"Well," he added sheepishly, "that's what they said."

"*They* said?" she asked. "Who is *they*?"

He didn't answer, and she could almost sense him shrugging his shoulders on the other end of the line.

"You can come back as a stunt double," he said. "Just not as coordinator."

This was wholly unacceptable to Julie. It was like telling an actress on a hit TV show that her acting services were no longer wanted but that she could come back as an extra.

It wasn't pride that held her back. Julie is a proud woman, but not a prideful one. There was a principle at stake. They had lied to her.

"All right, Ronnie, thanks," she said. "I'll call Aaron and get this straightened out."

She hung up and called Spelling's office. An assistant answered the phone.

"Hello," she told the assistant. "This is Julie Johnson. I'm the stunt coordinator on *Charlie's Angels*. I'd like to speak to Mr. Spelling, please."

"He can't talk to you," the assistant said. "He's in pilot season."

The way he said it sounded to Julie like Spelling had been expecting her call and had given his assistant this pat answer.

Over the next few days, she tried several more times to get in touch with Spelling, but each time she was turned away. No one would ever show her anything she'd done on the show that was substandard. No one would ever show her where she had overpaid for adjustments. No one would ever show her anything to justify her termination.

Julie, of course, already knew the *real* reason she'd been fired. She'd complained too much about safety; she'd complained too much about drug abuse on the set. They saw her as a troublemaker. And making matters worse, she was a *woman* troublemaker.

The good old boys' club had spoken.

My main mentor Richard Ziker

Chapter 6

The Toughest Little Girl in Fullerton

In the summer of 1954, Julie's mom and stepfather moved to Venezuela. It all happened very suddenly. He'd gotten a good-paying job repairing equipment for an American oil company down there. Julie was sad to see her mother go, but she was relieved as well. She couldn't take much more of her drinking. And now she'd get to live full-time with her father in Fullerton.

Not long after her mom left, when Julie was thirteen years old, she performed her seventh stunt. This one involved a basketball, a slippery roof, and a very hard concrete driveway. This one almost killed her.

Julie was a tomboy. When she was a kid, she'd much rather play with a ball than a doll. She had no interest in playing dress-up or hosting tea parties for her little friends. Give her a rock and a stick to hit it with, and she was happy.

"My mother spent hours and hours knitting and crocheting little outfits for these beautiful dolls she bought me," Julie recalls, "but if you showed me a doll and a ball, my eye would go right to the ball."

La Habra, where Julie'd lived with her mother and stepfather, may have been the perfect place for a tomboy to grow up. There were plenty of open fields for boys—and tomboys—to play in and lots of trees to climb. There were oaks and elms, sycamores and cottonwoods, and a sprinkling of jacarandas, which blossomed in the spring and then shed their purple petals on the streets and sidewalks.

But mostly there were miles and miles of citrus and avocado groves and strawberry fields that seemed to go on forever.

In 1954, La Habra—population five thousand—was the sticks. The town, snuggled in the northwestern corner of Orange County, was famous for only two things: it was the center of avocado production in Southern California, and it was where Richard Nixon—who was then vice president of the United States—had opened his first law office in a building that's subsequently been demolished. Not much to brag about.

As a kid, Julie loved to climb trees. It was a perfect escape when her mom and stepfather, after an afternoon of drinking, would start quarrelling

47

"When they'd start their arguing—and it was usually about money—I'd head out the backdoor, over the fence, into the park, and up a tree," she recalls. "I had a couple of favorite trees over there that I'd go climb. That was my favorite thing to do."

One of her favorite games was Tarzan and Jane.

"Anytime we'd play Tarzan and Jane, I had to be Tarzan," she laughs, "because I was the only one who could leap from branch to branch."

She never got hurt climbing in trees, but she almost got killed that summer climbing on the roof of a neighbor's garage.

Julie loved to play basketball, but she hated the rules for girls' basketball. In those days, girls could only play half-court, and they could only dribble the ball twice and take two steps before having to pass it or shoot it.

"That was one of my favorite sports," she says, "but girls' rules were so frustrating. So I practiced my hook shot, which I could make from anywhere outside the key."

Two steps and a shot, two steps and a shot. One time she made eight hook shots in a row from outside the key, a feat that stunned her teammates and coaches and is rarely equaled today in college or pro basketball—women's or men's.

Julie had her own basketball, but she didn't have a backboard and hoop. But there was one at a neighbor's house just down the street from her father's house, and she practiced her hook shot there whenever she could.

One day that summer, she was shooting hoops in the neighbor's driveway when the ball hit the rim, bounced way up, and came down behind the backboard and got stuck up there. She looked around for a broomstick or a pole, something long enough to poke the ball down with, but she couldn't find one. She realized that she'd have to go up and get it herself or leave it up there and wait for one of the neighbor's boys to come home and go up there and get it for her. It was an easy choice.

She scaled the chain-link fence next to the garage and then, balancing carefully on the top of the fence, slowly pulled herself up onto the roof. Cautiously, as if on a tightrope—her arms spread out for balance—she walked across the garage roof's slippery asphalt shingles to the backboard and picked up the ball that had come to rest there behind it.

Turning to leave, she hesitated and then returned to the backboard. The hoop was tantalizingly close, right there, just below her feet. This would make a great dunk shot, she thought. Unable to resist, she raised the ball above her head to slam it through the hoop below. She heard the sweet sound of the ball swooshing through the net, but then her feet suddenly slipped out from under her and she skidded into the backboard. For a moment, time seemed to stop and then sped up as if to make up for the lost moment.

Everything happened so fast. The backboard, which was fastened to the garage by a few long nails, creaked and then, in an instant, gave way. Suddenly, Julie found herself falling.

It was a long way down, headfirst.

With her arms reaching out to break the fall, she belly flopped on the cement driveway. She was knocked out cold.

When she came to, her father was kneeling over her. Blood and foam was bubbling from her mouth.

"I can't wait for an ambulance!" he was yelling at someone standing nearby. "I can't wait for an ambulance!"

Julie couldn't see—she couldn't even open her eyes—but she could hear what was happening around her. She remembered where she was and what had happened—she'd fallen off the neighbor's roof. And she remembered something else; she remembered that just before hitting the pavement, something cushioned her fall. It wasn't her arms, and it wasn't the basketball or the backboard, which was now crushed and lying under the lower half of her body. It was something else. It was something miraculous.

"There is no reason for me to be alive," Julie laughs about it now. "When I fell off the roof, just before I hit the ground, I felt that there was something under me—like a pad of air or something—that cushioned my fall. I felt that then, and I've always felt that."

Julie has a word for it; the word is "placed."

"For some reason," she says, "I got placed. How I got placed and why I got placed, I don't know. All I know is that I got placed."

To Julie, "placed" means being spiritually placed in the right place at the right time. It may not seem like the right place at the time, but in the end, it always seems to work out. It's like a guiding hand that has put the pieces of her life's puzzle into the right places.

It's being guided. It's being protected. It's being "placed."

Someone or something had placed a cushion of air under her to break her fall from the roof that day; someone or something would place her in the stunt business; someone or something had placed her here for a reason.

The lady who lived in the house, it turns out, was a nurse; and when she returned home just before dark, she found Julie lying unconscious in her driveway. She quickly checked Julie's pulse—the kid was still alive—then she checked her airway for any obstructions. Then she yelled for one of her boys to run over to Art's house to bring him here as fast as he could.

"Tell him to hurry!" she yelled as he ran off to get him. "Tell him his daughter's hurt real bad!"

Art got there a few minutes later. The lady who owned the house had waited for him and then turned to go into the house to call an ambulance. And that was the first thing Julie heard when she came to—her father telling the neighbor lady that he couldn't wait for an ambulance.

Carefully—very carefully—he lifted Julie up from ground, cradling her head in the crook of his left arm. He'd been a coach long enough to know that you shouldn't move somebody with a possible neck injury unless it was a life-or-death situation; and this, he rightly concluded, was just that.

He carried her to his old station wagon, and with the neighbor lady holding the backdoor open, gingerly—very gingerly—laid Julie down in the backseat.

"Hold on a minute," the lady said and ran back into the house. Thirty seconds later, she returned with a pillow under her arm and twirling a towel into something that could pass for a neck brace. She came around the other side of the car, opened the backdoor, and carefully—very carefully—placed the makeshift brace around Julie's neck, and placed the pillow under her head for extra support. Thank God she was a nurse.

Julie moaned, but she didn't cry. She was the toughest little girl in Fullerton.

Art was already behind the wheel, and when the neighbor gently shut the back door, he slowly—very slowly—backed the car out of the neighbor's driveway. He then drove to the nearest hospital as fast as he could, careful not to hit any turns too fast, careful not to stop at lights too quickly.

Art stayed at the hospital with his injured daughter all night. The doctor took x-rays, and Julie's neck was all right, but both wrists were shattered. She'd suffered a concussion and had two black eyes, but she'd live. It was a good thing the neighbor found her when she did though. Julie, the doctor said, could have choked to death on her own blood.

A month later, when school started, Julie showed up for the first day of her freshman year of high school with both arms in casts and two black eyes.

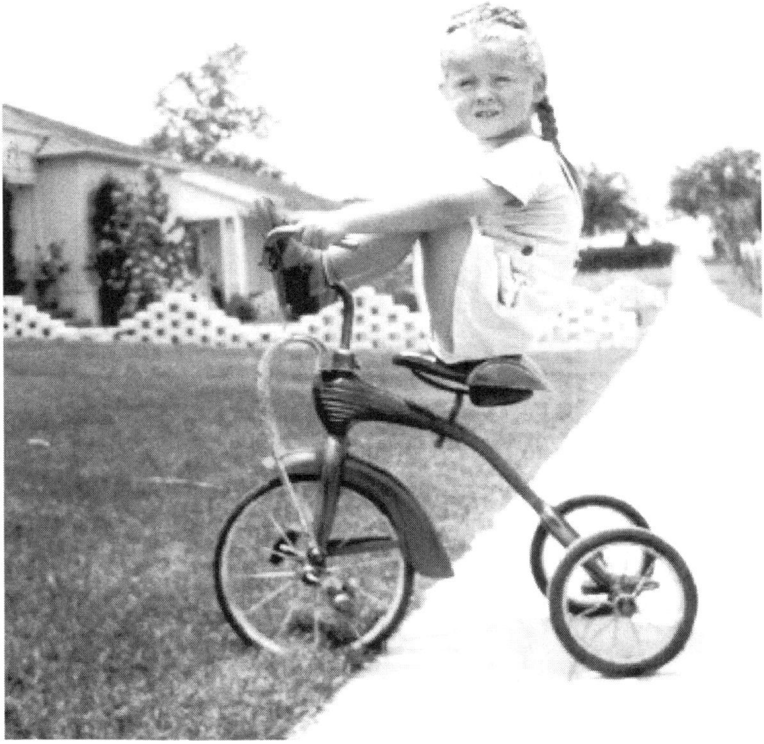

First golf lesson

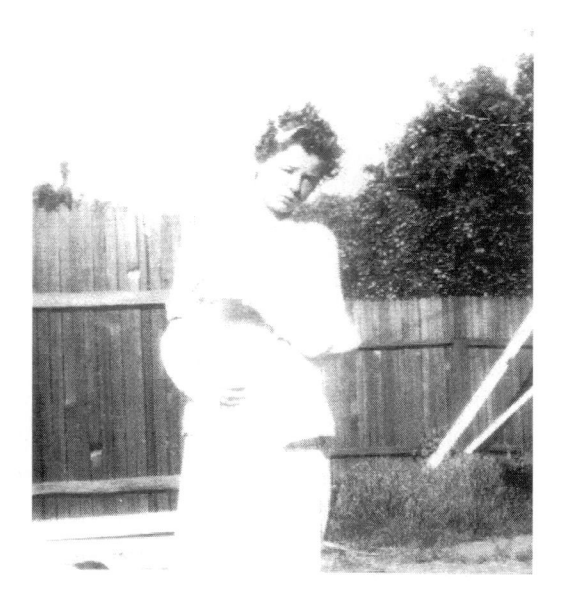

After the fall

Chapter 7

Sexism Is Not Sexy

Charlie's Angels was one of the highest rated TV shows of the 1970s, but there was trouble on the set almost from the beginning. Farrah Fawcett, the show's breakout star, quit the series after the first season and was promptly sued for breach of contract by the show's producer, Aaron Spelling, the richest and most powerful man in television.

Charlie's Angels, a show about three female private detectives, was one of the first to feature women in roles usually reserved for men. There were lots of stunts and action scenes and plenty of opportunities for stuntwomen, and when Julie was hired as the show's stunt coordinator in its third season, she became one of the first female stunt coordinators in the history of series television. It was a major crack in the glass ceiling, but old habits die hard in Hollywood, especially in the male-dominated stunt community.

Hollywood has always been a sexist town, and this was especially true in the 1970s, when men held nearly all of the top jobs at the film studios and TV networks. Hollywood wouldn't get its first female studio president (Sherry Lansing at Paramount) until 1980, and there wouldn't be a female president of a major network's entertainment division until 1996 (Jamie Tarses at ABC, followed two years later by Nancy Tellem at CBS).

In the 1970s, nearly all the directors of major motion pictures were men, as were the vast majority of screenwriters. Year in and year out, annual Screen Actors Guild earnings reports showed that male actors were being paid twice as much their female costars.

The first breakthrough for women in the modern era of Hollywood came in 1975 when Kathleen Nolan was elected president of the Screen Actors Guild—the first woman to hold SAG's highest elected post. The next breakthrough came a few years later when Julie was hired as stunt coordinator on *Charlie's Angels*.

For Hollywood's stuntwomen, the show was a bonanza. Nearly every stuntwoman in town worked on the show at one time or another. But they didn't have to compete just against each other for jobs doubling actresses, they had to compete against stuntmen for those jobs as well.

As a group, stuntmen are the most macho men in Hollywood—maybe in all of America—but even they are not above putting on dresses and wigs to double for women; they'd been doing it since the days of silent movies. After all, a paycheck's a paycheck.

In 1980, SAG finally got the industry to agree to add some tepid affirmative action language to its contract covering women and minority stunt performers. In the 1980 contract, the producers agreed that "women and minorities shall be <u>considered</u> for doubling roles . . . on a non-discriminatory basis."

They would consider it. They might not do it, but at least they would think about it.

In 1981, Julie tried to get the guild to do more. As cochair of SAG's Stuntwomen's Subcommittee, she was getting more and more reports about stuntmen doubling women.

"There has been a shocking increase in the use of stuntmen to double for women," she wrote in a letter, dated December 4, 1981, to SAG president Ed Asner. "The increase in the use of men to double women shows total disregard for the professional competence of stuntwomen. The excuse being offered by stunt coordinators is that their conscience won't allow them to put a 'lady' in danger. This is no longer acceptable to us."

"The status of today's stuntwoman is at a critical stage," she told Asner. "Qualified stuntwomen are being denied important jobs that would further their potential and expertise. We are being excluded from our chosen career, which results in great financial hardship and diminishes the stuntwoman's role in the industry."

To stop this blatant form of discrimination, Julie and the Stuntwomen's Subcommittee urged SAG to take a tougher stance at the bargaining table. They proposed that the guild bargain for contract language requiring that "no stuntman shall double for a woman unless previously cleared by the SAG Stuntwomen's Subcommittee. If clearance is not obtained, liquidated damages should be levied against the stunt coordinator."

"For several years," she told Asner, "we have asked SAG for assistance in abolishing this discrimination. We request that the SAG board of directors act upon this critical motion. Our future depends heavily upon it."

Julie had experienced this kind of discrimination firsthand during the winter of 1978 while shooting a *Charlie's Angels* episode in Vail, Colorado. Her friend and hero, Kathleen Nolan—who was then president of SAG—was guest-starring on the show, and Julie was her stunt double. They'd worked together many times before, and whenever Nolan was on a job that involved stunts, she always asked for Julie. They both admired each other's work.

In this particular episode, called "Terror on Skis," the Angels are sent on a special assignment to find the terrorists responsible for killing one of the president's top aides at a Colorado ski resort.

One of the scenes called for Nolan's character to flee the terrorists on a snowmobile. Julie wanted to do the scene, but the producers wanted a man for the job. Producer Ed Lasko gave her the news the night before the stunt was to be shot.

"I was called to Ed's room at about eleven o'clock at night and was told that I would not be doing the snowmobile job," Julie recalls.

"Why not?" she asked, taken completely by surprise.

"We don't think you can do it," Lasko told her.

Julie was dumbfounded. Driving was her specialty, whether it was cars or trucks, and driving a snowmobile wasn't much different. Her crew had been on location at Vail for nearly two weeks, and she'd driven the snowmobiles in several scenes already. The stunt in question was no big deal; it called for the snowmobile to hit a ramp, launch into the air, and come down safely.

Julie tried to get the Lasko to change his mind.

"If I say I can do it, I should have the opportunity—to wreck like a stuntman would wreck if I'm gonna wreck it," she said.

But Lasko wouldn't budge, and the next day, one of the stuntmen put on a wig and a woman's ski outfit and doubled for Nolan in the snowmobile "gag."

For Julie, it was a sexist slap in the face and a personal affront to her professionalism. Worse yet, it was being done right in front of her hero, SAG president Kathleen Nolan. And everyone on the set knew about it.

"It was upsetting," Julie says. "Very upsetting."

It was Julie's first taste of overt sexism on the show, but it wouldn't be the last.

Hollywood is a union town. It has been since the 1930s, when most of the major entertainment industry unions were formed. In Hollywood, there's a union for almost everybody: actors, writers, directors, cameramen, editors, art directors, hair stylists, makeup artists, costume designers, sound technicians, electricians, painters, plumbers, prop makers, lighting technicians, set decorators, truck drivers, gaffers, grips, and extras.

The most powerful union in Hollywood is the Screen Actors Guild—which not only represents actors but stunt performers as well.

Hollywood is also a liberal town. It has been since the days of silent movies. Actors, artists, and writers have always tended to be more liberal than the rest of society, and it's no wonder since their craft is considered part of "the liberal arts."

The vast majority of SAG's members also tend to be liberal—even the richest and most powerful stars. But there is one significant pocket of conservatism within the guild's ranks—the community of stuntmen. They are Hollywood's true action heroes—men that action stars like John Wayne, Harrison Ford, Tom Cruise, Bruce Willis, Sylvester Stallone, Errol Flynn, Sean Connery, and Arnold Schwarzenegger only pretend to be like.

"Stuntmen—I'm a huge fan of theirs," Burt Reynolds once said. "I never wanted to be John Wayne. I wanted to be Hal Needham," the legendary stuntman.

Stuntmen are a tight-knit group. To them, everyone in Hollywood is either a cowboy or an Indian. They're the cowboys; everyone else is an Indian.

Many stuntmen are great guys: fearless, fun to hang out with, and cooler than Steve McQueen. But back in the 1970s and '80s, they were the worst bunch of sexist in the film and TV industry. Many still are today.

They even have their own organizations, and up until the 1980s, they wouldn't let women join. Some won't let women join today. On December 28, 1983, *Daily Variety*, the "bible of show business," published a front-page article about this under the headline "Okay on the Job, but No Room for Women in Two of Three Stuntmen's Orgs."

The story began, "The Stuntmen's Association of Motion Pictures, Hollywood's oldest, largest and most prestigious stuntmen's organization, does not allow women to join as members. It never has and, according to its president, it never will."

According to Stuntmen's Association president Bill Lane, the reason was simple: "It says '*stuntmen*,' it doesn't say 'stuntwomen,'" he told *Daily Variety*, referring to the title of his organization. "It doesn't say 'stunt persons' either."

According to Lane, who at the time was also the head of SAG's stunt and safety investigating team, the Stuntmen's Association is a "fraternal organization. It's a California corporation. It was set up that way (to be for men only) twenty-two years ago. "At that time, they didn't have the Equal Rights Amendment or any other shit like that."

"We have enough of our own problems," Lane told the newspaper. "We don't need the women's. If they ever let one in, I'll resign and probably the whole outfit will too."

Trouble is, the Stuntmen's Association and all the other stuntmen's groups—such as Stunts Unlimited and the International Stuntmen's Association—are not just fraternal organizations; they also act as employment agencies.

"The stunt coordinator does all the hiring of stunt performers," said a well-known casting director. "They are the ones who know all the guys. They run their own small empire. It's the most incredible fraternity I've ever seen."

When a stunt coordinator needs a stunt performer, he makes his recommendation to the unit production manager, the director, the line producer, or the first assistant director, who in turn tells the casting department to hire that person.

"Stuntmen and coordinators do the recommending," Lane said, acknowledging that the coordinators "try to suggest their own guys. That's what a fraternity is for."

In fact, the stuntmen's organizations function more like hiring halls than fraternities, and therein lies the problem: under Title VII of the 1964 Civil Rights Act, it's illegal for employment agencies to discriminate on the basis of gender or race.

The day after the article appeared in *Daily Variety*, Julie Johnson called the Stuntmen's Association to ask about joining. Roy Clark, a veteran stuntman and an official of the stuntmen's group, answered the phone.

"I'd like some information on how I'd join the Stuntmen's Association," she told him.

"Oh god," he said. "Who is this?"

"Who is *this*?" she asked. "This sounds like Roy."

"Yeah, it is. Is this Julie?"

"Yeah," she said. "I'd just like to know how I could join the Stuntmen's Association. I have twenty years in the business, and I feel I'd be an asset to your group. I'd also like to continue working in the business, so it would help if I could join your group."

Roy laughed, realizing what she was up to.

"I guess I'll have to give you to Bill Lane," he said.

"Okay," Julie said. "Whatever. I'm just trying to find out how to join."

Roy handed the call off to Bill Lane.

"Well, as you've read," Lane told her, "it's 'stuntmen'—not 'women' or 'persons.'"

"So you have to be male, huh?" she asked.

"Yep," he said, "you have to be male."

"Fine," Julie replied, as courteous as ever. "Thank you very much for your time."

A few weeks later, on February 21, 1984, Julie filed a class action sex discrimination suit against the Stuntmen's Association, two other stuntmen's groups, the Screen Actors Guild, and the Alliance of Motion Picture and Television Producers—the organization that represents Hollywood's producers at the bargaining table.

In her complaint, filed with the federal government's Equal Employment Opportunity Commission and with California Department of Fair Employment and Housing, Julie charged that qualified stuntwomen were being denied employment solely on the basis of their gender. Sometimes, she said, less qualified stuntmen were being used to double for actresses; and if stuntwomen were hired, they were often paid considerably less than men with the same experience doing the same job. The problem, she said, is cyclical: SAG routinely recommends that prospective employers hire stunt performers and stunt coordinators through one of the three main stuntmen's organizations, which in turn refuse to accept qualified women as members.

A few months later, two African-American stunt performers—stuntwoman Jade David and stuntman Marvin Walters—met with EEOC attorney Margaret Ryan to complain about rampant racial discrimination in Hollywood. As a result, the EEOC launched a major investigation into Hollywood's hiring practices. Ryan, the lead investigator on the case, found a widespread and systemic pattern of discrimination in Hollywood's hiring practices, including blatant and illegal discrimination against stuntwomen.

Ryan spent more than a year working on the case, interviewing hundreds of people to get an accurate picture of Hollywood's hiring practices, which are unlike any other major industry in America. What she found was that for many workers—especially stunt performers and so-called below-the-line workers who toil behind the cameras—hiring is done almost exclusively on a who-you-know basis.

"The people who were doing the hiring were doing it by who they knew and by word of mouth," Ryan said in an interview for this book. In such a system, in an industry dominated by white males, she said, "You would never get women and people of color."

This was especially true of the stunt business.

Ryan was preparing to litigate the case when she was informed by the district director of the EEOC's Los Angeles office that an outside litigation expert was being brought in to handle it. When he arrived, Ryan recalls, he told her, "You don't have to worry about me stabbing you in the back. I'm going to stab you right between the eyes."

Alarmed by his attitude and concerned that she could not protect the many confidential sources who'd confided in her during the course of her investigation, Ryan quit the EEOC in 1985 and has never spoken publicly about the case until now.

Her case was strong, and "everyone, on the surface, was behind it," she said.

EEOC director Clarence Thomas, who would later become a Supreme Court Justice, had supported Ryan's investigation all the way; but after she left the EEOC, the investigation withered and died.

Politically, Ryan's investigation of Hollywood's racist and sexist hiring practices had been a long shot from the beginning. Ronald Reagan was in the White House, and he was adamantly opposed to affirmative action, which the EEOC had used since the late 1960s to counterbalance past discrimination by giving preferences in hiring and college admissions to qualified women and minorities.

During his very first press conference as president, Reagan told reporters in 1981 that affirmative action programs had been "distorted" into quota systems and that he was going to put an end to that.

"I'm old enough to remember," Reagan said, "when quotas existed in the U.S. for the purpose of discrimination, and I don't want to see that happen again."

Reagan, a former actor and a former SAG president, had been governor of California the last time the EEOC turned its spotlight on Hollywood's discriminatory hiring practices. It was 1969, and after a lengthy investigation, the EEOC found that the film and television industry had been engaging in a "pattern or practice of discrimination" against minorities seeking work in dozens of behind-the-scenes job categories. To remedy this violation of Title VII of the 1964 Civil Rights Act, the studios agreed to take affirmative action by establishing a set of "goals and timetables" to recruit and employ more minorities.

Nothing much came of it though. In 1976, acting EEOC chairwoman Ethel Walsh wrote that the agency "found very little progress had been made" toward ending discrimination in Hollywood.

When Reagan became president in 1981, he still had strong ties to Hollywood. Sources close to Reagan said he read the Hollywood trade papers—*Daily Variety* and *The Hollywood Reporter*—in the Oval Office nearly every day. And his old friend and former agent, Lew Wasserman, the head of Universal Studios, was widely regarded as the most powerful man in Hollywood. Certainly, Wasserman would not have welcomed another far-reaching prosecution of Hollywood's hiring practices.

To this day, Ryan's report and recommendations remain a government secret.

Thomas remained the head of the EEOC until 1990, when President George H. W. Bush appointed him to serve on the U.S. Court of Appeals for the District of Columbia, the second most powerful court in the land. Eighteen months later, Bush named Thomas to the U.S. Supreme Court to succeed the legendary civil rights crusader Thurgood Marshall, the first African American to serve on the Supreme Court.

Over the next twenty years, Thomas worked tirelessly on the Supreme Court to undo everything that Marshall had accomplished—with a special emphasis on destroying affirmative action, even though he has acknowledged that he got into Yale Law School in the early 1970s because of the school's affirmative action policies.

Today, Hollywood's stuntwomen are still discriminated against, and stuntmen still put on wigs and dresses to double for actresses. In 1980, SAG's contract required that stunt coordinators "consider" hiring stuntwomen to double for women. More than thirty years later, they are now only required to "endeavor" to hire stuntwomen for those jobs.

Not much has changed.

Chapter 8

The Blacklisting Begins

Julie never wanted to sue Aaron Spelling, but he left her no choice. All she wanted was a meeting with him so that she could thank him for having given her the opportunity to coordinate and to tell him why she'd *really* been fired—not the trumped up reasons Ronnie Rondell had given her. Filing suit, she believed, was the only way to salvage her reputation.

In order to sue Spelling-Goldberg Productions for sex discrimination, however, she'd first have to get a right-to-sue letter from the California Department of Fair Employment and Housing. That took nearly a year and would set in motion the events that would lead to her blacklisting.

In the spring of 1982, a few months after she filed suit in Los Angeles Superior Court, Julie, Jeannie Coulter, and a few of the other more outspoken stuntwomen in town decided to break away from the Stuntwomen's Association of Motion Pictures, which Julie had helped found back in 1967. Now she would cofound a new organization called the Society of Professional Stuntwomen.

"The other women in the association didn't want to make trouble," Julie recalls. "They were happy with the way things were. They didn't like it when we brought up problems. They wanted to keep their mouths shut."

There were lots of problems to discuss: men doubling for women, sexual harassment on the job, drugs and safety issues, just to name but a few.

Some of the best stuntwomen in Hollywood joined the new group. Besides Julie and Jeannie, there was Jadie David, a fearless, second-degree karate black belt and one of the few African-American stuntwomen in the business; Debbie Evans, the best female motorcyclist in the industry; Glory Fioramonti, one of the busiest stuntwomen in Hollywood; Stevie Myers, famous for her stunt work on *The Blues Brothers* and *The Black Hole*; veteran stuntwoman Regina Parton; Leslie Hoffman, who a year later would become the first stuntwoman elected to the SAG board of directors; Mae Boss, one of the grande dames of the stunt community, and Jeannie Epper, who in hair and makeup was a dead ringer for Lynda Carter, for whom Epper doubled on *Wonder Woman*.

In April of 1982, Jeannie Coulter hosted a meeting of the Society of Professional Stuntwomen at her home in Calabasas. It was the organization's first meeting since Julie had filed her lawsuit, and almost everyone gathered around the table in Jeannie's dining room that day supported her; almost everyone, but not everyone.

"Excuse me," Epper said. "I've got to go to the bathroom."

The women kept talking and encouraging Julie to fight the dirty bastards. A few minutes later, Epper returned.

In Julie and Jeannie Coulter's court testimony, they told what happened next.

"I've got something to say," Epper said, standing near the table around which the others were seated. "Julie, I've been sent here to tell you that if you don't stop making waves and drop this lawsuit, none of us are going to work in this business."

Julie was stunned.

"What are you talking about?" she asked. "Who told you to say that?"

"Never mind who told me," Epper replied. "It was relayed to me to tell everybody at this meeting."

"Who told you to say that?" Julie insisted.

Epper just stood there, glaring at Julie, her arms folded in defiance.

"She wouldn't say," Jeannie Coulter recalled seven years later during her deposition as a witness in Julie's lawsuit. "She never told us."

The other women, not knowing what to say, looked at one another and then at Julie.

Julie couldn't believe it, and yet coming as it did from Jeannie Epper, she knew it was true. In Hollywood's stunt community, Jeannie Epper was royalty. Her father was legendary stuntman Johnny Epper, who'd double for Gary Cooper, Henry Fonda, Ronald Reagan, and Errol Flynn. And her brothers—Tony, Gary, and Andy—were famous stuntmen as well. In fact, her brother Gary had succeeded Julie when she was fired as stunt coordinator on *Charlie's Angels*. Jeannie Epper was connected, and a threat from her was a threat from the entire good old boys' stunt establishment, and maybe even from the god of television himself—Aaron Spelling.

Ironically, Epper would later fall victim to sex discrimination herself.

"If my name was Gary Epper instead of Jeannie Epper," she said in 2004, "I probably would be second unit directing and stunt coordinating jobs all the time."

But for now, she was content to do the men's bidding.

Julie looked at her friends and then got up from the table.

"All right," she said, "if that's how it is, I quit. I'm leaving the group so that you can all continue to work. Just tell the guys that I'm gone, that you no longer associate with me."

And before anyone could tell her not to go, she was gone. She left and drove home; and on that day, the Society of Professional Stuntwomen, which Julie had cofounded only a few months earlier with a bunch of her closest and dearest friends, ceased to exist.

On that day, the blacklisting of Julie Johnson had begun.

She fell into a nine-month-long depression. She went for days without leaving the house, and she didn't see anyone or go anywhere but to the corner market for groceries. Sometimes she was too depressed to eat or to even get out of bed, and she lost twenty-five pounds. Most days she sat in the den with the drapes closed. Usually, she didn't know if it was day or night. Either way, it didn't matter.

CHAPTER 9

Granddaughter of Greatness

In the summer of 1957, Julie's grandfather—her mother's father—was inducted into the Baseball Hall of Fame. His name was Sam Crawford, and he was one of the greatest baseball players of all time. To this day, he holds the record for career triples and most inside-the-park home runs in a single season—records that will probably never be broken.

Beginning in 1899, Sam played four seasons with the Cincinnati Reds, leading the league in home runs once and triples twice and then was traded to the Detroit Tigers, where he played outfield for the next fifteen seasons, the last thirteen with the best hitter to ever play the game—Ty Cobb. For most of their years together on the Tigers, Sam and Cobb played side by side in the outfield—Sam in right field and Cobb in center, Cobb batting third and Sam batting cleanup. They'd gone to three straight World Series together, and finally won it in 1909.

When Julie was a kid, her dad used to drive her out to Pearblossom, a dusty little desert town in the Antelope Valley, to see her grandpa. Sam had a shack out there that he liked to sneak off to get away from Mary, his second wife. She was a jealous and overprotective shrew who tried to keep everyone away from her husband—even his family. Sam's first wife—Virginia's mother—had died before Julie was born, so Julie never got to know her real grandmother.

Julie loved those trips to see her grandpa. Sam was funny and playful, and he always took time to play a little catch with her when she came to visit. Her dad loved Sam too, and the two men would sit in a shady spot outside the shack talking for hours about old-time baseball. Julie would listen, dreaming of the faraway, romantic places Sam had visited on his travels through the major league circuit. And when Sam talked, she could almost hear the clatter of the railroad tracks in his voice.

Born in Wahoo, Nebraska, in 1880, Sam was a star high school athlete, leading his team to two state football championships. But his life at home was horrific. His father was a violent drunk who beat him mercilessly.

At sixteen, Sam had had enough and ran away to play baseball with a semipro team that traveled from town to town, playing ball by day and sleeping under hay wagons at night. In the spring of 1898, Sam's speed and skill with the bat caught the eye of a scout, who hired him to play for the Chatham Reds of the Canadian League for $2 a day.

"That's an odd thing, having to get out of the country to get your start," he'd tell Julie's dad. "The Canadian League was just a little shrub of a league. It folded up in July of that year. Then I went to the Western League. I was in there from July 'til September."

He played so well, the next year the Cincinnati Reds called Sam up to the majors.

"That was in the fall of 1899," he'd tell Julie's dad. "Those were tough days. Things were different."

"How's that?" Art would ask.

"Well, everything was different. We'd play a whole game with the same ball if it stayed in the park." Sam would laugh. "It'd be lopsided, black, and everything else. Everything was different. The traveling. The trains. You know, you'd have two guys sleeping in an upper. Things like that. It was altogether different."

"Ball players in those days were considered pretty rough," he'd laugh, and when he told his stories, he'd always laugh. "You'd go into a dining room in a good hotel, or as good as you could get, and they always sat you way down in the corner somewhere."

"You saw some mighty good pitching back then," Art would prod.

"Yeah. I hit against Walter Johnson in the first game he ever played in the American League."

Walter Johnson, of course, was one of the greatest pitchers to ever play the game. A right-handed hurler for the Washington Senators, he still holds the record for most shutouts and is second only to Cy Young in career wins.

"I hit a two-run home run off him that first day. We beat him three to two. That was in nineteen-seven. He was just a string of a kid, ya' know? Tall and lanky. Walter had just reported from Idaho or somewhere. Didn't have a curve. But he had that fastball. He had a swish on it. It swished." And Sam would make a swishing sound with his mouth.

Julie and her dad would always leave before sundown and then make the long, sleepy drive back home.

Sam was at his shack in Pearblossom in the summer of '57 when he got the news that he'd been selected to the Hall of Fame. It had been forty years since he'd last played in the majors. A reporter found him there, pushing a wheel burrow.

"Hey, are you Sam Crawford?" the reporter called out. "You're in the Hall of Fame!'"

Sam greeted the news with a characteristic grin and, a few months later, traveled back to Cooperstown for his induction. He gave a brief speech, but overcome with emotion, had to cut it short and sit down with tears in his eyes. Ty Cobb, who was on hand for the induction, put his arm around Sam's shoulder and they both cried together a little.

Julie couldn't be with her grandpa that day. She wanted to, but her parents wouldn't let her go. She had to go to summer school, so she stayed behind in Orange County and fell in love instead.

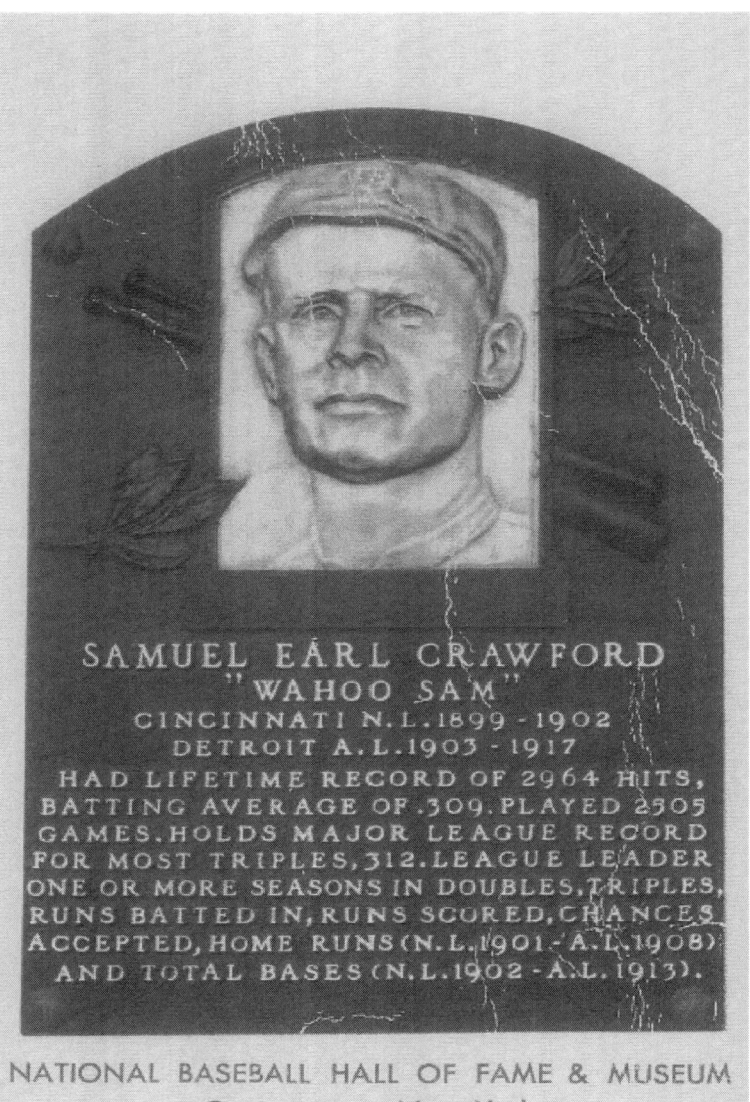

Sam's Hall of Fame Plaque Cooper's Town, NJ

The Glory of Their Times

Chapter 10

Julie and Eddie

Three years after she fell off the roof, Julie fell in love. And just like everything else she did, she fell hard. Only this time she didn't break her arms—she broke her heart. It was her eighth stunt, and for Julie, falling in love would prove the highest high fall of all.

It was the summer of 1957. Julie had just finished her junior year of high school. She was sixteen, with blue eyes and blond hair, and at 5'7" she was fully grown—at least vertically—but still coltish.

He was twenty-one; he'd just finished his junior year at UCLA, where he was a yell leader and a big man on campus. His name was Eddie, and he was absolutely gorgeous.

It hadn't been easy growing up as the coach's daughter. Julie was more athletic than most of the boys in her school, and those who weren't intimidated by her were intimidated by her father.

"None of the boys in school would have anything to do with me," she says with a laugh many years later, although it wasn't very funny back then. "They'd say, 'Stay away from the coach's daughter.' It was just known, 'Don't mess with the coach's daughter.'"

But Eddie was a college man, and he wasn't intimidated by anybody.

If there was a more handsome boy in Southern California, Julie had yet to meet him. He was cuter than any of the boys she saw in *Seventeen* magazine—cuter than Tab Hunter and way cuter than Ricky Nelson, cuter than Pat Boone for sure, and almost as cute as James Dean—but he'd been killed in a car crash two years earlier, so he didn't count.

And Eddie was cool, way cooler than Paul Anka or Frankie Avalon and almost as cool as James Dean—but he was dead, so again, that didn't count.

Tan and lean, with the build of a gymnast, Eddie was a fraternity man—Beta Theta Pi—majoring in business administration. But he didn't look like any businessman she'd ever seen. He had the prettiest green eyes and the sexiest smile. He looked like he'd just stepped out of a race car—not the kind of souped-up hot rods the kids drove back in those days, but something hotter, something they raced at Le Mans, a Porsche maybe or a Jaguar or an Aston Martin.

And he smelled good too. Not like the cheap aftershave that many of the boys in her school wore before they could even shave—but like magnolias, with just a hint of musk and cigarette smoke.

Eddie smoked. A lot of the guys did back then. But it was the *way* he smoked, the way he held a cigarette in his hand, so casual, so sexy.

And his hair was perfect—thick and full, without any gobs of grease that was popular among boys back then. Eddie was just different.

They'd met that summer at Big Corona, the state beach in Corona del Mar. For most teenage girls in Southern California, the summer ritual was pretty much the same in those days: pile into a car, go down to the beach, lie in the sun, and talk about cute boys. And if they were lucky, a cute boy would talk to them. One day that summer, Julie got very lucky. She was sunning herself on the beach with some friends—Robin, Dawn, and Myrna—when Eddie walked by, wearing nothing but bathing trunks and a magnetic smile. Their eyes met; and somewhere down the beach, Johnny Mathis's no. 1 hit song, *Chances Are* was playing on someone's transistor radio.

> *Chances are, 'cause I wear a silly grin*
> *the moment you come into view,*
> *chances are you think that I'm in love with you.*

Eddie didn't know it yet, but that would be *their* song. Julie knew it. She knew it the moment he came into view.

She looked at him as only a sixteen-year-old girl who's fallen instantly in love for the first time can look at a boy. Eddie smiled back at her, and she melted. She broke eye contact, and when she looked back up, he was walking away. He was even beautiful from behind.

She watched as he slowly strolled away; and then he looked back over his shoulder, caught her eye, and smiled again. Julie smiled back and blushed.

Julie's friends turned their collective gaze from Eddie to Julie, who was sitting there beside them, smiling as if she were completely alone.

Then her friends all burst into girlish laughter.

"Did you see that?" Robin said, amazed at the silent scene that had just played out before them.

"Julie's got an admirer," Myrna said, beaming at Julie.

"Romeo and Julie," Robin giggled.

"Julie's in *love*," Dawn said derisively, as only someone who's never been in love can say.

"Don't be silly," Julie said, snapping out of her trance. "Let's go swimming!"

The next weekend, Julie was back at the beach with her friends. It was hot, and her brown skin glistened with sweat and baby oil. She decided to go to the fresh-squeezed orange juice stand for a drink. She was standing there in line, barefoot in a one-piece black bathing suit when Eddie got in line behind her.

"Hi," he said.

She turned and their faces were only inches apart.

"Hi," she said, her eyes visibly widening. It didn't seem possible, but he was even prettier close up.

"I'm Eddie," he said, smiling broadly.

"I'm . . . ," Julie stammered. "I'm Julie."

"Hello, I'm Julie," he joked. "Pretty hot, huh?"

"Yes, you are," she said. She knew instantly that she'd said the wrong thing.

Eddie laughed so hard everyone in line turned around to see what was so funny.

Julie was really embarrassed now.

"Don't mind them," he said, putting his hand gently on her bare shoulder to reassure her. His hand was soft and cool. It was the first time a young man had touched her bare skin. It was electric.

"Listen," he whispered. "I'd like to see you. Can I have your phone number?"

"Yes," she said instantly, mesmerized by the movement of his lips as he spoke.

For a long moment he looked at her eyes looking at his lips.

"Well," he chuckled. "What is it?"

"Oh," she said, embarrassed again. "Do you have a pen?"

"No," he said. "Just tell me. I'll remember."

"Remember." Such a beautiful word. And she knew that he would.

"Where's my orange drink?" Robin asked when Julie returned to her friends.

"What?" Julie said, still in a daze.

"You were going to get me an orange drink," Robin reminded her.

"Oh, yeah," Julie said sheepishly. "I forgot."

"You forgot?" Robin said, puzzled that someone could forget something so easy in such a short amount of time.

"You look different, Julie," Myrna said, sensing something had happened.

"Different?" Julie asked. "How?"

"I don't know," Myrna replied. "Older, maybe. Wiser . . . taller. Something . . ." Then Myrna's face brightened as she realized what it was. "You met a boy, didn't you?" she chirped. "You're in love!"

Julie turned away to hide her face.

"That's it!" Myrna said, amazed at her own powers of deduction. "Julie's in love!"

The girls pulled Julie down on the beach blanket beside them and coaxed her into giving them all the details.

"Who is he?" they asked in unison.

"His name is Eddie," she said. "We saw him here last week. He was the boy who smiled at me."

Julie's friends looked at one another knowingly, their eyes wide in amazement.

Then, after recounting her encounter with Eddie at the orange juice stand, she told them how they'd left it.

"He asked for my phone number," she said.

"And . . . ?" Dawn prompted.

"And I gave it to him," Julie said matter-of-factly.

"Oh my god!" Robin said. "Did you write it down for him?"

"No," Julie replied. "He said he'd remember it."

All three of Julie's friends squealed at the delicious idea of such a romantic thing to say.

"Well," Robin said, barely able to control her glee, "if you go to the movies with him, ask him to buy popcorn—a big bucket—so his hands are occupied!"

They all laughed again, and then Robin asked, "So do you think he'll call you?"

Julie thought for a moment. "Yes," she said. "I think he will."

A few days later, Eddie called Julie at her dad's house in Fullerton. She answered it on the first ring. Her father was standing right there.

"Hello?" she said. "Oh, hi, Eddie . . . Why yes, I'd love to."

Uh-oh. She'd said the L-word, and right in front of her father.

"Was that him?" her father asked, sounding a bit more disapproving than he'd intended.

"Yes," Julie said. "He's going to pick me up tomorrow night for dinner and a movie. You'll lo . . . You'll like him." She'd almost said the L-word again, but quickly changed it to "like."

Their first date was dinner and a movie, *An Affair to Remember*, the classic story of star-crossed lovers, starring Cary Grant and Deborah Kerr. For Julie, it was the perfect first-date movie—not only because of the timelessness of the love story but also because of a word in the title. The word was "remember," the word Eddie had used when she asked him if he had a pen to write down her phone number. It would always be the word she would remember him by.

They dated all that summer, the summer of 1957. Sometimes they'd go to the beach and walk along the shore, holding hands, or sit on the sand, holding hands, staring up at the stars. Sometimes they'd go to Oscar's Drive-In for burgers and fries and listen to the car radio. Every song, it seemed, had been written just for them: *Love Letters in the Sand, Kisses Sweeter than Wine, Young Love, You Send Me*, and of course, *Chances Are*.

And of course, there were movies. Drive-in theaters were popular among teenagers in those days. A young couple could go there, watch a movie and *neck* in the privacy of their own car without some brat in the row behind them kicking the back of their seats.

Julie had been to drive-ins with her girlfriends, but never before with a boy.

"When the girls would go to a drive-in," she laughs, "one or two of us would get in the trunk so we could get in free."

One night, Eddie took her to the Highway 39 Drive-In Theatre in Westminster, which was so fancy it called itself a theatre—spelled the British way. As they approached the *theatre*, Julie could see the beautiful flood-lit mural painted on the back of the drive-in's giant outdoor screen, depicting sailboats gliding across a bright blue sea. Many years later, the screen and its lovely seascape would be torn down to make way for a Wal-Mart.

As they got a little closer, Julie could see the marquee, and in large red letters, the name of the movie they'd be seeing that night. It was "Hot Rod Rumble"—or something like that. Julie can't remember for sure. The exact title has been lost to the years and to other memories that have crowded it out. But aside from its forgettable title, it was a memorable movie because it first gave Julie the idea that she wanted to be a stuntwoman.

Eddie paid their admission, parked the car, rolled down his window halfway, and hung the speaker on it. Julie slid over next to him, and they necked for a little while to the accompaniment of a cheery little drive-in ditty:

> *Come on down to the snack bar,*
> *Come on down to the snack bar,*
> *Come on down to the snack bar and get yourself a treat.*

The movie, whatever its title, had to do with boys and girls in hotrods. In one scene, two open-topped hotrods were racing down the highway, side by side, when one of the teenagers stood up in the front passenger seat and jumped into the backseat of the other speeding car.

"I would love to do that," she told Eddie, pointing at the screen.

"What? You want to jump from car to car in a movie?" he said incredulously.

"Yes!" she said, excited by the very idea of it.

"Women can't do that," he huffed. "Only guys do that."

There it was again—sexism, although it would be years before anyone would give it that name. She'd experienced it on the playground when she was a kid, and now she felt its sting again here at the drive-in with her boyfriend.

"I know," she said. "I just wished."

She was disappointed that he would say something like that, but she didn't say anything; she let it go. But the seed had been planted, and the dream of one day becoming a stuntwoman had taken hold, even though at that time she didn't know what a stuntwoman was.

When school started in September, Eddie went back to college and Julie entered her senior year of high school. They talked on the phone and saw each when he came home to Garden Grove to see his parents on weekends and holidays.

They'd been going—if not steady, then steadily—for several months; and in all that time, on all those moonlit nights, Eddie had never pressured her for sex. She was only sixteen, and she wasn't ready for that yet. They kissed deeply and petted softly, but he always knew when to stop without her having to tell him. He was kind and gentle and shy, and she loved him all the more for it. They loved being in love, even though they hadn't said the word yet. Sex could wait; there was plenty of time for that later. Or so they thought.

Julie didn't have a car in high school, and UCLA was so far from Fullerton it might as well have been in Texas. So they wrote letters—tender missives full of youthful enthusiasm, heartache, misunderstandings, and bitter-sweet love. To this day, Julie keeps his, tied with a white ribbon, in a desk drawer by her bed.

"Gosh, Julie, right now I'm so tired of all this confusion and loneliness that I want to get up and hit something or hold someone," he wrote from his frat house in Westwood. "I miss you very much, but there's not much I can say. Just now, Vic Damone began the introduction to *An Affair to Remember*. I shall never forget that night as long as I live, and every time I hear this album, I will relive it in my mind."

He signed it, "Always with love, Eddie."

They hadn't spoken the word to one another yet, but she loved seeing it in writing.

Julie had given him the record, hoping he would play it when they were apart. The lyrics were so beautiful and so meaningful, and Vic Damone sang them so well.

> *Our love affair, may it always be*
> *A flame to burn through eternity.*
> *So take my hand with a fervent prayer,*
> *That we may live and we may share*
> *A love affair to remember.*

He'd given her a record too, called "Julie Is Her Name," by the Four Freshman. After she finished reading his letter, she put it on and started to cry.

They never talked about marriage, but sometimes they talked about the future, and there was always a place for her in his.

His dream, he wrote her, "is to be drifting on a peaceful sea with the soft, warm, salty breeze caressing two figures on the deck of a sailing yacht that is lit by a moon that was meant for the girl on the deck. Our destination will be life itself, and the sweet purity of the breeze will make it a lasting memory. And if we can take that trip, then, Julie, you will know that I have arrived."

Eddie was studying economics at UCLA, but what he really wanted to be was an actor. He certainly had the looks—and the smile and the playful green eyes and the body of a gymnast. Julie so loved his beauty, but it troubled her as well.

"I just never felt that I was pretty or attractive enough for him," she recalls. "And he was always surrounded by beautiful college cheerleaders."

One night, when she was feeling blue, she wrote him a letter saying that they might not ever see one another again, that maybe he would be happier with someone else, someone more beautiful than she.

Eddie was happy to get her letter, but shocked and confused when he read it.

"I just received your letter and I was very happy and very disturbed," he wrote. "I want to tell you, Julie, that I don't mind being alone because I'm not really. I will never be alone as long as I have your picture, and I still receive your letters.

"Julie, I have never told a girl the things that I told you and meant it with such deep feelings. As for the girls up here, maybe they are outstanding in some respects and some of them may be beautiful, but for all I care they all have three eyes. I haven't stopped thinking about you and this summer, but what really hurts is the way you keep saying we may never see each other again, because unless you tell me that you don't want to see me, then I will find you no matter where you go or what you do."

That made her feel better, but still, she wasn't sure. Still needing reassurance, the next time they talked on the phone, she told him that she thought maybe she was standing in his way.

"Julie, you are not standing in the way of my happiness," he told her. "Quite the contrary. You *are* my happiness. I want very badly to see you, and that's an understatement. It is being with you that makes me happy."

Julie's senior year was hard. Eddie was away at college, and she was struggling with her studies just to get B's and C's—she'd had to go to summer school every year to make up for the poor grades she got in math and English. The only A's she got were in art and physical education. But she excelled in sports; she was always the first one picked, no matter what the sport. She was one of her school's fastest swimmers, an ace tennis player, and a leader on her softball, basketball, volleyball, and field hockey teams. For good measure, she received the Girl's Athletic Association Award for top female athlete at her school that year.

Athletics kept her busy, but she still got lonely and was so looking forward to spending the summer with Eddie. But then, the day before she was to be photographed for her high school yearbook, the bottom of her world fell out.

That night, Julie was in her bedroom reading a movie magazine when the phone rang.

"Julie," her father called out from the living room. "Eddie's on the phone for you."

Julie fairly sprinted into the living room where her father handed her the phone.

"Hi," she said, watching as her dad walked off to his bedroom.
"Hi," Eddie said.
"I miss you," she said.
"So do I," he said.
"I thought you had to study tonight," she said.
"I'm supposed to," he said, "but I can't stop thinking about you. Julie, what are we gonna do?"

Just then, there was a knock on Julie's bedroom door.

"Julie? Could I talk to you?" her father asked through the closed door.

"Just a minute," she called out to her father, covering the mouthpiece with her hand.

Then, whispering into the phone: "I have to go, Eddie. My dad's at the door. Bye."

"Come in, Dad," she yelled, quickly hanging up the phone.

Art came in and stood in the doorway.

"Julie, you are not even eighteen," he said. "Eddie is twenty-three. What does he want from you?"

"Dad, we're just friends," she replied, a bit surprised that her father, who she loved so much, would put it so crudely.

"He calls here every night," her dad said. "What am I supposed to think?"

"We're just friends," she insisted, knowing that it wasn't the whole truth, but not exactly a lie either.

"Well, your mother called today," he said. "She would like you to visit her."

"What?" Julie said, more an expression of shock than a question. "Visit her? Where?"

"In South America," he said. "Venezuela."

"When . . . ," she started to ask, suddenly realizing that decisions had been made about her future without her knowledge or consent.

"As soon as you graduate," he said.

"But that's only two weeks away," she moaned. "What will I tell Eddie?"

"Tell him that you are going to visit your mother for the summer."

"The summer . . . but . . . Venezuela . . . all my friends are here," she stammered.

"I'm sure they all go away for the summer," he said, sitting down on the bed beside her.

She could have said no. She'd be eighteen in just a few months, and she could have just refused to go. But it didn't even occur to her to disobey her father. She loved him and trusted him. Defying him was not an option. And besides, it would only be for the summer. Even so, she wasn't happy about it—not at all.

The next day, Julie had her yearbook photo taken. She looked like the saddest girl in Orange County.

On graduation day, she wore a black gown and black mortar board with a white tassel. Her dad was so proud, but he was also concerned. Her grades weren't good enough to get into a four-year college, and Julie didn't have any clear notion of what she wanted to do with her life. Visiting her mother in Venezuela, he thought, might do her some good. It would certainly keep her away from Eddie and keep her from getting pregnant.

The days after graduation were some of the saddest in Julie's young life. All the songs on the radio seemed to be about heartbreak and loss: *Oh, Lonesome Me, Tears on My Pillow, Summertime Blues,* and of course, the Everly Brothers' *Bye Bye, Love.*

> *Bye bye, love.*
> *Bye bye, happiness.*
> *Hello, loneliness.*
> *I think I'm a-gonna cry-y.*

How was she going to tell Eddie?

She went to Bullock's the next day to buy Eddie a good-bye gift. She was only supposed to be gone for the summer, but somehow she knew it would be much, much longer. She bought him a watch and told the jeweler the inscription she wanted to put on it. It would be ready the next day, he told her.

Eddie called a few days later. He was at his parents' home in Garden Grove and wanted to see her.

"Yes," she said. "Friday night at six. I have something to tell you."

"What is it?" he asked, concerned by her tone. "Have you found someone else?"

"No, no," she said. "Never. I'll tell you when I see you."

"All right," he laughed. "I love a woman of mystery."

There was that word again.

He picked her up Friday at six and drove her to Andree's, the best French restaurant in Laguna Beach. Along the way, she sat close.

Eddie was buoyant, happy to see her. Julie was pensive and nervous. *Oh, Julie* by the Crescendos, came on the radio; and Eddie, trying to cheer her up, mouthed the words to her, overacting for comic effect.

> *Oh-uh-oh-uh-oh Julie,*
> *You'll never know how I love yo-ou-ou.*
> *Oh-uh-oh-uh-oh Julie*
> *A teenage dream that can't come true*

He laughed, but it just about broke Julie's heart.

At the restaurant, they were escorted to a seat by the window overlooking the painfully blue Pacific Ocean. Eddie had made reservations. They ordered, and when the waitress left, Eddie turned serious.

"All right, we're here," he said. "Are you going to tell me what was so important that you couldn't tell me on the phone?"

"I want to give you a birthday present," she said, suddenly brightening.

"But it's not my birthday," he protested, but happy to see her smile again.

"I know," she said, casting her eyes downward, "but I won't be here to celebrate it with you."

"Why not?" he asked, now sensing that something terrible was happening.

"I'm going to Venezuela for the summer," she said, looking deeply into his eyes to see his reaction.

"What? When do you leave?"

"Tomorrow," she said.

"Tomorrow? You're leaving Tomorrow? For Venezuela?"

Julie reached into her purse, pulled out a small package—tied with a pink ribbon—and sat it before him.

"What is it?" he asked.

"Open it."

Slowly, he untied the ribbon and then unwrapped the gift, careful not to tear the paper. He opened the box inside, revealing a beautiful watch with a leather band.

"A watch," he said, genuinely surprised.

"Look at the inscription," she said.

He turned the watch over and read the words inscribed on the back: "Time Remembered—Love Always, Julie."

There. She'd said it, the L-word.

"When we saw *An Affair to Remember*, you said that would be us one day," she reminded him.

"I remember," he said.

There was *that* word again.

"Put it on," she said cheerily, fighting back tears.

He did and they held hands across the table until the waitress came with their salads. He looked at his new watch. It was five past seven. Julie had set it to the correct time.

After dinner, they went to a drive-in. It didn't matter which one. It didn't matter what was playing. They parked but didn't even bother with the speaker. They got into the backseat and held each other for the last time.

When the movie ended, he drove her home and walked her to the door. High above, the full moon shone down on them like a porch light. Holding her tight, he kissed her deeply.

"Will you write me?" he asked.

"I will," she said. It was all she could do to keep from crying.

"I'll write you too," he said. Then, looking into her eyes, he whispered, "I'll always remember this moonlight on your face."

He kissed her for the last time, then turned and walked to his car. As he drove away, he could see her still standing there, her tears glistening in the moonlight.

Chapter 11

The Phone Call to Monty

Julie had already been through two lawyers—both of whom had dropped her without doing anything to advance her case—when she found a third attorney to represent her.

"The first lawyer filed my case wrong," Julie recalls with a sigh. "She held out for a year and then would not return my phone calls. My second lawyer held my case for *over* a year, then harassed me to make a settlement and, when I refused, walked out on me."

Julie was running out of time. She was going broke—she had only $44 left in the bank—and couldn't afford to get stuck with another attorney who would let her down. So she decided to do some research; she'd try to find a lawyer who wouldn't be afraid to take on Aaron Spelling—she'd try to find one who was already suing him.

In April 1986—five years after she'd originally filed her lawsuit—Julie went downtown to the Los Angeles Superior Courthouse on Hill Street to see if she could dig up any records. A clerk directed her to the Records Section, where she started rummaging through recent filings looking for someone—anyone—who was suing Spelling.

After several hours, she finally found a screenwriter who claimed that Spelling had stolen a story from her. Court records showed that her lawyer was a guy with the highfalutin name of Monty Greenwood Mason II.

Julie drove back home to the Valley and called his office; it was just down the road on Ventura Boulevard. He answered the phone himself on the third ring.

Julie introduced herself and told him about her case and the trouble she'd had with her two previous attorneys. She told him that if she could just get her case before a jury, she was sure she would win.

"I think when a jury hears what I've been through," she said, "it's just gonna be unbelievable. It's been a nightmare."

"Well," Monty said in a deep, mellifluous voice, "that's the whole point—to have the jury like you and to like your witnesses."

"Yes," Julie said. "And that jury is going to be determining the future of stuntwomen. Stuntwomen today have to prostitute themselves. It's horrible. I've been around twenty-three years, and I know. We're as important as the women athletes—our Olympians—and if the jury knew how we've been treated by this industry, I think they would find it unbelievable."

Julie was on a roll. It was so nice to have someone to talk to about it all.

"Something has to be done," she continued, "and whether it takes me five or ten years more, I don't care. I'm gonna try very hard not to starve. I don't have a penny to my name right now. I am facing bankruptcy. But I'm a very strong person and have a lot of faith in justice, and maybe that's wrong. I've been told that the justice system stinks."

"You are right, Julie," Monty chimed in. "You are quite right. There is no justice."

Julie was taken aback. There is no justice? That was a strange thing for a lawyer to say, a very strange thing. And besides, that's not what she meant at all.

"But you have to hold on to your faith," she said with a nervous laugh.

"Well," he said cynically, "you have to hold on to the faith that *maybe*, on occasion, yours can be the exception, and that a jury will come to your rescue. That's the faith involved."

"If they do," she said, ignoring a major red flag, "they come to the rescue of the future of this business. I think that's the most important thing that has to be sold to the jury. Which is: Do they want their daughters to have to prostitute themselves? Do they want their daughters to have to go on drugs? Do they want their daughters to have to be maimed and killed? Because that's how we leave the business. We leave the business one of five ways: killed, maimed, drug addicts, alcoholics, or suicides. This is how we leave it. And it does not have to be that way. But it has to be brought out and explained that way to a jury."

"It could make a hell of a case," Monty said with some enthusiasm.

"Oh, it's a beautiful case," she said, warming to him. "I've known this from the beginning. But I've run into some very crooked attorneys."

"Well, sometimes it's more misunderstanding than crooked," he said, defending his profession, although he knew more than a few crooked lawyers himself.

"Yes, I don't mean to use that word," she said apologetically. "It's just that after six years of where I've been, I'm very, very bitter, and I'm very angry, and I have not had a day without anger for six years—not a day without rage. I guess that's what it takes to keep beatin' down the door."

"It does," he assured her.

"But they've picked the wrong girl to do it to," she said earnestly, which got a hearty laugh from Monty. "I mean, these guys trained me! And my father, being a coach, and my grandfather, being in the Baseball Hall of Fame. I come from that kind of stock. When you're right, you fight for it. When you're wrong, you accept it and go do something else. Well, this was something that you just don't go do something else. As a stuntwoman, I am one of the tops in the business. I've built my reputation on doing tough jobs. I've never prostituted myself, but now, after twenty years, they've asked me to prostitute myself."

"Well," Monty said, "you still have men with the attitude that women are inferior and it's their private game reserve."

"Yeah," Julie said. "And all I'm trying to tell them is, 'I am not your enemy, sir.' Ignorance is the enemy, not me. I'm trying to fix things, and it would be very simple to fix these things if they would listen."

"Except, you're asking men to give up the old casting couch," Monty said, completely missing her point. "And they're not going to do it. Believe me, there's no chance that they're going to give up the best thing they've got going for them."

"I know," she said, even though she wasn't talking about sex or casting couches. "But they have to see the havoc and the devastation they're reaping."

"They couldn't care less," he said flatly. "It's like talking to a rapist."

A rapist? Where did that come from? His buttery voice sounded so smooth and persuasive, but he didn't seem to be listening to what she was saying.

"I guess so," she said, agreeing with him rather than arguing. "I guess you're right."

"Believe me," he said. "The simple reality is, whether it's a molester, a rapist, or a casting couch type, they only think of themselves. They are incredibly selfish. And don't think for one moment that you can hold a mirror up to their behavior. It won't happen. All you can do is punish them financially and hope to scare the hell out of the producers and make sure they know they'll get sued if they play this kind of game."

That made sense, she thought—except for the stuff about rapists and molesters. Julie was starting to like this guy.

"You're right," she said. "This is a precedent case, and that's why it's probably more difficult to get off the ground. But I have to press on. I have to take care of my future and the future of others. Nobody's ever gone against the system like I'm going against it."

"That's because most people have some kind of vested interest in not attacking the system," he said.

"I had two homes," she said, reflecting on everything she'd lost by taking on the system. "I had a good savings account. I had $10,000 in the bank and was building on that, and I had a good career that was booming. And then, bang! Now I end up with nothing. I end up with $44 in my savings account, and that's it. And I don't have next month's mortgage. You know, I never wanted more than what I was worth or what I was deserving of. And it was never about money in the beginning. I just wanted justice. I just wanted to make it safe and fair for the young women coming into the business. But they wouldn't listen. Spelling wouldn't see me. He wouldn't even talk to me on the phone! Instead, they chose to destroy me. But they can't use any weapon against me anymore, because I'm a ghost at this point, and they've stripped me of everything, and I'm just as naked as can be. But I've kept my body in shape, and even at forty-five, I don't mind standing in front of 'em."

They both had a good laugh about that and then Julie finished, "They can nail me up there, but it's gonna be blood on their hands. And they're not gonna be able to wash it off, and they're not gonna like that."

"Well," Monty said, "there is no attack that you can make that will hit anyone as hard as an attack on the wallet. That's just the simple truth of it."

Julie knew he was right about that. Yes, he was cynical, and no, he didn't listen very well; but his voice was so beautiful, so soothing and reassuring. It was a great voice—a great lawyer's voice—and after hanging up, she knew that that was the voice she wanted to represent her case to a jury.

A few days later, Monty called and told her he would accept her case. He told her he thought he could win it.

But what he was really hoping for was a quick and easy settlement.

Chapter 12

Julie and the Shrink

On November 3, 1986, Julie drove over to North Hollywood Park—a bucolic retreat in the heart of the San Fernando Valley. She parked her car and walked to the picnic area and sat at a table under the shade of an old black walnut tree. It was cool and breezy, a refreshing change from the stifling heat that had baked the Valley for the past five months. It was a lovely autumn day, but Julie wasn't there for the scenery.

After a while, a distinguished-looking man about her age, wearing a suit and a tie, approached her.

"Julie?" he asked.

"Yes," she replied, rising to greet him.

"I'm Robert Matirko," he said, extending his hand.

They shook hands and then sat at the picnic table, facing one another. They spoke for about an hour; she did most of the talking. A casual observer might have thought they were lovers—or ex-lovers. She was upset and occasionally broke down in tears. But this was not a lovers' quarrel. This was a professional meeting. Beginning on that day, he was to be her psychotherapist.

A park isn't the usual setting for psychoanalysis, of course, but Julie insisted and he agreed. For an outdoorswoman like Julie, it turned out to be the perfect setting.

She hadn't wanted to see him at all, but her new attorney, Monty Mason, insisted on it. He thought it would help her case to document the full extent of the psychological damage she'd suffered by being wrongfully terminated and then blacklisted in the entertainment industry for the past seven years.

"This client was referred to me," Matirko wrote of their first meeting, "for an initial interview and psychotherapy because of anxiety, difficulties in concentration, disturbances in sleep patterns, and depression over an alleged wrongful termination and discrimination dismissal from Spelling-Goldberg Productions in April 1980. This was exacerbated by the added stress of preparing for her impending court case and surviving on limited funds over the past seven years."

For Julie, it had been seven long years of struggling to survive on residuals, a few odd jobs, disability, and state assistance—seven years of fighting her way through the legal system to get her case before a jury. Seven years of anxiety, depression, and defeat.

But Julie had survived through will power and her unquenchable desire for justice. And sometimes that's all it takes. Still, she was not happy to be seeing a shrink.

"I don't think I need any psychological help," Julie told him that day in the park. "I'm used to toughing things out on my own. Because of my upbringing, I was told to keep my feelings in. So it's unsettling for me to even have to talk to a psychologist. I've never talked to one before. I always thought I could handle things on my own."

Matirko jotted all this down.

"Since the client perceives herself as needed and indispensable," he wrote in his initial report, "she found it difficult to admit to herself that she required any mental treatment. Also, the client was brought up to be self-sufficient and independent. Thus, there was the initial resistance to psychotherapy as well as its social stigma."

Over the next four months, they would meet twenty-three more times—once or twice a week. Julie poured her heart out to him, and afterward, he would take copious notes on their sessions together. He came to know her very well.

"Prior to coping with her practical and legal problems," Matirko concluded at the end of their many sessions, "Julie's basic personality structure was that of a reserved but forceful individual, who demonstrates above-average awareness, sensitivity, and intelligence in her interactions with others. She has a strong sense of individual and social justice, idealism, and motivated determination to follow through conscientiously on her basic beliefs and for the rights of others. She has always been concerned and dedicated to the welfare and safety of others."

In his unflinching and penetrating analysis of her personality, he wrote, "Since early childhood and the divorce of her parents, Julie was expected to function more independently and to accept responsibilities for herself and family beyond her years. She stoically accepted this fact, not only due to her life circumstances but also because of her needs to please. In this way she would feel worthwhile and loved by her family and others if she conscientiously performed as expected."

Matirko, however, didn't just see Julie as who she had been, but who she had become—a brave and selfless crusader for safety and justice in an industry that didn't care much about either.

"Thus, having acquired a strong individual and social sense of responsibility," he wrote, "she primarily developed through her own efforts the basic tenants and human values to resist moral and social injustice. Maintaining these basic values throughout her life, she unwaveringly upheld her integrity and diligence in the face of adversities."

"Her decision to challenge the injustices she discovered would test the limits of her courage and fortitude. Her goal was not only justice for herself and reinstatement of her stunt job but also to establish increased professionalism and safety regulations from which all stunt performers could profit. In the long run, both the producers and the television and movie industry would also benefit from a safer, more reliable, well-trained, and organized group of stunt performers."

But on the first day that they met in the park, Matirko saw a starkly different Julie—a demoralized Julie—a Julie who'd almost been beaten by life and the legal system.

"During the initial interview," he wrote, "she explained her frustrations and discontent with herself over not functioning as before. She is very upset as she describes her anxiety level and depressed moods. The client repeats throughout the session that nothing matters to her like it use to. Her enthusiasm and motivation have depleted significantly, to such an extent that she cannot function as adequately as she should. In fact, she is becoming progressively withdrawn and isolative, except for a few close friends and family. Her attitude tends to be negative, and she feels basically demoralized. Because of all her life struggles and the litigation involved over some past seven years, she is experiencing 'burn out,' frustration, and a sense of futility.

"The client admits to feeling depressed for a long time and has frequent crying spells. In this therapist's opinion, her feelings of helplessness and despair are very genuine."

And yet, Julie refused to take any medications to lift her mood. She was determined to tough it out without drugs. And in that way, she was much tougher than so many of the tough-guy stuntmen she knew who had turned to cocaine to lift their moods and to give them the courage they lacked to do their jobs.

"She refused antidepressants," Matirko noted, "fearing a chemical dependency upon an unnatural substance that she believed she did not require in either case. She firmly felt she could cope with her emotional problems independently as she had always done throughout her life."

The ongoing and never-ending legal case only added to her burden.

"Initially," Matirko wrote, "she had to interview over fifty lawyers, and the one she finally chose, she had to discard for incompetence after two and a half years of service before she discovered her present legal representative."

Unbeknown to Matirko and to Julie, her "present legal representative"—Monty Mason II—would cause her more grief and despair than she could imagine.

"Throughout the years," Matirko wrote, "there were notices of depositions that had to be filed in relation to her case. While she was attempting to find employment, all this added litigation was disruptive and time-consuming and counterproductive to the client's well-being. Any social or recreational time she may have had available was not fully appreciated because of the intermittent stress she had to endure. At this point, she only desires the case to be finalized in her favor, eventually to be free of anxiety and depression, and to become reinstated as a stunt coordinator once again."

CHAPTER 13

A Settlement Offer

Monty Mason was a settlement specialist. Taking cases to trial was time-consuming and expensive, and you never knew if you were going to win or not. A settlement, on the other hand, was a sure thing, quick and easy and guaranteed to put money in the client's pocket—and his.

Monty was busy, but he figured Julie's case wouldn't take long to settle. He had another case he had to settle first and was in talks to settle a pair of class action suits down in San Diego involving some real estate ventures that'd gone bad. But they wouldn't take much of his time. They'd be a piece of cake. Or so he thought.

A few months later, the San Diego cases would turn into a quagmire that threatened not only to end his career and land him in jail but also to undermine Julie's case and get her killed. The confluence of Julie's case and the class actions in San Diego—which had been underwritten by the same insurance carrier—would change Monty's life forever, and Julie's as well.

A trial date had been set for Julie's case—March 17, 1987—and as Monty battled to salvage his career from the imploding cases in San Diego, he struggled to respond to the mountain of motions the attorneys for Aaron Spelling were heaping on him.

In an attempt to get out of this jam, Monty came up with a plan: he'd get Julie to drop her suit in exchange for a nominal cash settlement. Julie wasn't interested in the money, so to get her on board, he'd get Spelling to take out ads in the Hollywood trade papers—*Daily Variety* and *The Hollywood Reporter*—attesting to Julie's integrity and professionalism as a stuntwoman.

Julie, he knew, would go for that deal. She'd already tried—three times—to get a meeting with Spelling to settle the case.

"This letter—my third one—is to request a meeting to discuss the possibility of dropping my lawsuit against your company," she'd written to Spelling in 1985. "I have weathered almost six years of blacklisting partly due to your company and some of the people associated with *Charlie's Angels*. I am sure if you knew from me why this is happening you would agree to end this matter promptly and therefore release us both from any further litigation. I am approaching you with a hopeful and open heart that you will grant me an appointment to try and end this madness."

She never heard back from him. Maybe he'd talk to Monty.

The ad that Monty had in mind would appear under Spelling's letterhead and over his signature. It would state:

> I feel compelled to give a response to Ms. Johnson for the adverse treatment she has received over the last seven years by my production company and the industry in general. In my busy schedule, I failed to realize the importance of Ms. Johnson's plight. She must be commended for her superb service to the industry over the last two decades.
>
> As a producer, it is my duty to foster and nurture our stunt persons into better, safer and more educated stunt people. Ms. Johnson's expertise and profound caring has re-reminded me of this important issue.
>
> I will personally do all I can and will impress upon the producers to restore Ms. Johnson's integrity and to return her to her craft as a stunt coordinator. Her dedication to her craft knows no boundary.
>
> Very sincerely,
> Aaron Spelling

Julie loved the idea. It would be an admission that she had indeed been blacklisted and might get her back in the business.

"I would have taken just the letter," Julie insists. "I didn't care about the money. The letter would have validated my claim and got my career back for me. That's all I wanted."

But Spelling refused. He wouldn't sign it. There would be no settlement.

So with the trial set to start in only a few weeks, Monty hurriedly began taking depositions. One of the first, and probably the most important, would be Jeannie Coulter's.

Jeannie, like Julie, had been one of Hollywood's premier stuntwomen. Like Julie, Bobby Bass had nearly killed her that day out by Magic Mountain in 1979 while shooting a stunt, high on cocaine, for *Charlie's Angels*. Like Julie, she'd been appalled by the vast amount of cocaine being consumed by stuntmen and women in the late '70s and early '80s. And like Julie, she never touched the stuff. Back in those days, Jeannie was married to a cop and didn't run in those circles. But she'd seen plenty of it around.

"It made the stunt guys feel invincible," Jeannie recalls. "When I worked on *The Blues Brothers*, they had bowls of cocaine for everybody. The guys all talked about it. I talked to Jim Belushi on the set afterward, and he was so depressed."

Cocaine use was so rampant in Hollywood in those days that Johnny Carson even joked about it while hosting the 1981 Academy Awards show. "The biggest moneymaker in Hollywood last year," he quipped, "was Colombia—not the studio—the country."

Jeannie's deposition, which was taken on March 7, 1987, at a Holiday Inn in Fresno, would be explosive. She'd tell how she'd witnessed two of the key figures in Julie's case—stuntmen Ronnie Rondell and Roy "Stuffy" Harrison—sniffing cocaine and how she was there when Julie was blacklisted for daring to file a wrongful termination suit against Aaron Spelling. These were serious charges and could sway a jury to find in Julie's favor. So naturally, Spelling's lawyers would try to make sure that a jury would never hear them. His lawyers would say that they were hearsay and irrelevant and try to get the judge to rule them inadmissible.

But more damaging still would be Jeannie's testimony that she'd witnessed sex discrimination against Julie when she was the stunt coordinator on *Charlie's Angels.*

"How many times did you see this?" Spelling's lawyer asked her at her deposition.

How many times? How could she answer? It seemed like just about every day.

"I don't know how many times," Jeannie replied, "but you hear a lot of things on the set. When I was working, I'd hear guys saying, 'Oh, well, she's a woman. What do you expect?' Those are just things that people say."

"Who were the guys who said that?" the lawyer asked.

"Well, I've heard stuntmen say negative things about her," she said. "I've heard people working on the set say different things—whether its electricians, general workers, or grips laughing in the back—you hear certain things on the set."

"And that was because she was a woman?"

"Yes," she answered. "They would say, 'What do you expect? It's a woman doing it. If you had a man in there, he would take care of everything.' But it wasn't that she wasn't doing the same job that the man would do, it was just that she wasn't a man. It's real strange and very difficult for me to explain, but if you were a woman, you'd probably understand. It was just that the men put her down as stunt coordinator because I really feel that they felt a woman should not have that job."

Jeannie knew what she was talking about, and she said it with such clarity and sincerity that any woman—any woman on the jury—would probably understand what she was saying. Clearly, the best Aaron Spelling could hope for would be to have the sex discrimination portion of the complaint thrown out of court before Jeannie's testimony could be heard by a jury.

And that's exactly what happened, and it happened in a most unusual way: At the request of Spelling's attorneys, and without Julie's knowledge or consent, Monty Mason dropped Julie's sex discrimination charge shortly before the case was to go to trial. And he would later swear under oath that he'd done so on orders from the mob.

Chapter 14

The Bombshell

Monty Mason was coming unhinged. The class action cases he'd been handling in San Diego that were supposed to be an "easy settlement" had turned into a lawyer's worst nightmare and now the district attorney down there was investigating him. There were accusations that Monty was involved in a ring of crooked lawyers who'd schemed to defraud insurance companies out of millions of dollars in legal fees through the systematic manipulation and prolongation of complex civil litigations.

Monty flatly denied it. He claimed he'd been set up by sinister forces operating in the shadows—that the Mafia was involved, and that he was the patsy.

It all came to a head on April 28, 1987—a few weeks after Monty had flown up to Fresno to take Jeannie Coulter's deposition, and just a few weeks before he was set to take Julie's case to trial—when he called Julie and told her he had to talk to her in person. He told her to meet him that evening at a coffee shop in Van Nuys. He had urgent news.

Julie was there, seated in a booth in the back of the cafe, when Monty showed up.

"Hi, Monty," she said as he pulled up a chair across from her. "What's going on?"

"We have a settlement offer from Spelling," he told her in his deep, mellifluous voice.

"Really? That's fantastic!" she said, thinking that her long battle for justice might finally be coming to an end. "And . . . okay. What's the settlement?"

The waitress came to the booth and asked if they'd like some coffee.

"Yes," Monty said.

"I'll have an iced tea," Julie said.

When the waitress left, Monty laid out the deal.

"They're offering $37,500," he said. "And you have to sign a confidentiality agreement—you can never reveal the amount of the award or use Spelling's name or likeness in any book or movie that you may plan to write about this case."

Julie was broke and desperate for money, but $37,500 wouldn't even cover the residuals Spelling had cheated her out of, much less compensate her for all the years of income she'd lost since being blacklisted. There was no way she was going to let them get away with what they'd done for a measly $37,500; and in fact, she wouldn't even get that much. After Monty deducted his expenses and 40 percent contingency fee, she'd be lucky to walk away with $15,000.

But more importantly, she wanted future generations of stuntwomen to know what she'd been through, and for the industry to treat them better than it'd treated her. She wanted her day in court.

And she certainly wasn't going to sign a confidentiality agreement that would strip her of her right to write a book about her life. She'd been working on a book ever since she'd broken into the stunt business back in the 1960s. It was a book she'd known she was going to write ever since she was a kid.

In 1947, when she was seven years old and living in La Habra with her mother and stepfather, they had a neighbor who lived across the street named Aleene Zane, who was an amateur fortuneteller. Julie would run across the street every chance she got to have her fortune told.

"I would go over and sit on her porch, and she would read my palm," Julie recalls.

"Hey, Aleene, read my fortune again," little Julie would beseech her neighbor.

Aleene would take her little hand, study the lines on her palm, and tell her what she saw in the little girl's future.

"You're going to have one serious illness," her neighbor told her. "See here? Your lifeline is broken. But don't worry. You'll pull through just fine."

Little Julie breathed a sigh of relief. "What else do you see?" she implored.

"I don't think you're going to get married or have children," she answered, studying Julie's little palm carefully. "But you're going to write a book one day!"

"Really?" Julie said, instantly over her disappointment about never marrying or having children. "What am I going to write about?"

"I don't know," the palm reader replied. "It's a long, long time from now."

And it all came true. She did have a major illness—a hysterectomy that nearly killed her—and she never did get married or have any kids. And she was indeed writing a book—a book about her experiences as a stuntwoman. And there was no way she was going to stop writing it now.

"No way, Monty," she told her lawyer that night in the coffee shop. "I'd rather take my case to trial."

Monty looked at her sternly. "You don't know who you are dealing with!" he snapped.

Several customers, hearing his outburst, turned around and looked to see what was going on in the back booth.

Julie was shocked. He'd never raised his voice to her before. "What do you mean, Monty? Who am I dealing with?"

Monty looked around nervously to make sure that the other customers had returned to their own business. Then, in a whisper, he said, "The Mafia."

"What?" Julie asked, dumbfounded.

"I've done some checking around," Monty continued in a low voice, "and I've discovered that Spelling is involved with the Mafia."

Over the years, Hollywood has had long ties to the mob. Bugsy Siegel, Johnny Roselli, Sid Korshak, and Mickey Cohen were just a few real-life gangsters with ties to Tinsel Town; and Universal's Lew Wasserman, Columbia Picture's Harry Cohn, and Paramount's Robert Evans were just a few movie moguls with proven ties to gangsters. But Aaron Spelling's name had never been publicly linked to the mob, not by any intrepid investigative reporter or by any law enforcement agency anywhere. Monty Mason, however, was saying he'd found out something that everyone else had somehow missed—that Spelling was "connected."

Julie was stunned. She didn't know what to say.

"Well . . . ," she stammered, but Monty cut her off.

"We don't have a choice," he told her. "And if we don't do it, we don't have a chance. They have threatened to kill us both."

For a moment, the restaurant seemed to spin. It was like a doctor—someone she trusted completely—had just told her that she has cancer and only has a few days to live. When the room stopped spinning, Julie looked into Monty's eyes and could see that he was serious—dead serious.

"I've got a gun," he said, "and you should take steps to protect yourself too."

"Who told you this?" she asked, finally collecting her thoughts enough to ask the obvious question.

As Monty would say many years later in a sworn affidavit, he'd been warned of all this by his paralegal on the class action cases he was handling in San Diego. Her name was Shelly Tyson, and her ex-husband was an assistant district attorney for Los Angeles County.

The assistant DA, he told Julie, "was in a special position to have contact with important people. He had a message that his ex-wife delivered to me. She said that as a DA, he was in touch with the Mafia and that Aaron Spelling was 'connected.' Spelling had requested a favor from the Mafia, which was that I was to drop your case or settle it at whatever figure might be given to me by the attorneys for the Fireman's Fund."

As it turned out, the Fireman's Fund—which today is the largest insurer and underwriter of Hollywood movies—was the insurance company for the defendants in the class action cases Monty was handling in San Diego, and for the defendant in Julie's case, Spelling-Goldberg Productions.

As Monty would later write in his sworn affidavit, "This message, her ex-husband said, was now being relayed to me and that if I wanted to live I must do as ordered. Because of the circumstances of the class action cases, I believed her. I believed that both Julie and I were now Mafia hit 'targets' and that I had no means of defense, or that anyone, especially the authorities, would believe me. At first I decided not to do as ordered. I made arrangements to defend myself, to have another friend of mine hide me during the expected combat, and to die ultimately. Shortly thereafter, I decided that a scorched earth policy was fruitless and would involve innocents. My only other choice was to capitulate."

The waitress brought their coffee and iced tea.

"Can I get you anything else?" she asked chirpily.

"Not for me," Monty said glumly.

Julie just shook her head.

When the waitress left, Monty handed Julie a piece of paper. Julie slumped back in the booth and stared at it. It was the proposed settlement agreement—$37,500 and a strict confidentiality agreement.

"They won't pay a dime more," Monty told her, sipping his coffee, "and they don't want anyone to know that they even paid that. They don't want to look weak and encourage more lawsuits."

Julie looked blankly at the settlement agreement.

"I'm not gonna sign this," she said. "I'm not gonna give up my right to write a book."

"If you don't sign it," he said dolefully, "we're dead."

"I don't care," she said firmly. "They can kill me if they want. I'm not gonna sign it."

Julie's stomach turned at the thought of Spelling cheating her out of her day in court, but she wasn't afraid. She'd never been afraid a day in her life. She'd been depressed and distraught and worried, but never afraid. And she wasn't afraid now. But Monty was.

"He was scared," Julie recalled many years later. "I could tell that he was sweating. This was not made-up."

"I was scared shitless," Monty said years later in an interview for this book. "When this finally came down, I believed it. Julie definitely believed it too, but she was confident. She's gutsy. She's a fighter. She had a steely eyed gaze that any stuntwoman would have been proud of."

All these years later, Monty isn't sure anymore if the threat was real or not.

"I thought I'd be assassinated, seriously," he says. "I really thought they were after me." But now, he says, he believes that the threat "could possibly have been false" and that Shelly Tyson, the paralegal who he swore had warned him to quit the case—or else—"could easily have been lying to me." But it seemed very real to him and Julie at the time.

Julie sat gloomily at the table and then suddenly brightened.

"We could call a press conference!" she said. "I know at least *one* reporter who would cover it. We could tell the world what these bastards are doing."

"No," Monty replied coolly. "No newspaper in the country would print that Aaron Spelling had hired the mob to kill a lawyer—not without proof anyway. And hell, even I can't prove it."

Julie slumped back in her seat again.

Monty finished his coffee. Julie hadn't even taken a sip of her iced tea. She wasn't going to sign the settlement agreement, so there was nothing more to say. Monty paid the bill and left a dollar tip; and as they left, Julie wondered if men were sitting in a car parked outside, waiting to gun them down when they walked out of the coffee shop.

Chapter 15

Three-Card Monty

Two days after his meeting with Julie in the coffee shop, Monty and Spelling's attorneys attended a status conference in Department 68 of the Los Angeles Superior Court—the Honorable Judge Alexander R. Early III, presiding.

But there'd be nothing honorable about the proceedings that day.

After clearing up a few routine matters, Monty made a move—at the request of Spelling's lawyers—that would change the course of the upcoming trial. Without Julie's knowledge or consent, he agreed to dismiss the sex discrimination portion of her suit, which was the very heart of her case.

"I have the authority of my client to dismiss the third cause of action, without prejudice," Monty told the judge.

"It is ordered dismissed," the judge said.

In fact, Julie had never given Monty the authority to dismiss any part of her complaint, much less the sex discrimination charge. But he'd done it anyway, and the judge had let him do it without even calling Julie to court to ask if she had, in fact, approved of it.

"The employment discrimination claim was dismissed upon the motion of counsel for plaintiff shortly before the commencement of trial," Spelling's attorneys wrote in a subsequent brief, without offering any further explanation.

Many years later, Monty explained in a sworn affidavit why he'd done it.

"Believing that I had to do as I was ordered and in fear of my life and hers," he wrote, "I dismissed her discrimination cause of action in an effort to show 'compliance.'"

The claim of sex discrimination was the most important part of Julie's case, and given the specifics of her case and the history of the stunt business, it probably would have been the easiest to prove. But now it had been thrown out by Julie's own attorney, who decided to sabotage her case on what he believed were orders from the mob.

It was the grossest kind of attorney misconduct and intentional misrepresentation imaginable, punishable by disbarment, at the very least.

But Monty wasn't through yet.

A few days later, he met with Spelling's lawyers for a court-mandated settlement conference. Right away he told them there'd be no settlement. He told them that while he thought their offer of $37,500 was fair and reasonable, his client did not. And then he told them that he'd heard something scurrilous about their client.

It was a gamble, he knew—one that might make Spelling even madder at him than he already was. But he had a plan, as he always did, and he thought it just might work.

He told them he'd heard that Spelling was connected to the mob.

Spelling's lawyers were dumbfounded. What kind of stunt was this, they wondered.

They'd soon find out.

Monty was planning to withdraw from the case, but he knew that no judge would allow a lawyer to drop out on the eve of a trial without a very good reason. So this was Monty's: he told Spelling's lawyers that under Section 6068 of the California Business and Professions Code, he was duty-bound "to advance no fact prejudicial to the honor or reputation of a party or witness, unless required by the justice of the cause."

He told them that he couldn't continue to represent his client without, at the same time, violating his duty not to bring dishonor to Spelling.

Spelling's lawyers looked at each other like this guy was crazy.

May 10, 1987, was a Sunday—a beautiful spring day in the Valley. Julie was puttering around the house on Van Noord, talking to her mother and looking through boxes of court records she'd accumulated over the years. She was excited about the upcoming trial. Jury selection was to begin the next day.

She was making sandwiches when the phone rang. It was Monty Mason.

"Hi, Monty," she said, cradling the phone in the crook of her neck and spreading mayonnaise onto a piece of bread.

"Hello, Julie," he said. "I have some bad news."

Julie's heart sank. What could it be? More death threats? Was he sick? Was he dying?

"I'm withdrawing from the case," he said.

"What?" she said, although she had heard him very clearly. After everything she'd been through, this was the last thing in the world she expected to hear.

"Jury selection begins tomorrow," she said. "How can you quit on me now?"

"I have to," he said, ashamed of his cowardice. "They're going to kill us both if I don't."

"Monty . . . ," she started, but he cut her off.

"Take care of yourself, kid," he said. "I'll see you in court tomorrow."

Then he hung up. Julie was left standing there in her kitchen, a jar of mayonnaise in one hand, the phone in the other, and no one on the other end of the phone to talk to. Her mother was in the other room, but Julie couldn't have felt more alone.

The next day, Julie drove downtown to the courthouse on Hill Street, where a year earlier she'd found Monty's name while digging through court records looking for a lawyer brave enough to take on Aaron Spelling.

Monty and Spelling's lawyers were already there when she got to the courtroom. She took a seat next to Monty without even saying hello.

The judge entered from his chambers and took his seat on the bench. It was 2:34 p.m.

"I understand you want to make a motion, Mr. Mason?" the judge inquired.

Monty stood up next to Julie for the last time. "Yes, Your Honor," he said. "I'd like to make a motion to withdraw from the case and, at the same time, ask for a continuance so that my client can seek other counsel."

The judge looked at Monty for a long moment. "All right," he said. "Is there any reason, Ms. Johnson, I shouldn't grant Mr. Mason's motion to be relieved as counsel?"

Julie rose and stood next to her cowardly lawyer.

"I don't really understand what you're asking me," she told the judge.

"He doesn't want to be your attorney anymore," the judge told her, as if explaining it to a child. "He's asking the court to permit him to withdraw from this case as your attorney. That means you'll have to get a new attorney or handle the case without the services of an attorney. Is there any reason I should refuse to let him withdraw?"

Julie understood all that. Monty wanted off the case. That much was clear. What she did not understand about the judge's question was something else altogether different. It posed a moral dilemma to which there was no easy answer. Should she insist on Monty staying on as her lawyer even if it meant putting his life in jeopardy?

Finally, she answered the judge's question. "That is confusing to me," she said, "because in light of the fact that my attorney has been threatened, that's very difficult for me to answer. I would like him to be on the case and take it to trial, but under the circumstances, I'm concerned about his life too. So naturally, I don't think that I can say to him, 'Continue with my case even though your life is going to be in danger.' You put me in a very, very difficult position here."

Slowly, the judge removed his reading glasses and looked first at Julie and then at her lawyer. "Let me ask you, Mr. Mason, what are the reasons that you desire to withdraw, on what is substantially the eve of the trial?"

Monty had his lie all set up.

"There's a variety of reasons, Your Honor," Mason said. "First, there has been no threat against my life. The threat, if you can call it that, is simply a statement that opposing counsel feels that its client would be wronged by the information which I would attempt to place into evidence—that it would constitute slander."

Julie listened in disbelief as Monty went on and on in what she now realized was just an elaborate and cowardly ruse to save his own neck. Her attorney, whose voice had once sounded so strong and noble to her, now sounded like a blustering windbag.

"My client," he continued, "has indicated on some occasions that she would be more than willing to hold a press conference about matters about which, during my last court appearance, I had offered to make various offers of proof *in camera*, and I have refused to give press conferences or make that material available.

"I cannot help but think that their offers, which are commensurate with the liability of this case, are adequate on the contract measure, while my client continues to press for the tort. And there is every doubt in my mind that the matters which I have disclosed to the court *in camera* would necessarily ever pass muster in motions *in limine* and see the light of day before twelve jurors."

Julie had now completely lost track of what Monty was saying. It sounded Greek to her, but in fact, it was partly Latin, with a little French and a lot of legalistic bullshit thrown in for good measure.

A *tort*, which is based on a French word, is "a civil wrong."

In camera is a Latin phrase meaning privately, "in the judge's chambers."

In limine is another Latin phrase meaning "at the threshold," and in law, a motion *in limine* is a motion for a protective order against prejudicial questions and statements.

Had she gone to law school, or majored in Latin, she might have understood that what Monty was saying was that he thought that Spelling's settlement proposal was fair and that a judge would probably never allow a jury to hear the secret about Spelling that Monty had privately disclosed to Spelling's attorneys in the judge's chambers.

"Therefore," he continued, "on the one hand, I don't want to face either legal liability for what might be a useless act and end up with nothing more than something tried in the papers without adequate and admissible evidence to get before a court, having in mind my duty to my client and my duty also to the defense client. Because under the Business and Professions Code, I can bring no dishonor to him except when necessity compels me to do so.

"And I have my doubts that I'm going to be able to get the evidence that I think would backstop the only possible way to prove her wrongful termination. All I'm going to wind up with is a notorious matter on the outside of court, and nothing relevant and admissible inside of court.

"And yet, I'm being compelled to do that by my client, and at the same time, there's a reasonable and fair offer on the table with respect to her contract action. So I'm trying now to do duty between two masters and I'd just as soon withdraw."

Julie was now beyond shock, beyond disbelief. She could understand that Monty was afraid and wanted off the case. But she didn't understand why he had to concoct such a ridiculous lie to do so, and she would never understand why he felt that he had to tell the judge that that he thought the settlement offer Spelling had made was "reasonable and fair."

It was all a horrible, shocking lie, made all the more unfathomable coming from a man who, only a few weeks earlier, she'd regarded as her hero, a knight in shining armor who'd rode to her rescue after she'd been abandoned twice by unscrupulous lawyers.

Now she felt ashamed of him and for him. It must be horrible, she thought, to be such a coward. She'd rather be shot where she stood than live in fear like that.

"Ms. Johnson, have you reported this threat to law enforcement authorities?" the judge asked her solemnly.

"No, sir," she replied.

"The motion to withdraw is granted," the judge ruled. "The court finds the relations between Mr. Mason and his client have reached a stage of complete incompatibility, and I do not think that under the circumstances he could do the best possible job of representing her interest in this court."

And that was it. Monty was gone. He'd fooled Julie, and now he'd fooled the judge. It was all so astonishing, but what really astounded Julie was how easy it had been to fool a judge. He only asked her one question: "Have you reported this threat to law enforcement authorities?"

She should have said, "Really? That's all you want to know? You don't want to know who threatened my attorney? Or when he was threatened? Or where he was threatened? Or how he was threatened? Or why he was threatened?" Any first year journalism major would have known to ask those basic five questions. But apparently they didn't teach that in judge school.

But what amazed Julie the most was that here she was, with only a high school diploma, standing among all these learned and educated men of the law, and she was the only one who really wanted the truth to come out. She was the only one who really knew what was going on. She was the only one who wanted justice.

She was also the only one there who wanted to keep this fight going. She'd been alone in this fight before, and she hadn't given up then. Now she was alone again, and she still would not give up.

Chapter 16

"Some Thoughts about Loss"

Julie had to find a new lawyer fast. The judge had granted a continuance until August, but she only had a month to retain an attorney and prepare for the trial. So she employed her tried-and-true method—she headed downtown to the courthouse and poured over old court records looking for somebody who'd already sued Spelling.

What she found was a case in which one of Spelling's own lawyers had sued him after she'd been fired for uncovering the fact that Spelling had cheated actor Robert Wagner, who had a 50 percent ownership stake in *Charlie's Angels*, out of $500,000 in profits from the show. The firm that represented her in that case was called Simke, Chodos, Silberfeld & Anteau, with offices on Wilshire Boulevard in the Miracle Mile.

The next day, she called and made an appointment; one of the partners, David Chodos, would see her.

Her meeting with Chodos went well, but he was too busy to handle her case; so he handed it off to one of his associates, Richard Grey, a former high school teacher turned attorney.

"I was first consulted by Julie when her lawsuit was within thirty days of coming to trial," Grey recalled. "After conducting a hurried investigation, the firm agreed to represent her at trial."

Actually, his firm expected a quick settlement. "But that didn't happen," he said, "so the only option was to go to trial."

One of the first things Grey did was to get Julie to a psychiatrist for a second opinion. He figured it would be good for her and good for her case. He was right on both counts.

The psychiatrist he chose was a remarkable man named Dr. William M. Lamers, whose unique field of expertise was the treatment of people trapped in the grip of sorrow and grief. Over the course of his long career, he'd become a world-renowned expert on the psychological treatment of the dying. His specialty was loss, which made him the perfect psychiatrist for Julie, who felt that she'd lost everything.

Julie first met with Dr. Lamers at the Los Angeles offices of Grey's law firm. They would only have three sessions together there, but during that short time, Julie poured her heart out to the good doctor and would come to believe that he understood her sense of loss better than anyone ever had or ever would.

After their last meeting, Dr. Lamers wrote up an eight-page report that he titled: "Some Thoughts about Loss." It perfectly captured how Julie felt—about everything. It even contained flashes of poetry.

For Julie, Dr. Lamers's report was a lifesaver—literally. Over the years, in her darkest moments, she would take it out and pour over it, consoling herself that at least one person on earth understood what she had been going through.

"That really saved me," she recalled many years later, "because for the first time I saw in print what I had lost. When I felt that horrendous empty feeling coming over me, I'd go read his report, and it was right there in black-and-white."

"There is a sense of sadness about what happened to Julie," Dr. Lamers wrote. "She gave her life's energies to improving her craft, her profession. She risked her life many times for well-known stars. She would have been pleased to have had the chance to continue to do so. But she was *dumped* at the peak of her career. Had she been younger, there would have been a number of opportunities open to her. But she had devoted herself to this one career."

In his report, he then quoted an appropriate verse from Edna St. Vincent Millay.

> *If I had loved you less or played you slyly,*
> *I might have held you for a summer more.*

"Had Julie been less than ethical, if she had 'played the game' with the crowd that was abusing drugs," he wrote, "she might still be working. It would have meant compromising her integrity. But she was ethical and, moreover, was responsible for the safety of her stunts. She could not tolerate unnecessary risks in an already-risky business. She 'blew the whistle.' And an unsupportive management, bowing to the influence of those abusing drugs on the set, blew her away. Julie was expendable."

By the time Julie had come to see Dr. Lamers, she'd worked only twenty-three days as a stuntwoman in the seven years since she'd been let go by Spelling-Goldberg.

Dr. Lamers realized that her blacklisting only intensified when she filed suit and then took her complaints about drugs and safety to the Screen Actors Guild. She was a pariah in the stunt community—seen by the stuntmen who ruled it as a troublemaker and a threat. As a result, she lost nearly everything.

Dr. Lamers saw an apt comparison between Julie and Ulysses, the hero of Greek mythology. Both had risked their lives for others in one heroic adventure after another, and both felt an overwhelming sense of loss of purpose when they could no longer do what they wanted most to do. And he found just the right line from Lord Alfred Tennyson's poem "Ulysses" that expressed that feeling.

How dull it is to pause, to make an end,
to rust unburnished, not to shine in use.

He also understood the nature of the conspiracy that had led to Julie's downfall. It was not the elaborate and farfetched "conspiracy" of UFO cover-ups and JFK assassination plots, but rather, one rooted in the very origin of the word "conspiracy," which is derived from the Latin word *conspirare*, meaning "to breathe together." And that's exactly what had happened to Julie. The macho, chauvinistic, and sexist community of Hollywood's stuntmen, whose powerful fraternities decided who would work and who would not, had "breathed together" and decided that Julie would not.

"Julie was injured," he wrote, "because of the careless performance by a stunt driver who was apparently under the influence of cocaine. Julie took responsible action in calling this dangerous behavior to the attention of those who should have helped remedy the situation. Julie was trying to see that she and others would not be subject to added risks because of the use of illicit drugs on movie sets.

"The logical outcome of her stand would be that the leadership of the film company would take action to see that illicit drug use was stopped on production sites. Instead, she was faced with an 'illogical' outcome. She was suspended from her job. When she protested, she was openly blacklisted."

Chapter 17

Norma Connolly Testifies

"Call your first witness," Judge Savitch told Julie's attorney.

"Thank you, Your Honor," Richard Grey said. "The plaintiff calls Norma Connolly."

The clerk walked out to the hallway and motioned to Norma, who entered the courtroom and took the witness stand.

"Do you solemnly swear that the testimony you may give in the cause pending before this court shall be the truth, the whole truth, and nothing but the truth, so help you God?"

"I do," Norma replied, and nobody could tell the truth better than Norma Connolly.

An accomplished actress on stage, screen, and television, Norma is perhaps best known in the role of Aunt Ruby, who she played for twenty years on *General Hospital*. But among her fellow actors, she is best loved for a different role she played—as the hard-charging, no-nonsense national chairwoman of the Screen Actors Guild's Women's Committee. It was a role she was born to play, and a role she relished.

A fierce supporter of women's rights, she championed the concerns of actresses to anyone who would listen—and to many who wouldn't. She worked tirelessly against ageism and sexism and spoke out about the limited roles provided actresses to such organizations as California's State Commission on the Status of Women and the City of Los Angeles' Commission on the Status of Women.

To her many fans, Norma was a TV star; but to many TV stars, she was a hero.

"Are you presently acquainted with Julie Johnson, the plaintiff in this case?" Grey asked her.

"Yes," Norma replied.

"How did you first come to be acquainted with her?" he asked.

"Through my work at the Screen Actors Guild," she said.

Norma had appeared on the very first episode of *Charlie's Angels*, but Julie hadn't joined the show until the sixth episode. They'd first met at SAG's offices in 1978, when Julie and a group of stuntwomen came in to urge the union to do something to the help stuntwomen. Norma, a former SAG vice president, was then cochair of SAG's Stunt and Safety Committee, and she subsequently met with Julie once a month for nearly a decade to address the plight of stuntwomen.

"What were the concerns that Julie expressed to you about stuntwomen?" Grey asked.

"They were underemployed," she testified, "and they were deeply concerned about safety conditions on the set."

Then Grey asked Norma a question at the center of Julie's case, "Did Julie express her concern about being retaliated against for bringing these concerns to public attention?"

Julie had good reason to be concerned. Once one of the busiest stuntwomen in the business, job offers ceased entirely after she complained about drugs and safety. She'd been branded a troublemaker, and as brave as stuntmen are, that's the thing they fear the most—troublemakers.

"Yes," Norma replied. "Julie was very concerned about her own employment, as were the other stuntwomen."

"What was Julie's reputation in the industry when she was employed by Spelling-Goldberg Productions?" Grey asked.

"She was one of the most respected women in the stunt community and in her profession," Norma answered.

"Have you seen any significant changes in Julie's personality over the years?" Grey asked her.

"Objection!" Koska said, rising from his chair. "Irrelevant!"

But it was very relevant. The destruction of a personality is always relevant to a jury when considering damages.

"Overruled," the judge declared.

"Yes, I have seen a change," Norma replied.

"What change have you seen?" Grey asked.

"Objection!" Koska interjected. "No foundation! Speculation!"

"Overruled," the judge said.

"She was a very strong woman," Norma replied. "Very sure in her work, very sure of herself, and a leader within the stunt community."

Norma had seen Julie in action—not on the set—but at the bargaining table. Norma had served on SAG's Wages and Working Conditions Committee, which negotiates SAG's major contracts every three years. Julie was part of the negotiating team in 1977 and 1980, and Norma had been very impressed by Julie's performance.

"There was Julie and three stuntmen representing the stunt community," Norma testified. "But in the past few years, and with her unemployment and related problems, I have seen Julie's competence and strength and sureness whittled away."

This was the Julie Johnson that Norma now saw sitting across the courtroom at the plaintiff's table: a less confident Julie, a less hopeful Julie, but not a defeated

Julie. After all, Julie was here, wasn't she? She'd fought her way through the legal system, overcoming every hurdle—even overcoming an attorney who confessed he tried to throw her case on orders from the Mafia. She was here, and she was here to win, and Norma was going to do everything she could to help her.

"In your work with Julie Johnson," Grey asked, "did you become familiar with her reputation in the industry as an advocate of safety procedures?"

"She had a reputation of fighting for safety, for the proper equipment and for it to be properly maintained," Norma responded. "Car, seat belts, brakes, every piece of equipment that had to do with safety she fought for."

"Ms. Connolly, do you have any knowledge of Julie Johnson's efforts to obtain employment opportunities in the entertainment industry after she was terminated by Spelling-Goldberg?" Grey asked.

"She was *very* unemployed," she said, emphasizing the word "very."

Koska jumped from his seat. "Move to strike the response as nonresponsive to the question asked," he declared.

"Overruled," the judge said.

There. Now it was out there. A witness had testified that Julie was unemployable after being fired for whistle-blowing. If the jury came to understand that Julie had been blacklisted for trying to make Hollywood a safer place to work, the damages could be doubled or tripled.

"Did you encounter any of the difficulties that Julie Johnson was experiencing in her efforts to obtain employment after her termination?" Grey asked.

"Yes," she replied.

"On how many occasions did that come to your personal attention?"

"At various times," Norma answered. "On my television show, *General Hospital*, when we employed stuntwomen, they would speak to me about Julie and her problems."

What Norma had heard was that Julie'd been blackballed because she was considered a troublemaker. She didn't get to say so in court because hearsay is not admissible.

But it was true all the same.

Norma Connolly

Chapter 18

"A Piece of Cake"

When Norma stepped down from the witness stand, Judge Savitch excused the jury.

"Ladies and gentlemen," he told the jurors, "there are times when there are things that have to be done outside your presence. This is one of those times."

After the jurors filed out of the courtroom, Julie's attorney set up a video monitor to show the judge and defense counsel a videotape of scenes of Julie working on various episodes of *Charlie's Angels*. Grey wanted to get the judge's permission to show it to the jury the next day to give them an idea of the kind of work Julie did on the show. But one of the scenes held a deeper meaning—a hidden message about the importance of safety on the set. That footage featured an actress who, two years after the scene was shot, would be terribly injured in a stunt that went horribly wrong during filming of the movie *Cannonball Run*. Her name was Heidi von Beltz.

"Your Honor," Grey told the judge, fiddling with the videotape equipment, "I have taken excerpts from *Charlie's Angels* showing stunt work in which Julie Johnson was involved, mostly as stunt coordinator. But Julie can tell us specifically what these episodes were. I'll run it. And forgive my technical bungling here."

Richard Grey was not the most tech savvy of guys.

"If I have a question," the judge said, "Ms. Johnson can clarify it."

Grey pushed a button on the remote control device and started the videotape.

"The first scene," Grey said, "is a fall from a golf cart where Julie did the fall and was doubling for Cheryl Ladd."

After that scene played, a shot of a speedboat was shown racing through choppy waters.

"This second scene has to do with jumping off a boat. And you're doubling for whom in that one?" he asked Julie.

"Shelly Hack," she said.

"The next one will be a fight scene in a women's locker room," Grey said, "with Julie doubling for Jaclyn Smith. And the other girl is Heidi von Beltz, an actress and stuntwoman at that time."

"That is the girl that was crippled in *Cannonball Run* without a seat belt in the car," Julie told the judge.

The judge turned to Julie and scolded her for talking out of turn.

"Ms. Johnson," he said sternly. "Don't make any comments until you are asked to."

She winced at the rebuke but didn't say anything.

Julie first met Heidi just before Christmas 1977 on the set of *Charlie's Angels*. Julie was doubling for Jaclyn Smith in a ferocious fight scene with Heidi, who played a bully on a woman's professional football team. Julie had seen Heidi around—she was Bobby Bass's fiancée, but they'd never worked together or been introduced until now.

"She was a nice kid," Julie recalls. "A beautiful girl with her whole life ahead of her."

Heidi had been given a speaking role on this particular episode in which the Angels go undercover on an all-female pro football team that's being terrorized by a motorcycle gang. Kate Jackson plays the team's quarterback and Cheryl Ladd her tight end.

On the practice field, as the team gets ready for their big game, we see Kate Jackson, being doubled by Julie, dropping back to pass and then throwing a perfect spiral to Cheryl Ladd, who is tackled by a strappingly beautiful six-foot linebacker played by Heidi.

After the tackle, Heidi rubs Cheryl's nose in the dirt.

"Did precious fall down and go boom?" Heidi mocks her.

After practice, Heidi, wearing only flip-flops and a white bath towel, confronts the much smaller Cheryl Ladd in the locker room.

"Well hello, precious," Heidi sneers. "Gonna wash some of that dirt off your nose?"

"How would you like some skin off of your nose?" Cheryl shoots back.

"Cutie pie, you're about a foot short and forty pounds shy of doing me any damage," Heidi says, sauntering menacingly over to her.

Then, as Jaclyn Smith enters the locker room, Heidi shoves Cheryl and walks away.

"Hey," Jaclyn barks at Heidi, grabbing her arm and spinning her around. "How about me? Think I can do you any damage?"

Heidi takes a swing at her, but Jaclyn's character—now being doubled again by Julie—blocks it. Julie then throws a right hook that sends Heidi flying across the room.

Described by one critic as "the most physics-defying fight scene in TV history," the knockdown, drag-out fight lasts nearly a minute on screen—which is a very long time on a one-hour show. In the end, of course, Julie wins and Heidi is held under a cold shower to cool her off.

It was a great scene, and to this day, Julie uses it in her demo reel—film clips to show the best of her work.

A year later, on January 3, 1979, Heidi was on the *Charlie's Angels* location shoot out by Magic Mountain when Julie and Jeannie Coulter nearly lost their lives because Bobby Bass, flying high on cocaine, was driving way too fast.

Heidi wasn't working on the show that day. She was just there as Bobby Bass's girlfriend.

"Heidi was there when we got hurt," Julie recalls. "She was standing on this little slope up above us. I was told, 'There's Heidi von Beltz.' She was there because Bobby was doing the stunt with us."

A little more than a year later, on June 25, 1980, Heidi was shooting *Cannonball Run* in the desert outside Las Vegas when a stunt went horribly wrong. Heidi was doubling in a scene for Farrah Fawcett. It was an easy job. They told her that it was going to be "a piece of cake." All she had to do was sit as a passenger in the front seat of the stunt car as it weaved its way through a line of speeding, oncoming cars.

It could have just as easily been Jeannie Coulter doubling that day for Farrah.

"I was offered that job on *Cannonball Run* but turned it down to do *Jaws II*," Coulter says.

It could have been Julie too.

"It could have been me because I was one of Farrah Fawcett's better doubles," Julie says. "The only reason Heidi was there is because she was Bobby Bass's girlfriend. They told her, 'Oh, it's a simple job. You're just gonna ride in the car. Put the Farrah wig on. That's all you have to do. It's a piece of cake.'"

"Well," Julie muses, "when they say 'a piece of cake,' that's when I was always the most nervous, because 'a piece of cake' was the one where you got hurt."

And Heidi got hurt—real bad.

Heidi didn't know it, but the car she was going to be riding in had been plagued by mechanical problems. The clutch and steering barely worked, and the speedometer didn't work at all. To make matters worse, the car had no seat belts.

Bobby Bass, the film's stunt coordinator, assured Heidi that everything would be okay. His judgment, however, was badly impaired. He was high on coke.

The driver, Jimmy Nickerson, wanted to wait until the car could be repaired, but he was told that the parts from Los Angeles had not arrived and that he'd have to "make do."

"The last thing I remember before the crash was somebody yelling, 'Faster! Faster!' over the walkie-talkie," Heidi recalled.

Then her car slammed head-on into an oncoming car, and she was hurtled into the windshield. When members of the crew got to the scene of the accident, the car was on fire, and they found Heidi unconscious, her head hanging limply on her chest, her neck crushed. In that moment, her life changed forever. She was paralyzed from the neck down, and remains so to this day. After six months in the hospital, Heidi filed a wrongful injury suit and won a $4.5 million jury award.

In those days, most stuntmen observed the code of silence when they saw a fellow stuntman screw up. They might talk about it quietly—or even heatedly—among themselves, but rarely was anyone called out for being too drunk or too stoned to work.

Many stuntmen are like that even today.

Hal Needham—Hollywood's most famous stuntman—is no different.

Needham was the director of *Cannonball Run* and was the chief defendant in Heidi's civil suit. But reading his 2011 book, *Stuntman*, you'd never know that the accident—or the subsequent trial—even happened.

Needham does write of a "big mishap" during filming of *Cannonball Run*, but it had nothing to do with Heidi or the accident that left her a quadriplegic.

"A few days into the shoot," he writes, "we had a big mishap . . . We were shooting at the motel where we were staying. It was a night scene, and the cameraman brought in a twenty-ton truck crane. He hung a bunch of lights on it to light the parking lot where we'd positioned all the cars that were in the race, plus some exotic cars as background . . . The operator raised the crane arm with the attached lights and swung it to one side to place the lights over the parking lot. As the rig's weight shifted, the outriggers—the legs that balance the crane—sank into some mud, and down it came. The crane arm landed on a Ferrari, which was suddenly only three feet high, about $12,000 worth of lights scattered across the parking lot, and the crane lay on its side. The only good thing was, nobody got hurt."

No mention in the entire book of Heidi von Beltz—just a funny story about a crane that fell over. No mention of the fiery crash that nearly killed her, crushed her spinal cord, and left her in a wheelchair for life—just a funny story about a Ferrari that got squashed. No mention of the subsequent civil trial and verdict, in which a jury ordered Needham and his corporation, Stuntman, Inc., to pay Heidi $4.5 million in damages—just a funny story about $12,000 worth of lights that got broken.

In the Mafia, it's called omertà. In Hollywood, it's called the code of silence.

Julie had worked with Needham many times throughout their long careers. She never got seriously injured working with him, but she nearly got killed four times.

She first worked with him in the late 1960s on a shoot-and-run for a TV show that needed footage of a car nearly going off a cliff in the Hollywood Hills. The producers needed the shot done fast, so they didn't bother obtaining the permits required to film on the streets of Los Angeles. Needham would be the driver and Julie the passenger.

"It was just me and Hal, the cameraman, and a production manager," Julie recalls. "We were sneakin' a shot somewhere in the hills off of Mulholland Drive—one of those white-knuckle jobs where you hang on for dear life."

The producers needed a shot of a car roaring down a mountain road, skidding into a U-turn, and then barreling back up the hill.

"The production manager came over to me on the passenger side of the car and says, 'Oh, you got the white-knuckle job, huh?'" Julie recalls with a laugh. "I didn't know what that meant until after the shot."

They did two practice runs, and then they shot the scene.

"On the third run," Julie recalls, "Hal came down the hill and threw the car into a skid. The wheels were spinning, and he went off the road and was in the dirt. The ass-end of the car was so close to the cliff—I looked out my window, and if we'd gone six inches farther, we would have been off the road and down the cliff."

"Oh my god!" Julie thought as she looked out the side window at the one-hundred-foot drop stretching out below. "Then, for some reason, the tires grabbed the road. Hal hit the gas, and we were out of there."

It was her first brush with death with Hal Needham—but it wouldn't be her last.

A year later, Julie was filming *Little Big Man* in Calgary, Canada, during one of the coldest winters there on record. One day it hit fifty below zero.

The film, which stars Dustin Hoffman, tells the fictional story of the only white survivor of the Battle of Little Big Horn. Julie was hired for stunts, and Needham was the stunt coordinator.

One day, they were shooting a scene in which the cavalry rides in to massacres an Indian village. Julie, playing an Indian woman, got her directions from Hal: she was to run toward the camera and then, simulating being shot, fall and slide to within five feet of the camera position—with horses galloping all around her.

Preparing for the stunt, she placed a rock where she was supposed to fall, and when the director yelled "Action!" she ran toward the camera. When she hit her mark, she fell in front of the camera and lay there for a moment.

"I did it," she says, "and the last thing I remember hearing was someone yelling, 'Bring the horse through here! Bring the horse through here!'

It was so cold that day that all of the horses' hooves had become caked with mud that had turned to ice. The ground was frozen solid, and the horses, each with balls of ice on their hooves, were sliding around as if they were on a skating rink.

"Well, there's five feet between my head and the camera," Julie recalls, "and these horses are running around on balls of ice, and they're slippin' and slidin' and their feet are going every which way. It's a wonder they could even stay on their feet. Some of 'em went down. But this one that came through between me and the camera clipped the side of my head with its hoof, and I got spun around 180 degrees."

Julie was knocked unconscious, and the next thing she remembers was somebody yelling to her, "Don't get up! Don't get up!"

"What happened?" she asked, still in a haze.

"You got kicked in the head by a horse," a man's voice told her, and to this day, she doesn't know who it was—whether it was Needham or the director, Arthur Penn, or the second unit director. She just doesn't know.

"Oh, okay," she said blithely.

"We got the shot," he said. "You can go get warm in the bus, and we'll see you tomorrow."

She went to the bus and sat there in a daze. No one came to give her any medical attention, and the next day she went back to work. Fortunately, she'd been wearing an Indian wig when she was kicked, and that padded the blow to her head. But to this day, she still has a dent in the side of her head where the horse kicked her.

And it could have been much worse. Had the horse's hoof hit her an inch or two more squarely on the head, it could have easily fractured her skull or broken her neck.

Two years later, Julie was working with Needham again on the pilot of a short-lived NBC TV series called *The Magician*, which starred Bill Bixby as a wealthy illusionist who uses his conjuring skills to help people in trouble.

Julie had been swimming in her backyard pool one day in 1973 when she got a call from Teddy's—the phone service that nearly everyone in the stunt community used back in those days.

"Hello?" Julie said, toweling herself off.

"We have a request for you from Hal Needham," Teddy told her. "He wants you to fly to Michigan. He has a job for you. It's a transfer from a boat to an airplane."

"When is it?" she asked.

"You would have to leave tomorrow morning from LAX."

"Well, okay," she said.

"Let me call them back to confirm," Teddy said. "I'll give you a buzz as soon as I know the time of your departure and your hotel. Oh, I almost forgot. Dress warm. The temperature there is twenty-eight degrees. Bye."

Julie caught a flight to Detroit the next morning and was taken by a company car to the location on the shores of Lake Michigan. As Teddy had warned her, it was freezing.

She checked in at the wardrobe trailer, where she changed out of her warm clothes and into a skimpy little dress, stockings, a coat, and shoes with low heels. She walked over to the makeup trailer and, looking down toward the lake, noticed Needham, the show's stunt coordinator, talking to a couple of the crewmembers.

After hair and makeup were done, she walked down to the set. There was a boat and a seaplane and, spreading out before her as far as she could see, Lake Michigan. It was cold, but the lake was beautiful. There was no wind, and the water was smooth as glass.

Hal was talking to the boat driver.

"How fast have you done in this boat?" he asked.

"Forty miles an hour," the driver replied. "Maybe forty-five."

"I know you're not a stunt driver," Needham told him, "but you'll have to go eighty-five to have the same speed as the plane at the time of transfer."

"Eighty-five?" the driver asked, his eyes widening in disbelief. He knew, theoretically, that under the right conditions—under perfect conditions—the boat could probably go that fast. But it would be awfully risky. Not just for the boat and its engine but also for anybody who was in it—or in its way.

Julie took all this in as she stood on the dock, watching a worker remove the door on the seaplane that would lift her and Needham out of the boat—at eighty-five miles an hour. The plane's pontoons, she noticed, were covered in ice. That was not good. She kicked at the ice on the skid, but it wouldn't come off. It was frozen solid. Needham, hearing the thud of her shoe on the icy skid, turned and was pleased to see her.

"Hey, Julie," he said, a big smile spreading across his ruggedly handsome face. "What's up?"

"Hey, Hal," she said. "You know, there's ice on the pontoons. We won't have a good footing. Could we get a strip of corrugated rubber?"

Hal looked down at the skid, a dumb look on his face. He obviously hadn't noticed that before. He gave the ice a kick with a heavy boot, but only a small chip flew off.

"Harry," he said authoritatively to the guy removing the plane's door. "Remove the ice on the pontoons and lay a strip of corrugated rubber on there for the lady."

Turning back to Julie with a wry smile, he said, "This is going to be a bitch and a half of a stunt—no cable, no harness, and both the pilot and the speedboat driver are locals!"

They both laughed, even though there was nothing funny about the situation.

Half an hour later, Julie, Hal, and the driver were in the boat, cruising along the calm waters of Lake Michigan, preparing to start the rehearsal run.

Hal picked up the two-way radio and said something to the pilot, whose plane Julie couldn't see, but could hear somewhere above and behind her.

Then, turning to Julie, he filled her in on how the stunt was going to work.

"I go first," he said in a loud voice, which she could barely hear above the roar of the boat's engine. "I had special effects rig an extra strut on the plane so I can wrap my leg around as a support to grab you safely. Then, when both of us are on the pontoon, I'll get you into the plane and follow you in."

Julie nodded. At least she thought she did. She was shivering so hard it felt like her whole body was nodding. It was twenty-eight degrees, but out on the lake, with the spray and the cold air rushing past them, it felt like twenty-eight below.

Suddenly, she saw the plane swoop down behind them, moving into position for the trial run.

"Get up to speed!" Needham yelled at the boat driver. "And don't look back at the plane, or we'll have one hell of a wreck!"

The driver gunned the boat's engine, and Julie swayed backward, steadying herself against the thrust. Looking over at the boat's speedometer, she saw its needle hit seventy-four knots—eighty-five miles per hour.

The seaplane roared up from behind them, and the pilot brought the pontoon right up to eye level—close enough to grab on to. The boat and the plane held their positions for a few seconds, and then the plane peeled away, climbing back into the crystal blue sky.

"That was perfect!" Needham yelled. "Too bad the cameras weren't rolling. We should have shot the rehearsal!"

The driver eased back on the throttle, bringing the boat back down to cruising speed.

"Okay," Needham told the driver. "Let's go back to our start point."

A few minutes later, they did it again—only this time the camera on shore was rolling.

As before, the boat got up to speed and the seaplane swooped down from behind. When the plane and boat matched speeds, the pilot descended just enough so that Needham could clamber onto the pontoon. Now safely secure on the skid, he reached down and took Julie's hand and then, with all his might, pulled her up onto the pontoon next to him.

It was freezing cold out there on the landing skid of the seaplane. They were both soaked with icy water from the spray of the boat, and the air was rushing past them at near-hurricane speed. It was like being bit by a tornado in an Antarctic carwash.

Suddenly, the plane began a steep ascent, sheering away from the speedboat below. The hard tug of gravity nearly pulled them off the pontoon and into the frigid lake one hundred feet below. Had they lost their grip, they would have been killed for sure—neither was secured to the plane by a harness or wire.

When the plane leveled off, Needham gave Julie a good push on the rump, shoving her through the plane's open door. A few seconds later, he scrambled in behind her. Whew! They both breathed a sigh of relief. Needham reached out his right hand to shake Julie's; their hands were so cold, they nearly stuck together.

The next day, back at their hotel, Hal, Julie, the camera crew, and the show's unit production manager were looking at a monitor watching the dailies. As the footage of the boat-to-plane transfer scene was played, Needham became increasingly upset. Finally, he could no longer control his anger.

"Where's the stunt?" he exploded. "Where was the camera? You can hardly see what we did! Where is the second angle?"

Nobody said anything.

"You mean there was not a second angle?" he bellowed. "Great! We'll have to do it again."

"You can't," the UPM answered timidly. "It's too expensive."

"Oh yes, we can," Needham shot back. "You pay the lady, and I'll do it for free. I won't have my work being second-rate!"

"We would have to move," the UPM answered, even more timidly than before. "We only rented the location for one day."

"Then find another location and get an extra boat to follow us," Needham ordered.

Two days later, they were at it again. Only now the wind had come up, and the lake was very choppy—like the Pacific Ocean having bad day. And it was even colder than before.

Julie and Hal were back in the boat, and the driver was trying to get it up to speed. To Julie, the air rushing by, mixed with bow spray, felt like frozen needles slashing at her face. Looking out over the dark lake, she half-expected to see icebergs floating by.

"Remember, eighty-five!" Needham barked at the driver. Then, into his two-way radio, he yelled at the camera crews, "Shoot the rehearsal!"

The driver gave it full throttle, and the boat bucked like an untamed rodeo horse. Behind them, a chase boat and camera crew tried to keep up.

Between the howl of the wind and the roar of the engine, Julie didn't even hear the seaplane when it swooped down and settled in right over their heads. The waves buffeted the boat up and down, and the wind did the same to the plane. The pilot and the boat driver were going to have to time their ups and downs just perfectly if Hal and Julie were going to be able to make the transfer.

Hal reached up for the pontoon, but the plane moved just out of his grasp. On the second try, as the boat and plane jockeyed for position, he grabbed the pontoon; but a gust of wind turned the plane sideways, the massive, whirling propeller coming only inches from his head. Instinctively, Julie grabbed him by the back of his coat and pulled him back into the boat.

"I wonder if they got *that* on film," she wondered.

Hal gave it another try. This time, when the boat and plane aligned, he grabbed hold of the pontoon and pulled himself out of the boat. Wrapping his leg around the added strut, he reached out and took Julie's hand, but the wind blew her back into the boat. Finally, Julie reached up and grabbed his forearm and he yanked her onto the pontoon. And when they scrambled in through the open door to safety, the camera team in the chase boat burst into spontaneous applause.

"Hal was relieved when it was over," Julie recalls. "You could see it on his face."

Julie was relieved too. They'd defied death, and all for the sake of a silly little TV show that nobody even remembers today.

Three years later, in 1976, Julie was working with Needham again on a movie called *Nickelodeon*, a comedy about the early days of silent movies. Once again, the scene called for Julie—doubling for actress Jane Hitchcock—to be dangling high in the air, only this time, instead of from an airplane, it would be from a hot-air balloon. Needham, doubling for Burt Reynolds, would be in the gondola, pulling her to safety.

It was a great scene; the studio even used it in the poster for the film.

But it almost got Julie and Hal killed—again.

In the film, Julie's character is accidentally pulled into the air by the balloon when the rope securing it to the ground comes loose and wraps around her leg. Hal's character has to pull her into the basket to save her from a fatal fall.

In real life, there was no real danger of Julie falling. She was suspended, hanging upside down, by a cable secured to a harness around her waist. The cable, in turn, was attached to an electric winch in the gondola, which would pull her up, while looking like Hal's character was pulling her, hand over hand, into the basket.

But there was an unforeseen danger that day—the wind. It was breezy at ground level, but higher up—where the balloon would be—it was really blowing, with gusts up to forty to fifty miles an hour. The ground crew, however, wouldn't realize it until the balloon, tethered to the ground by three strong cables, began its ascent, with Julie dangling upside down ten feet below.

Halfway up, the basket started rocking in the high wind. Julie was being tossed around like a puppet hanging from a string in a wind tunnel.

Then, when the balloon got about one hundred feet up in the air—stretching the three cables tight—one of the cables holding the balloon to the ground snapped, falling uselessly to the ground. This sent the balloon—and Julie—careening across the sky until the other two cables took hold. Then the second cable snapped.

Needham, in the basket, saw that they were in serious trouble. He started winching Julie back into the basket, while at the same time yelling into the two-way radio, "Get us down! Get us down!"

If the third cable broke, there'd be no telling where they'd come down—miles away, perhaps, tangled in power lines or snagged by tree branches or slammed against the side of a building. Fortunately, Hal was able to pull Julie back into the basket, and the ground crew was able to pull the balloon safely back down to the ground.

"It was dicey," Julie recalls. "Real dicey."

And another close call working with Needham.

"Hal was one of the best in the business," she says. "It was a pleasure and a privilege to work with him. He knew his craft, and I learned a lot."

In his book, he doesn't even mention Julie or their many harrowing adventures together. But Julie doesn't mind. The life of a Hollywood stuntwoman is pretty unheralded anyway. And besides, she has her own story to tell.

"Nickelodeon" with Stuntman Hal Needham, Columbia Pictures

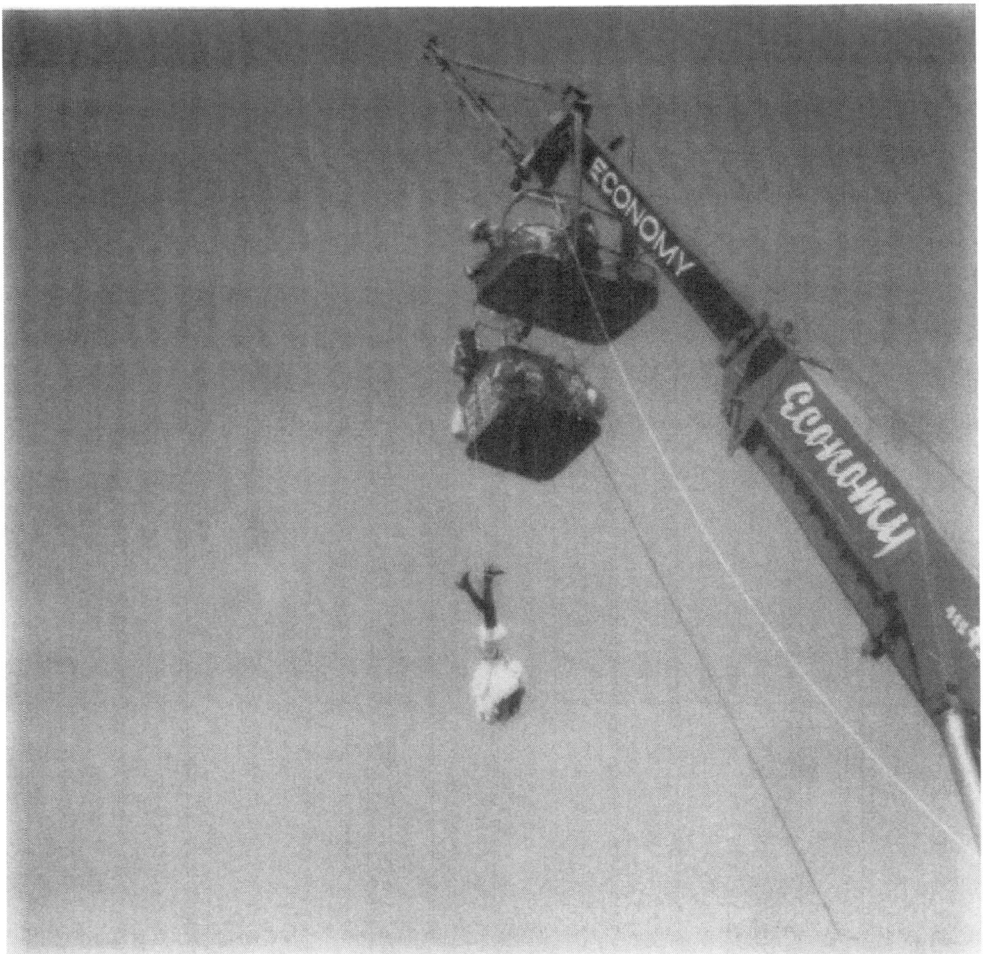
ECONOMY
Economy

Chapter 19

A Sad Good-bye

Julie's ninth stunt began the day after she kissed Eddie good-bye, when her father and stepmother, Margo, drove her to the airport and put her on a plane bound for Caracas, Venezuela. She might as well have been flying down to hell.

Julie had been thirteen years old—not yet in high school—when her mother left for Venezuela, where Stan had a job working as a maintenance man for an American oil company. Julie hadn't seen or talked to her mother in four years. That would have been a hardship for most teenage girls growing up in the 1950s, but for Julie it was a blessing. She loved her mother dearly, but her mother's drinking had become too much for her to bear. For four years, Julie'd lived a normal life, with sober parents, in a middle-class town in Orange County. Now she was being sent to live with two drunks in the middle of a bug-infested jungle in South America.

"I'd finally become used to not having a mother, and it pained me to have to see her again," Julie recalls many years later. "I wondered if she and my stepfather still drank as much as they used to. Was I headed there for more of the same thing? I would have to get to know my mother all over again. It was a very unsettling time."

Her dad and stepmom waved good-bye as she boarded the plane, the flagship of the American Airlines fleet—a four-engine DC-7—for the first leg of her trip to Venezuela: LAX to New Orleans. She took her seat by the window, placed her carry-on bag under her seat, and buckled up. Pretty stewardesses stationed around the cabin gave a prepared safety speech, pointing in unison to the emergency exists, and demonstrating, as if in a silent movie, how to use the oxygen mask if the plane suddenly lost cabin pressure.

Julie looked out the window and saw the giant twin engines on her side of the plane roar to life, spewing clouds of black smoke as the propellers spun into action. The plane taxied down the runway, and when it took off, Julie was thrust back hard in her seat. She stared down as the runway fell away below her, and then they were out over the blue Pacific. Up ahead, she could see Catalina, where she'd spent a happy weekend with her mom and dad when she was a kid. Still gaining altitude, the plane banked hard and turned back over the city. Far below she could see the hills of Palos Verdes and, off in the distance somewhere, Orange County. One of those specks out there, she knew, was her little house in Fullerton.

Cityscape turned to desert, then mountains, then vast stretches of farmland—a giant green quilt stitched together by dirt roads.

She pulled her carry-on bag out from under her seat and took out her high school yearbook. All the kids had signed it. "Stay as sweet as you are," one of her friends wrote. "You're going to be the first girl to play for the Yankees!" wrote another. But most of them wrote on the same theme: "Have a great summer!" If only they knew.

Julie turned to the page with her photo. She was a beautiful girl, although she didn't think so anymore. Her hair was perfect, and the little fake pearl necklace was just the right touch. But the look on her face was so sad. Everyone else on her page was smiling but her. Just the day before the picture was taken, she'd been told that she was being sent to stay with her mother in Venezuela and that she wouldn't be seeing Eddie for the whole summer. She looked like the saddest girl in Fullerton. She looked like the homecoming queen of the Class of Nineteen-Fifty-Sad.

It was six o'clock when the stewardesses pushed the food and beverage cart down the aisle to begin serving dinner. At least it was six o'clock back in Orange County. She had no idea what time it was in whatever time zone they were in now.

Julie put her yearbook in the little pouch in the seatback in front of her, which contained the emergency evacuation instructions and a *Trailways* magazine. She pulled down the tray table. and when it was her turn to be served, the pretty young stewardess asked her if she'd like chicken or beef. She asked for the beef, but it tasted like chicken.

She picked at her salad and sipped her Coke. There was no one to talk to. The plane was half empty, and there was no one else sitting in her row.

It was dark outside when the stewardess came back to pick up her tray. Far below, Julie could see the twinkling lights of some small town, and high above, a crescent moon, with the planet Venus hanging nearby, and more stars than she'd ever imagined possible. It would have been beautiful if she hadn't been too lonely to notice.

Looking out the window, she wondered what was awaiting her in Venezuela. She wondered where she'd sleep, what she'd eat, what she'd wear. But mostly she wondered if her mother was still drinking. She wouldn't have to wonder long.

She looked at her watch. It was half past seven. She hadn't changed the hour hand; she was still on California time. She wondered if Eddie, at that moment, was looking at *his* watch—the one she'd given him before she left. She closed her eyes and thought about him, hoping that he was thinking of her too. She remembered their first kiss at the drive-in—long and tender and sweet—and wondered if he remembered it that way too.

She fell asleep thinking about Eddie and woke up when she heard the captain's voice come over the intercom.

"Ladies and gentlemen," he said in a thick Texas twang, "I've turned on the fasten-seat-belt sign. We'll be starting our descent on approach to Moisant Field. Local time in New Orleans is ten fifteen. Please remain seated until the plane has landed and we've come to a complete stop. Thank you, and thanks for flying American Airlines. Y'all have a real good time in the Big Easy, now, 'ya hear?"

Julie wouldn't be having a good time in New Orleans. And she knew that if anyone on the plane was coming home for their father's funeral, or to visit their dying mother, that they wouldn't be having a good time either. It was hard for her to imagine that she'd ever have another good time.

The plane landed hard and taxied to the terminal. Julie pulled her carry-on bag out from under her seat and got off the plane, walked down the portable staircase, crossed the tarmac, and entered the terminal. She'd only been in two other airport terminals in her life—the one at LAX and the one in Mexico City—and this one was much more like the one in Mexico City, except all the signs were in English. Named after a local hero she'd never heard of, it was shabby and empty. It looked more like an abandoned bus terminal than an airport.

She looked at her ticket; it said, "Avensa—Flight 16, Gate 4, 11:50 p.m." She had an hour to kill. She walked through the hangar-like terminal to Gate 4, found a seat, and waited for someone from Avensa Airlines to start boarding passengers. Before long, she fell asleep curled up in a ball as best she could in the small, hard seat, her head resting uncomfortably on the padded arm rest.

Half an hour later, she was bounced awake by a little kid and his mother who'd sat down beside her. Groups of people were milling about, waiting for the departure.

Husbands and wives, fathers and children, brothers and sisters, friends and lovers, all hugging and kissing, were saying their good-byes. Julie didn't have anyone to hug or kiss, and as far as she was concerned, there was nothing good about this good-bye.

A line had formed and Julie got in it. She showed her ticket and followed her fellow passengers through the doors back out onto the tarmac and up another portable staircase. The people in front of her stopped halfway up to wave good-bye to their loved ones. Julie didn't look back. She had no one to wave to.

On board the twin-engine Convair 340, she took her seat and starred gloomily out the window. The engines started, the plane taxied down the runway and then took off. Down below, New Orleans was lit up like fireflies on a Christmas tree.

Then darkness. The Gulf of Mexico, black as a Bible, stretched out ahead all the way to Havana, illuminated here and there by the running lights of a shrimp boat or an offshore oil rig.

The plane lurched. Lightning flashes lit up dark clouds in the distance. It started to rain. Water rolled down her window like tears. Julie was tired, but she couldn't sleep. Bored, she reached down under her seat and felt around in her carry-on bag for her yearbook. It wasn't there. It must have fallen out. She unbuckled her seat belt and got down on her hands and knees to look for it under her seat. It wasn't there either. Then she remembered. She'd put it in the little pouch in the seatback in front of her on the flight from LAX and forgotten it there when she got off the plane in New Orleans.

Her last link to the happy life she'd left only a few hours ago was now gone. Her boyfriend was gone, her friends were gone, and now her yearbook was gone. Overcome by despair, she felt like she'd disappeared, like her whole life had been erased, like she'd lost not only her yearbook but also everyone in it, including herself. But she didn't cry. She refused to cry. She would take whatever fate dished out, no matter what, without tears.

She was still on her hands and knees when a stewardess came by.

"You'll have to get back in your seat, ma'am," she said sternly. "There's severe weather up ahead."

Julie got up from the floor and sat back down in her seat. The stewardess buckled her in and left without saying another word. Julie watched as she walked away, holding on to the seatbacks to keep her balance as the plane bucked and bounced its way through the dark and turbulent sky. She'd never been called ma'am before, and now, on top of losing everything else, she felt like she'd just lost her youth.

After a bumpy seven-hour flight, the plane finally landed in Caracas. It was raining, and stepping off the plane, Julie could tell right away that the air was different. From her mother's letters, Julie knew that Venezuela was tropical, but now she could feel it, she could smell it. Back in California, when it rained, it was usually cold. But here it was raining and unbelievably hot at the same time.

As Julie and the other passengers descended single file down the portable metal stairway to the tarmac, airline workers rushed out with umbrellas to keep them from getting soaked. Julie got soaked anyway.

Standing in line, waiting to go through customs, Julie got her first glimpse of her mother in four years, and at first she almost didn't recognize her. Virginia's auburn hair was darker and shorter now, but the most striking change was that she appeared to be sober. She looked happy and healthy and smiled broadly when she caught Julie's eye.

After clearing customs, Julie lugged her carry-on bag out into the crowded terminal and embraced her mother warmly.

Virginia had flown in the night before from Anaco, the tiny oil town in the middle of the Venezuelan jungle where she and Stan had been living the last four years.

"It's good to see you, darling," Virginia said.

"It's good to see you too, Mom."

Virginia took Julie's hand and walked her out of the terminal. Several beat-up old taxis were lined up at the curb.

"Cuánto?" Virginia asked one of the drivers—"How much?"

"A dónde vas?" he asked—"Where you going?"

Virginia told him the name of the hotel.

"Quince bolívares," he replied—"About four American dollars."

"Diez," she bargained—"Three dollars."

"Okay," he said in English.

They put their bags in the trunk and got into the backseat of the cab. There were no seat belts. The driver, a man in his mid-forties, adjusted his rearview mirror so that he could see Julie's face whenever he glanced up. He pulled away from the curb and headed toward downtown Caracas. The streets were jammed with every kind of beat-up old American car imaginable. Bicyclists and scooters weaved crazily between the cars, which changed lanes without signaling. There didn't seem to be any crosswalks, and pedestrians crossed the streets whenever there was the tiniest opening in the traffic. Then it started pouring—monsoonal rain. It was coming down in sheets, like they were driving under a waterfall. The driver turned on his windshield wipers and then glanced into his rearview mirror. Catching Julie's eye, he grinned, exposing a dead front tooth. Julie and her mom rolled up their windows. It was sweltering, and there was no air-conditioning. Then, just as quickly as it had started, it stopped raining. In unison, Julie and her mom rolled down their windows. It was hot inside the cab, and the breeze helped a little, but not much.

They didn't talk much on the way to the hotel, and every question Virginia asked seemed to begin with the word "so"—a telltale sign of disinterest in the answer.

"So how was your flight?"

"So how's your dad these days?"

"So how was your graduation?"

"So how do you like our weather?"

Julie could have answered all of her mother's questions with the same word—"fine"—but she didn't want to be rude, so she tossed in a few extra words, all delivered in a monotone.

"It was fine. A little bumpy, but not too bad."

"Oh, he's fine. He says to say hello."

"It was very nice. Wish you could have been there."

"I've never seen rain like this."

Her only answer that was true was the last one.

When they pulled up to the hotel, a young bellhop in a snappy red uniform came out and opened their doors and helped Julie with her bags. Virginia paid the driver and took her daughter upstairs. Virginia tipped the bellhop, and Julie opened her suitcase and went into the bathroom to change. When she came out, she was wearing jeans and a T-shirt.

"So is this what kids are wearing these days?" her mother asked.

They went downstairs to the restaurant and seated themselves at a table by the window. When the waiter came, Virginia ordered a gin and tonic. It wasn't even noon yet.

"It's the tropics," her mom said in all seriousness. "You have to stay hydrated."

Such a fancy word for boozing, Julie thought, but didn't say a thing.

They ate lunch. Virginia had a salad. Julie had a cheeseburger and fries. It would be the last cheeseburger she'd have in a long time.

Later that evening at dinner, Virginia ordered another gin and tonic. After dinner, she ordered another. In four years, the only thing about her that had changed was her hair.

The next morning, they got up early, called a cab, and went back to the airport. It was only a short forty-five-minute flight to Anaco, but the landing would be hairy.

Not long after the twin-engine prop plane got into the air, a stewardess pushed the beverage cart down the aisle. Julie asked for a Coke. Virginia ordered a gin and tonic.

Julie didn't know it then, but the runway at the airport was notoriously short. Planes were always skidding off the runway and into the jungle. Sometimes, people got hurt. Sometimes they got killed.

Julie looked out the window as the plane began its approach. Down below, jungle stretched out as far as she could see. Up ahead, she saw the tiny runway that had been cut out of the tropical rain forest—a swath so narrow that it looked like the jungle could reclaim it at any moment.

The pilot said something over the intercom in Spanish that Julie didn't understand, even though she'd spent part of a school year in Mexico. She assumed it was "fasten your seat belts," but she feared it was "brace yourself for a crash landing." So she fastened her seat belt and braced herself for a crash landing.

The plane came in high and hit the runway hard. The brakes shrieked, and suddenly, the plane started shaking like it was coming apart. But it didn't. It was just the pilot reversing thrust to slow the plane down so it wouldn't skid off the runway.

The plane slowed and taxied to the terminal—a tiny building no bigger than her dad's house back in Fullerton. When the plane stopped, Julie and her mom got off and walked to the terminal to get their bags.

Stan was waiting for them at the gate. He pecked Virginia on the cheek and gave Julie a big hug. Then, holding her at arms' length, he said, "My, my my! You have turned into a lovely young woman!"

Julie blushed and smiled—her first real smile in South America. It was the nicest thing Stan had ever said to her. Maybe he'd changed. Maybe things weren't going to be so bad after all.

It was hot and humid inside the terminal, like a sauna. It was the rainy season, so everything was damp. Even the air was damp. Looking around, Julie noticed that there were puddles of water on the floor. Apparently the roof leaked when it rained, which was pretty much every day. The place smelled of mold and aviation fuel.

This was her fourth airport in two days—the airport at the end of the world. It really was a *terminal*—like a terminal disease, like terminal cancer. It was the end of the line, the end of the road, the end of the world.

They collected their bags, went outside, and got into Stan's car, an old Opel without air-conditioning. They pulled away from the tiny airport, and within half a mile, they were surrounded on both sides of the two-lane road by dense jungle. It started raining, and they all rolled up their windows. Stan switched on the windshield wipers, but the blades barely kept up with the pounding downpour. It was stifling hot inside the little car. Then, just as quickly as it had started, the rain stopped. In unison, they all rolled down their windows.

As they drove along, Julie saw an occasional clearing with three or four little cardboard huts with tin roofs and children playing in the mud. Sometimes there'd be a hammock strung between two trees. Sometimes there'd be chickens or a pig. Everything was wet.

"Jesus Christ!" Stan shouted and slammed on the brakes, thrusting Julie and her mother forward in their seats.

Two wet and scraggly cows, their ribs showing through their sides, had wandered out of the jungle onto the road, and Stan had to skid to keep from hitting them. Julie watched as they sauntered slowly across the road and disappeared back into the jungle.

"That happens all the time," Virginia whispered. "There are these half-starving cows down here that don't belong to anyone, just wandering around."

"Poor things," Julie muttered under her breath, feeling a sad kinship with the homeless cows.

A few miles down the road, Stan turned onto a side road you wouldn't know was there unless you knew it was there. A little ways farther, the Halliburton compound sprang up out of a clearing in the jungle. There were several little houses where the oilfield workers lived, a few shops, and a nine-hole golf course.

Virginia pointed to a large corrugated metal building with padlocked double steel doors, a sloping tin roof, and rusted, discarded pieces of indeterminate equipment scattered all around. "That's Stan's shop," she said, a false sense of pride in her voice.

It looked like a junkyard.

The road wound back into the jungle, and then Stan turned onto a muddy road that took them to their little three-room house. Stan stopped the car. They got out, unloaded their bags, and walked carefully along the muddy wooden planks leading to the front door. Julie stopped and looked around. She was surrounded by jungle on all sides.

"Welcome home, Splinter Butt," Stan said, and he and Virginia burst into laughter.

It *was* just like old times—except for the jungle and the monsoon rains, the ubiquitous mud and the starving cows, the strange insects and neighbors living in cardboard huts, the swarms of mosquitoes and the venomous snakes, the centipedes and flies and spiders and stinging red ants that seemed to get into everything.

In a few months, Julie would celebrate her eighteenth birthday in the middle of this steaming wilderness. A year after that, she'd turn nineteen down there, and then twenty. What she thought was going to be two and a half months in Venezuela turned into two and a half years in hell.

CHAPTER 20

Kathleen Nolan

"Call your next witness," the judge told Julie's attorney.

"Thank you, Your Honor," Grey said. "The plaintiff calls Kathleen Nolan."

Julie turned and took a deep breath when she saw the clerk escorting Nolan into the courtroom. At fifty-four, Nolan wasn't just beautiful, she was regal, her reddish blond hair combed straight back, an air of stately perfection about her. A crown wouldn't have looked out of place on her head at all—at least not to Julie. Kathleen Nolan was Julie's all-time hero.

Nolan looked like royalty, but she was actually a working class hero. As the first female president of the Screen Actors Guild, she'd fought for the little guy. She was a champion of the underdog, a crusader for women's rights, a heroine to all stuntwomen.

Julie's heart swelled with gratitude as the great woman walked past her. They shared a glance, and Julie smiled broadly. Kathleen Nolan was taking the stand—for her! To Julie, it almost made the horrendous ordeal she'd been through worthwhile.

Nolan, the daughter of show business parents, got her first acting job aboard a Mississippi showboat when she was only thirteen months old. At six, she negotiated her first contract, but she didn't just negotiate a raise for herself—she got one for everyone in the cast.

"When I was six years old," she later recalled, "I negotiated a raise for myself with the captain of the showboat because I was making fifty cents and everybody else was earning $2.50 a night, and I didn't think that was right. So I went to him on my own, and I not only ended up with my raise but everybody went up to $3.00. That was my first negotiation."

Disarmingly self-confident, with riveting green eyes, she was a born leader—and a born union leader.

She'd already enjoyed a distinguished acting career. She'd starred in her first Broadway play when she was sixteen, playing Wendy in *Peter Pan*. After that, she starred in four more Broadway shows, several movies, and dozens of TV shows. She was, in fact, one of the most sought-after actresses in television, guest starring on such shows as *Magnum, P.I., Quincy, The Rockford Files, The Bionic Woman, Bewitched, The Untouchables, Ben Casey*, and many, many more.

But she is perhaps best remembered, by those of a certain age, as Kate on *The Real McCoys*, a hugely popular TV show of the late '50s and early '60s, costarring as Richard Crenna's young wife.

Her most important role, however, was as a union leader—a real-life Norma Rae.

In 1964, she got into a public dispute with a talent agency that was taking advantage of its clients. That came to the attention of her famous friend, Charlton Heston, who was then second vice president of the Screen Actors Guild.

"He felt very strongly that I was the kind of person SAG needed on the board of directors because I wasn't afraid to fight back," she recalled.

Nolan was appointed to the SAG board and then quickly rose through the union's ranks. In 1972, she became the founding chairperson of the guild's newly created Women's Committee and, in 1973, became the first woman ever elected SAG first vice president. Two years later, she defeated four candidates—all men—to become the first woman president of the Screen Actors Guild. She won reelection to a second two-year term in 1977. A year later, she led a three-month strike that won better wages and working conditions for commercial actors.

On the Women's Committee, Nolan became a champion for fair treatment and equal pay for stuntwomen; and in 1978, while guest starring on a *Charlie's Angels* episode that was shooting in Vail, Colorado, she witnessed firsthand the kind of gender discrimination that stuntwomen face every day.

Julie was Nolan's stunt double on that show. They'd worked together many times before, and whenever Nolan was on a job that involved stunts, she always asked for Julie. They both admired each other's work.

One scene called for Julie to drive a snowmobile up a ramp and into the air, land safely on its skis, and then race down the hill. Julie wanted to do it, but the producers said no and replaced her on the job with a stuntman. It was a humiliating experience for Julie, made all the worse because it happened in front of her hero. But it would play an important role in Julie's case when Nolan was called to testify on her behalf.

The clerk read the oath, and Nolan swore that she would tell the truth, the whole truth, and nothing but the truth. And Julie knew that she would too.

"Would you please tell us your background and experience in the entertainment industry?" Grey asked.

Nolan had been working in show business all her life, so it took a while for her to tell it all.

"I suppose during the course of my television career I've done most of the major episodic series," she said, summing up.

"Are you personally acquainted with Aaron Spelling?" Grey asked.

"Yes," she replied.

"How long have you known Mr. Spelling?"

"Since the 1950s," she said. "I bought my first house in Los Angeles from him."

"Have you ever worked for Aaron Spelling as an actress?"

"Many times," she said. "I've worked for Mr. Spelling in his early days in television on *Burke's Law* to the present times of *Love Boat* and *Charlie's Angels* and have been acquainted with him personally over that period of time."

"Do you know Julie Johnson?" he asked.

"Yes," she replied, "since the early '70s. She was my stunt double on a miniseries at Universal called *Testimony of Two Men*."

Even before meeting Julie, Nolan said, she'd heard of her reputation as a great stuntwoman and a leader in the stunt community.

"How many times did Julie Johnson double for you?" he asked.

"At least ten times," she said. "I would always request her if she was available."

"Why did you request Julie Johnson?" Grey asked.

"Because she is a good double for me," Nolan replied, "and she had an excellent reputation, and as an actor . . . it's an extension of what you do and what you are seen doing on the screen, and it's very important in terms of what the public sees me doing on screen."

"Were you ever, in any way, dissatisfied with the quality of her work?" Grey asked.

"No," Nolan said emphatically. "Never."

Grey then asked her about the snowmobile incident in Vail.

"There were several stunts with snowmobiles," Nolan testified. "There was some snowmobile business about which there was great deal of talk, because they were using a man to double for a woman. So it was a very big deal because Julie was the coordinator."

"Did Julie tell you that she wanted to do this particular stunt?" Grey asked.

"Yes," she replied. "She very much wanted to do it. And I knew the stuntman. I know most of the stunt community, and he had doubled a lot of women and . . ."

"Move to strike the latter portion," Koska interrupted.

"The portion about doubling a lot of women is stricken," the judge said. "The rest of it stands."

Grey was fine with that. A judge might admonish a jury to disregard certain testimony, but there's no way a jury can forget everything it's heard. And this jury would not forget this example of the sex discrimination that Julie—or some stuntwoman in Hollywood—faced nearly every day.

Asked by Grey about her top priorities as SAG president, Nolan said that wages, working conditions, and safety on the set had been her primary concerns.

"With regard to the safety-related issues," Grey asked, "what particular group of SAG members did you turn to for assistance on those issues?"

"I turned to the experts," she said. "I turned to the stunt community."

"Throughout your career in entertainment," Grey asked, "have you had frequent contact with members of the stunt community?"

"I have had very frequent contact, and I am quite familiar with a large number of the 'best of the bunch,' as they are called," she testified.

She first came into contact with the stunt community in 1964 while working on a TV show called *Broadside*.

"There were a lot of stunts in it," she testified, "and at that time, I became quite familiar with a lot of the stunt people."

Grey then asked her to name just a few stunt performers she personally knew and respected in Hollywood.

"I would say Hal Needham, Ronnie Rondell, Julie Johnson, Mae Boss, Ron Stein, Chuck Roberson, Donna Garrett, Reg Parton, Jeannie Epper, Roy Clark . . ."

Grey had to stop her or she could have gone on all day. She knew them all. Then he asked her what she had done, as SAG president, to address safety issues in the stunt community.

"I formed the Stunt and Safety Committee," she answered.

"Did you chair that committee?" he asked.

"I did," she said. "If I was going to ask the top echelon to come and be a part of this group, then it was important for them to see that I thought it was significant enough for me to spend my Saturdays there too."

"Did the Stunt Committee remain active during both your terms as SAG president?"

"Yes," she said. "It remained active, but at the end of my second term, I noticed that some of the people that I had counted on weren't coming quite as frequently."

"Were you familiar with Julie Johnson's participation as a member of that group?" he asked.

"Oh, very much so," she said.

"How would you describe Miss Johnson's participation at those meetings?" he asked.

"Objection!" Koska interjected. "Irrelevant. Hearsay . . ."

"Overruled," the judge said.

"Well," she said, "it was quite significant. Actually, it was the impetus. Julie and three or four of the stuntwomen were really the impetus to get the Stunt Committee going."

"You mentioned earlier that some of the people stopped coming to those meetings," Grey reminded her. "Did Julie Johnson's participation ever lessen?"

"Never," she said emphatically.

"Did Ms. Johnson do other things for SAG on safety-related issues?" Grey asked.

"She served on a subcommittee to see if we could come up with solutions to safety problems," she answered. "She came to me personally many, many times about safety problems. She served on two Wages and Working Conditions Committees and two Negotiating Committees—which negotiated our contracts with the producers—specifically on the issues of stunt people and safety . . ."

"Move to strike as nonresponsive to the question asked," Koska barked.

"Overruled," the judge sighed.

"In these negotiations with the producers," Grey asked, "was Julie Johnson an advocate of safety and drug-related reforms?"

"Yes," Nolan said. "Her advocacy of what was best for her fellow stunt performers and actors on these issues was never a secret. She was very open and outspoken about it."

"Ms. Nolan," Grey asked, "what was Julie Johnson's reputation when you were president of the Screen Actors Guild?"

"Objection!" Koska said. "Hearsay!"

"Overruled."

"Julie had an excellent reputation," Nolan answered. "She was one of the top stunt people and was considered a leader in the stunt community."

"And what is her reputation today?" Grey asked.

"Objection!" Koska said again. "Hearsay!"

"Overruled."

"I think the feeling about Julie's reputation is that it's very sad that we've lost one of the best stuntwomen and coordinators in the business," she said. "I have seen a tremendous change in the person that I depended on a great deal as my connection with the stunt community and catalyst. I have seen a tremendous change in that human being over a period of years."

"How many times have you seen Ms. Johnson since she was no longer the stunt coordinator for Spelling-Goldberg Productions?" he asked.

"I saw her many, many times," she answered. "At least fifty times after that."

Laying the foundation for damages, Grey pressed in for the kill.

"Over the whole period of time that you have known Julie Johnson," he asked, "both before and after her termination by Spelling-Goldberg, have you observed any changes in her behavior, her attitude or other emotional responses that have caused you concern about her emotional well-being?"

Nolan's answer to this question was the last thing Koska wanted the jury to hear.

"Objection!" he shouted, rising from his chair. "Calls for a medical conclusion. No foundation. Leading. Suggestive and hearsay."

"Overruled," the judge said sternly. He wanted to hear the answer to this question, too.

"Yes," Nolan said, turning her gaze down to her hands folded on her lap. "I have seen a tremendous change."

"Please tell us what you have observed in that regard," Grey said in his quietest courtroom voice.

Nolan looked up from her hands and into the faces of the jurors, who all seemed to lean forward a bit in the jury box.

"I've seen Julie Johnson become somebody who's no longer as sure of herself—less confident, much more inclined to be dependent, where she was a very independent person, very much in charge," she said, the sadness showing clearly in her face and voice.

"I've seen sadness, a sense of loss of a life, because, after all, it is our work, but it's also our life. I was very surprised when I saw her when I came back from New York. And I saw her a few days ago. She's physically much thinner. I'm not sure she would be as good a double for me now. She just seems to be a lost soul where this vibrant human being existed before."

CHAPTER 21

The Jungle Years

Venezuela had been ruled by a military dictator until only a few months before Julie arrived in the summer of 1958, but the new democracy was fragile. Leftist guerillas were gaining strength in the countryside, and truckloads of armed *Federales*—Venezuelan national troops—regularly roared up and down Anaco's main road near the Halliburton encampment. There were bandits, and rumors of death squads, and deep in the jungle, headhunters.

At the compound's bar and four-lane bowling alley, the men often argued about which was worse: the outlaws or the *Federales*. But to Julie's way of thinking, it was an easy call; it was the headhunters, no doubt about it.

Closer to home, there were other dangers—venomous snakes, malarial mosquitoes, deadly scorpions, poisonous centipedes, and biting red ants that built anthills three feet high.

During the day, Julie worked with her mom at the little gift shop at the American center; and when she came home, the anthills would be a little higher. At night she read magazines and wrote letters home to Eddie. It took two weeks for her letters to reach him, and another two weeks for his to reach her. Time passed as slowly as the mail.

By September, they'd moved into a trailer behind Stan's tool shop, and Julie knew she'd be stuck in Venezuela a lot longer than three months. Her mother needed her down there to help her run the little gift shop. But mostly she wanted to keep Julie away from Eddie.

Julie's room in the trailer was just big enough for her bed and a nightstand. Stan and Virginia slept outside in a screened-in porch under a corrugated tin roof. It was so quiet at night that Julie could hear the ice cubes clinking in their glasses as they downed one cocktail after another. The impenetrable jungle was right outside her bedroom window now, and somewhere out there in the darkness, the headhunters.

It was the tropical season again, and the rain came down like bullets. Julie wrote to Eddie of her plight—that she might be down there for years—and on her eighteenth birthday, he wrote back.

"Today is your birthday," he wrote, "and I miss you so much. I can't help thinking back upon all the wonderful times we had together and then I realize how much I miss you. If everything goes right, I may be able to come and see you this summer. Julie, make the best of everything, and maybe it won't be too terribly long before I see you again—maybe only a matter of nine or ten months, which is better than three or four years."

Months passed. Eddie didn't come, but he kept writing. By the summer of 1959, she'd been stuck in that steaming jungle for a whole year. Stan bought a little record store adjoining the gift shop, and Julie split her time working there and helping her mother sell souvenirs and trinkets at the gift shop. Blonde and blue-eyed, she was easily the cutest girl in town, so she spent a lot of time fending off the advances of married oilfield workers.

To keep her sanity, she threw herself into sports. She bowled and, on the weekends, played golf at a nine-hole course down the road with hard-packed sand for greens. She could hit a five iron as far as most of the men, and she won several of the women's tournaments. But it was Eddie's letters that kept her alive.

"I haven't been to Big Corona since you left," he wrote that summer. "That beach just doesn't have it without you. I do wish you'd hurry home because I miss you very much."

Julie wrote back, telling him how much she missed him. That September, she turned nineteen in the Venezuelan jungle.

Eddie's letters were becoming more and more passionate. "Right now," he wrote in October, "I'm sitting alone listening to *An Affair to Remember*. The night is warm, windy, and clear, and I miss you so very, very much. I wait for you, for the time I can look upon my beautiful Julie, and most of all, to hold you again. You have come to dominate my thoughts and I don't know quite how to cope with it, but if I have nothing else, I have time—time given to me by you and 'remembered always.'"

Then, unable to conceal his feelings any longer, he wrote the words she'd waited so long to hear, "Oh, to hell with it. <u>Please</u> Come Home Soon. I LOVE YOU!!!"

There. He'd done it. It was out in the open now. He loved her, and she loved him. The only thing standing between them now was 3,640 miles, three time zones, two continents, and her mother.

A few weeks later, as the political situation in Venezuela continued to deteriorate, Julie wrote to Eddie and told him that it looked like her mother was finally going to let her go home after the New Year.

Eddie was ecstatic.

"I don't question how you've lasted the long blackout," he wrote in November, "and two and a half months, I know, is too long for you to wait, but it will seem twice that time, an eternity, for me. If it is at all possible to come home any sooner, PLEASE DO, and let me know. Johnny Mathis is right—you shall be home for Christmas, 'If only in my dreams.' This Christmas, every time I hear a bell, it will ring through my heart and soul, crying, 'Julie, Julie, please come to me. I need you Julie, my love.' I dream of you with such an obsession that it torments my very existence. No, there is no law against dreaming. I dreamed that I might come to you when you get home. You shall make me the happiest, Julie, by allowing me to make you happy. What I really want is you! With me! As soon as possible!"

"I'll be home soon," she wrote back, coyly adding that she'd put on a few pounds—"all in the right places"—since he'd seen her last.

On New Year's Eve 1959, Eddie wrote back.

"Sweetheart, according to my brilliant mathematical calculations, you should be home between January 12 and the 17. I don't know if I can take it, that's only three weeks away. God help me control myself. It's been two and a half years since we met, and you've never left me. Your big picture has always been in my room, and your little picture has always been in my wallet, and you have always been in my heart. Come home soon, darling. I love you.

"PS: More weight, hmmm? All the right places . . . hmmm? I'd better look into that situation very thoroughly!"

January came and went, and with it, the 1950s. But Julie was still stuck in Venezuela. Her mother said she needed her down there just a little bit longer—that she couldn't make it without her. A little bit longer turned into a lot longer. Eddie was disappointed, but he said he'd wait for her, and he kept writing. At night, alone and desperate in the still darkness surrounding their little trailer, Julie would look out her bedroom window into the impenetrable jungle and wonder if someone was out there, unseen, looking back.

The year 1960 was going to be an exciting one, and the beginning of an exciting new decade. Freedom was in the air. In Africa, seventeen nations gained their independence that year from their colonial masters, and in America, lunch counter sit-ins were sweeping the segregated South. But Julie felt like a slave stuck in this South American jungle. The world was going on without her. It was like she was dead, without having died.

In February, the 1960 Winter Olympics were held in Squaw Valley, California. The American hockey team won its first Olympic gold, and the gold medal in figure skating went to American Carol Heiss. Julie missed it all. In March, Elvis Presley returned home from Germany after two years in the army. Julie' been gone longer and didn't even know he'd left.

In May, Israeli secret agents captured the fugitive Nazi Adolf Eichmann in Argentina, and in June, Typhoon Mary killed a million people in China. In July, John F. Kennedy won the Democratic nomination for president. In August, Cuban dictator Fidel Castro nationalized all American businesses on the island—putting the two countries on a collision course. In September, a young boxer named Cassius Clay won the gold medal at the 1960 Olympics in Rome and sprinter Wilma Rudolph became the first American woman to win three gold medals in track and field during a single Olympic games. Julie turned twenty in the jungle that month, and two days later, JFK and Richard Nixon took part in the first televised presidential debate.

In October, Soviet premier Nikita Khrushchev pounded his shoe on the table at the United Nations, and in November, John F. Kennedy defeated Richard Nixon in the closest presidential election in American history.

For Julie, stuck in the Venezuelan jungle, it was like none of it even happened.

Year 1960 came and went, and with it, another year of Julie's young life. As 1961 began, the political situation in Venezuela began to deteriorate rapidly. Armed troop carriers raced up and down the main road outside the American compound, and at night, Julie could here gun battles raging in the distance. The American oil workers, fearful of the rebels *and* the *Federales*, began leaving in droves. Virginia and Stan were going to stay on, but they finally decided that it was time for Julie to go.

"It's time to send you back," Virginia told her daughter. "It's getting too dangerous down here."

It was the best news of her life.

Julie wrote to Eddie and told him she'd be home on the twenty-first of January. She hoped her letter would get there before she did. She hadn't heard from him in two months, but figured that the mail was getting slower as the situation in Venezuela deteriorated. With her luck, his latest letter would arrive after she left.

On the night of the nineteenth, as Julie was packing her bags, Stan knocked on her door.

"I have something I want to give you," he said. "It's a going-away present."

He handed her an envelope and a little box. The envelope was stuffed with cash, and inside the box was a little .22-caliber derringer pistol—one barrel on top of the other.

"It's loaded," he said, grinning widely.

"Thanks, Stan," she said and gave him a big hug.

After he left, she counted the money—$2,500! She put the envelope into a secret compartment in her purse, then took the gun out of the box, and felt its weight in her hand. She pointed it at an imaginary bad guy and pretended to shoot. Then she put it back in the box, stuck it down inside a sock, and tossed it in her suitcase.

The next day, Virginia and Stan drove Julie to the little airport where she'd first arrived two and a half years ago. It looked the same, only moldier. Julie checked her bags and hugged her mom. Virginia cried, and Julie cried too, although not for the same reason.

Julie walked out to the little two-engine prop plane on the tarmac and, climbing the stairs to the cabin, turned and waved good-bye to her mom and stepfather—good-bye to Anaco, good-bye to the jungle, good-bye to the mud and the rain and the venomous snakes and the biting red ants and the mosquitoes and the neighbors living in cardboard huts, good-bye to all this. Good-bye forever.

As the plane took off, Julie looked out the window. Down below was green jungle as far as she could see. Down below was two and a half years of her life. Soon, the flatness of the jungle gave way to the majestic Venezuelan costal mountain range called the Cordillera de la Costa and, beyond, the azure blue waters of the Caribbean.

When the plane landed in Caracas, Julie got off and collected her bags. The plane ride had only taken forty-five minutes; but now, standing here in the bustling airport of this emerald city by the sea, it seemed to Julie like she'd been transported hundreds of centuries through time: from the Stone Age to the Jet Age.

Her layover in Caracas was the happiest two hours she'd spent in the last two and a half years. There were people everywhere, hugging and kissing, saying their good-byes, or tearfully greeting loved ones just arrived from some distant land. She hadn't seen so many people—so many happy, healthy people—in years. There were fancy shops filled with beautiful clothes and exotic jewelry and newsstands with magazines and newspapers from around the world. Huge windows looked out onto the runways, where sparkling new jetliners—the first she'd ever seen—were taking on or disembarking passengers.

For Julie, it was a joyous reintroduction to the world. It was like being reborn.

Julie gathered her bags and proceeded through customs. Handing her passport to the customs agent, she'd forgotten that she had a loaded pistol in her suitcase. The agent unzipped the bag and rummaged around, but didn't find the gun.

"Tiene algo que declarar?" he asked. "Do you have anything to declare?"

"No," Julie said. She was fluent in Spanish now.

He stamped her passport and waved her through. Then she checked her suitcase at the airline counter, slung her carry-on bag over her shoulder, and boarded the plane to New Orleans. She was retracing the same route she'd taken coming here, only this time her heart was filled with joy instead of dread. After all these lonely years, she'd soon be in Eddie's arms again.

Her flight to New Orleans left at three o'clock in the afternoon, and three hours later, she enjoyed a spectacular sunset over the Gulf of Mexico. Dinner was served—some kind of Venezuelan beef stew—and it was the best thing she'd eaten in two and a half years. Maybe it was the altitude, maybe it was the food, maybe it was the little glass of red wine they served, but maybe it was just that everything tastes better when you're coming home than when you're leaving.

After dinner, she took Eddie's last letter out of her carry-on bag, flicked on the overhead light, and read his sweet words of encouragement and love.

"Come home soon," he'd written. "I love you."

Outside, a shining crescent moon rose over the Gulf. America lay just over the horizon.

The four-engine DC-7 prop plane bucked occasionally, but mostly it was a smooth seven-hour ride.

"Ladies and gentlemen," the pilot said over the intercom in perfect English, "please fasten your seat belts. We're making our approach to Louis Armstrong New Orleans International Airport. Local time is eight o'clock."

"Louis Armstrong International Airport?" Julie thought. Hadn't it been Moisant Field or something like that when she passed through two and a half years ago? Had they changed the names of everything while she was gone?

A few minutes later, the plane landed with a bump and taxied to the terminal. When the doors opened, everybody got up, collected their carry-ons from the overhead bins, and slowly marched, penguin-style, toward the front exit, where pretty young stewardesses smiled and said "buh-bye" to each and every one of the departing passengers.

Stepping out of the plane, Julie felt the cool, dry air on her cheeks—a feeling she'd almost forgotten. She held the handrail going down the metal staircase and, at the bottom, set foot on American soil for the first time since she was seventeen. She'd left as a teenager and returned as a woman. It was good to be back.

Walking through the terminal, the news racks were filled with papers that all featured the same front page story under slightly different headlines: "JFK Inaugurated!" It was January 21, 1961, and John F. Kennedy had been sworn into office the day before as the thirty-fifth president of the United States.

Julie bought a paper and then collected her luggage and went through customs, where a handsome young agent looked at her passport, opened her suitcase, and asked her if she was bringing any fruits or vegetables into the country.

"No," Julie answered.

"Do you have anything of value in excess of $250 that you're bringing into the country?" he asked, poking around the contents of her bag. "Any jewelry, cigarettes, or alcohol you want to declare?"

"No," Julie replied. "I don't smoke or drink."

And then she remembered the gun. *What if he finds the gun?*

"I see you've been out of the country for quite a while," he said in a pleasant southern accent. "Going to school down there in Venezuela?"

"No," Julie said, trying to conceal the fear rising from her gut. "I was helping out my mom. She has a shop down there."

The young agent looked her over carefully and then winked at her. "Welcome home, Ms. Johnson."

"Thank you," she said, smiling broadly. "It's good to be home."

Chapter 22

Home at Last

On the approach LAX, Julie looked out the window and noticed something new under construction at the airport below—something that looked like a flying saucer that had landed in the parking lot. She'd later learn it was the Theme Building, which would become an iconic landmark when it opened a few months later. She wondered what else had sprung up in her absence.

When the plane taxied to a stop, everyone got off and went into the terminal. Julie went to the baggage carousel and saw her old schoolmate Robin Randall waiting there for her. Overjoyed, Julie ran to Robin and embraced her amid the throng of people looking for their luggage. She hadn't hugged a friend in over two years.

Robin had received Julie's letter with the flight information and was right on time to pick her up. They talked excitedly for a while about all the girls they knew from school. Nearly all of them had gotten married and had kids since Julie left, and several had already gotten divorced.

When her suitcase finally came around, Julie picked it up and they headed for the door, where airport security guards stood checking baggage tags against ticket stubs. Fortunately, they didn't ask her to open her suitcase to reveal the loaded gun inside.

As soon as they got into her car, Robin started asking questions about South America.

"So how was it down there?"

"Hot," Julie said.

"Did you meet any boys?"

"Not really," Julie said.

"Have you kept in touch with Eddie?" she asked. Robin had never met Eddie, but everyone knew about him.

"Yes," Julie said. "He wrote to me all the time. I can't wait to see him. It's been two and a half years!"

"Oh, how romantic!" Robin said gleefully. "How perfectly romantic! Young lovers, separated by time and distance, finally reunited!"

"Not so young anymore," Julie sighed.

It was a long drive down to Robin's home in Fullerton—the 405 Freeway hadn't opened yet, so they took the scenic Pacific Coast Highway most of the way there.

The drive, the open road, the bright blue Pacific Ocean—it was all so beautiful. And the best thing of all: no jungle, no swarms of flying insects splattered all over the windshield, no cardboard huts with children playing outside in the mud, no cows or chickens or pigs sauntering across the road. It was good to be back in *North America*.

Driving along the coast, Robin caught Julie up on some of the things she'd missed in the last two and a half years.

"What do you think of Kennedy?" Robin asked.

"Kennedy?" Julie replied, not knowing who she was talking about.

"John F. Kennedy," Robin said. "Our new president. He beat Richard Nixon in the election."

"Oh, yeah," Julie said. She'd read about it in one of the two-week-old newspapers down there in the jungle.

"He is so dreamy," Robin said dreamily. "He will definitely be our cutest president."

They both laughed and talked the rest of the way about a cute guy Robin was dating.

When they finally got to Robin's place, Julie called her dad, who said he'd be right over to pick her up.

A little while later, Julie heard the familiar honk of her dad's old Buick. Some things, at least, never change. She kissed Robin on the cheek, picked up her bags, and ran out to the street. Art got out, opened the passenger door, and was turning to greet her when Julie bounced into his arms. They hugged for a long time. When he let her go, he backed up and stuck a boxer's pose. He'd taught her how to box when she was a kid and this had become their ritual greeting. He put up his dukes, and so did she. Then, bobbing and weaving, they threw a few fake punches and broke into laughter.

Art drove Julie back to his little house in Fullerton, the house she'd grown up in; and when they pulled into the driveway, Julie finally knew that she was home.

Her room was the same as she'd left it; only the bedspread had changed. She dropped her bags by her old dresser bureau, flopped down on the bed, and fell fast asleep. There really is no place like home. But she wouldn't be staying long.

The next day, Art took Julie to Home Savings and opened a savings account with the $2,500 that Stan had given her. Then he took her to a Chevrolet dealer, made the down payment, and cosigned for a car. She picked out a brand-new steel-blue 1961 two-door Chevy Corvair—the model with the engine in back that Ralph Nader would later describe as "unsafe at any speed." But unsafe or not, Julie loved it; it was her first car, and like her first love, she'd always remember her first car.

Later that evening, she called Eddie on the number he'd given her in his last letter—JEfferson-12701. In those days, they used the first two letters of a word as the first two digits in a phone number.

After a few rings, a woman's voice answered.

"I'm sorry, you have reached a number that is not in service at this time," the voice said. "If you need assistance, please call the operator. This is a recording."

A recording? That was something new. "When did they start that?" Julie wondered.

Figuring that she'd misdialed, Julie looked at the letter again and carefully redialed the numbers.

"I'm sorry, you have reached a number that is not in service at this time . . ."

Julie hung up and looked at Eddie's letter again. She dialed again, making sure she pushed 5 for the *J*, 3 for the *E*, and then 12701.

Same thing, same recording.

Deep in the pit of her stomach, something felt like it was rolling over. She dialed the operator, and after a few rings, a woman answered. This time it wasn't a recording.

"How may I help you, please?" the operator said in a stilted and distant tone, like she'd already said the same thing five hundred times that day.

"I'm calling this number," Julie explained, "but I keep getting a recording saying that it's not in service."

"What is the number, please?" the operator asked. Julie gave her the number.

"One moment, please," the operator said. Julie waited.

"That number is no longer in service," the operator said when she came back on the line.

"Not in service?" Julie asked. "What does that mean?"

"It means that it's not in service," the operator answered.

Julie was baffled. "Does that mean there's something wrong with the line?"

"No, ma'am," the operator said. "It means it's been disconnected."

"Disconnected?" Julie asked, her head beginning to feel like it had changed places with her stomach. "When was it disconnected?"

"I'm sorry, ma'am, I can't give you that information."

Julie gave the operator Eddie's first and last name. "Do you have a listing for him?"

"One moment, please," the operator said stiffly.

There was a longer pause this time as the operator checked the phone company's records. "No, ma'am," she said when she came back on the line "There is no listing under that name."

"No listing?" Julie said, a sense of panic rising in her voice.

"No, ma'am."

Julie didn't know what to say or do, so she poured her heart out to the operator.

"Listen," she said, "I've just come back after two and a half years in South America. This is my boyfriend's phone number. I was supposed to call him when I got back. Can you please help me? Can you please tell me what's going on?"

There was a long pause. "Listen, sweetie," the operator whispered tenderly, sounding for the first time more like a human being than a recording. "That number was disconnected over a month ago, and there is no forwarding number. That's all I can tell you. That's all I know."

Julie still didn't understand what was happening, but she understood that the operator had done everything she could. "Thank you," she said softly.

"Good luck, dear," the operator replied, as if she knew exactly what Julie was going through.

Julie hung up and looked at the phone. She felt dizzy, but after a few deep breaths, her head had cleared. Maybe he just forgot to pay his phone bill, she thought. Maybe that was it. Maybe it will be back on tomorrow. Yes, that's probably it, she thought. She started feeling better. She'd try again tomorrow. And besides, she still had his address on South Wright Street in Santa Ana.

She took out pen and paper and started writing Eddie a letter, telling him that she was back in Orange County, and about the funny mix-up she'd had with the phone company—leaving out the part about how scary it was. When she finished, she put it in an envelope, addressed it, and put a 4¢ stamp on it. She'd mail it first thing tomorrow, and he'd have it in a few days. She felt better now.

The next day, she drove her new Corvair to the post office, mailed Eddie's letter, and drove over to pick up Robin, who'd offered to help Julie look for an apartment in Corona del Mar. Julie had spent her entire life living with her parents and step-parents, and it was time to find a place of her own.

They drove around a while and found a place on Pacific Coast Highway with a For Rent sign posted outside. It was a lovely little one-bedroom cottage in a nice neighborhood not far from the beach. The owner, who lived next door, showed them around. It was small, but Julie loved it. "When is it available?" she asked.

"Right away," he said.

"How much?" she asked.

"Sixty-five dollars a month," he said. "Water's included."

That was a lot of money in those days, especially for a young woman without a job. But it was so charming and so near the beach. She just had to have it.

"Okay," she said and counted out six twenties and a ten-dollar bill for the first and last months' rent. They shook hands, and he handed her the keys.

"Welcome to the neighborhood," he said with a big smile.

The next day, she called the Edison Company, the phone company, and the gas company and had everything turned on and put in her name. Then her dad brought his van around. and they loaded it with furniture and household goods—a bed and dresser from the guest room, a fold-up card table and chairs from the garage, several boxes of pots and pans, linens and towels, and two suitcases full of clothes—and drove it over and unloaded it in her new apartment. It was sparse, but it would do until she could buy a couch and a few more pieces of furniture. And it was hers. And like her first love and her first car, she'd always remember her first apartment.

Later that day, she drove over to Sears and bought a phone. They had so many to choose from, and in so many colors. They even had pink girly ones called Princess Phones. They didn't have anything like that when she left for South America. Pink and girly, however, was not Julie's style; she settled on a standard black one instead. She took it straight home, plugged it in, and got a dial tone right away. The first call she made was to Eddie, to see if his old number was back in service. It wasn't.

"I'm sorry, you have reached a number that is not in service at this time . . ."

Julie hung up. It was not a good start for her new phone or her new apartment.

Then she called her dad.

"Hello?" he said.

"Hi, Daddy."

"Hello, sweetie. You got your new phone?"

"Yeah. You're my first call," she said, not meaning to lie, but not wanting to say that he was her second call either. And besides, this was the first call that went through.

"Honey," he said in a concerned voice, "your letter came back."

"My letter?" she said, not knowing right away what he was talking about.

"Your letter to Eddie," he said.

There was dead silence on the phone. She got it now. "I'll keep if for you," he said.

"Does it say anything on the envelope?" she asked.

"I'll keep it for you," he repeated, not wanting to tell her.

"What does it say, Daddy?"

Art picked up the letter and looked at the cold block letters stamped on the envelope.

"Return to sender," he told her glumly. "Address unknown."

"There must be . . ." she started to say "mistake," but realized that there'd been no mistake.

Her father, sensing his daughter's distress, said the one thing that would pull her back from the brink. "I'm sure he's moved and will be getting in touch with you real soon," he said confidently. "He has my address. He knows where to find you."

"Yes!" Julie agreed brightly, realizing that that must be the explanation. He'd probably come by her dad's place looking for her any day now.

"Thanks, Dad," she said. "I'm sure you're right."

She'd waited two and a half years to see him; she could wait a little longer. And while she was waiting, she couldn't sit around worrying. She'd have to get back into the swing of things. She'd have to find a job.

She started by looking through the help-wanted ads in the *Register*, Santa Ana's leading newspaper, but she didn't really know what she wanted to do, so she didn't know what kind of job to look for. Accounting? Nursing? Real estate? Sales? Secretarial?

"Well," her dad told her on the phone the next day, "there's the phone company, there's banks, there's department stores. You just gotta keep looking."

"Okay," she said. "I'll try the phone company."

The next day, she went down to Laguna Beach and put in an application at the phone company.

"They were ready to train me as a telephone operator," she recalls.

Her recent encounter with a phone company operator, however, had left a bad taste in her mouth. There was no way she could sit at a switchboard all day and say, "How may I help you, please?" So she went to the Bank of California in Corona del Mar and put in an application there.

They offered her a job and offered to train her. But she turned it down.

"I can't do that and handle all that money," she thought. "That would be too depressing."

She talked it over with her dad, who said, "Why don't you try Bullock's? They're in Santa Ana. They're bound to have work."

She did have some experience in retail, after all, even if it was only at a little gift store in the jungle.

"So I went to Bullock's, gave them my application, and they offered me a job as a sales person," she recalled.

This time she accepted the job offer, and they trained her to be a floater—a salesperson who would work in whatever department needed help.

"I worked a lot in housewares and then they sent me to children's wear and then they sent me to sportswear for women, and I always made my sales quota," she recalled. "I started at $40 a week for six days a week, Monday through Saturday."

It was her first real job, and her introduction to keeping her mouth shut when state and federal labor laws were being violated.

"The thing about retail in those days," she says, "was that you were only allowed eight hours. They didn't pay for overtime. But if you wanted to be good at your job, you knew you had to get in earlier and stay late. So if you came in at eight o'clock in the morning, you'd go down at nine o'clock and put your time card in. And then at five o'clock, you'd go down and put your time card in, but then you'd have to go back up and work another hour or two. If you wanted to be good at your job and make your sales quota, that's what you had to do."

The store's supervisors knew that all the sales workers were doing this, and by not paying overtime, they were violating state and federal labor laws.

"They all knew," Julie says. "And you had to keep quiet or you didn't work."

It was the same code of silence she'd encounter many years later in Hollywood.

After work, she'd go home and watch the new black-and-white TV she'd bought. She was sorry to see that *I Love Lucy* had been cancelled in her absence, but there were still lots of good shows on: *Route 66*, *Leave It to Beaver*, and *Ozzie and Harriet*. One of her favorites was *The Real McCoys*, which costarred Kathleen Nolan, who would one day play such an important role in her case against Aaron Spelling.

And no doubt, she'd also caught an episode or two of *Dragnet* or *Maverick* or any number of other shows costarring a young French actress named Lilyan Chauvin, who would one day play such an important role in Julie's life.

After work, she'd come home, make dinner, turn on the TV, and wait for the phone to ring. And every time it rang, she hoped it was Eddie. Maybe he'd gone off to Europe with his parents or something and would be coming right over to see her. But days and weeks went by, and each time the phone rang, it wasn't Eddie. she was starting to feel farther away from him than when she was 3,600 miles away in Venezuela.

A month after starting at Bullock's, Julie was working in the women's sportswear department when a saleswoman from the lingerie department she'd seen around came up to her and asked her if she was Julie Johnson.

"Yes," Julie said quizzically.

"You're Eddie's friend, aren't you?" she asked.

"Yes!" Julie said. "Do you know Eddie?"

"Yes," the lady said. "I'm his aunt."

Julie was astounded, almost speechless.

"Do you know . . . ?" she stammered. "How's he doing? Where is he?"

Eddie's aunt took a long look at the young woman standing before her.

"Don't you know?" she said, her eyes filled with sympathy. "He got married."

"Married?" Julie repeated, her astonishment turning quickly to shock.

"Yes," she said. "He's moved up north. I'm sorry. I thought you knew."

The department store began to spin; then the floor seemed to fall away.

"Are you all right?" the lady asked, placing her hand on Julie's shoulder.

Speechless, Julie could only nod. Managing a weak smile, she turned and walked away. Finding her supervisor, Julie told her she wasn't feeling well and then went downstairs to the basement and clocked out. She went out to the employees' parking lot, found her car, and drove to the first liquor store she could find and bought a bottle of vodka. She looked so gloomy, beaten down, and old that the clerk didn't even ask to see her ID. Then she drove home to perform her tenth stunt.

With tears rolling down her cheeks, Julie sat on the floor of her living room, her back against the wall, the half-empty vodka bottle at her side. Johnny Mathis's *Chances Are* was playing on her record player as she raised the .22 derringer to her head.

Then everything went black.

It was dark in the living room when she regained consciousness. Groggy at first, she raised herself up on one elbow and then remembered the gun. In a panic, she checked the side of her head. There was no blood. Then she felt around on the floor and found the pistol. It hadn't been fired. She'd passed out before she could pull the trigger. Maybe it was the vodka, but years later, she'd realize that it was something else. An unseen hand had intervened and spared her life that day.

She got up off the floor and turned a light on. Outside, she could hear a dog bark and children laughing. Through the window, between the branches of an old oak tree, she could see the moon rising over the San Joaquin Hills. A pleasant odor filled the room, a neighbor's cooking. She was hungry. It was good to be alive.

Chapter 23

A New Beginning

Julie went back to work at Bullock's the next day as if her world hadn't completely fallen apart. She had a terrible hangover, and the sour taste of vodka was still in her mouth. Her head hurt and her heart ached, but she knew now, more than ever, that she'd been "placed"—that she'd been protected and that everything happens for a reason. It was a new day; there were places to go and things to do and, on this day, children's clothes to sell.

Over the next few months, Julie worked hard, met her sales quotas, and avoided Eddie's aunt. After work, she'd go home, cook dinner, and watch TV. And every time the phone rang, she'd wonder if it was Eddie. It never was.

By this time, Julie had been promoted to assistant buyer and had gotten a raise to $45 a week, which was still barely enough to live on. Now, in addition to her sales duties, she had be at work before the store opened to make sure all the clothes were ready, that the racks were straight, and that everything was properly tagged. Then, at the end of her shift, she had to do all the bookkeeping for her department, which meant she was usually the last person to leave each night as well. It was a hard job with long hours, but she was good at it and took pride in doing her best every day.

Her work ethic and salesmanship didn't go unnoticed. Toward the end of the year, her bosses asked her to move to Sherman Oaks in the San Fernando Valley to help open the new Bullock's up there. The new store was going to be something different—not so much a department *store* as a department *palace*. It was going to be grand and luxurious, catering to a high-end clientele. And it would mean a raise—to $65 a week.

Julie didn't hesitate.

"Okay," she said, saying the word that would come to be her trademark.

She had become a can-do girl.

The money would be better in her new job, but more importantly, she was ready to leave Orange County. There were reminders of Eddie down there everywhere: the beach where they met, the drive-ins where they kissed, the streets they strolled, the fancy French restaurant where they said their last good-byes. Even the sunsets, there were sad reminders of happier days. And working at Bullock's made it even harder. Eddie's aunt worked there, and it was where she'd bought his watch and had it inscribed—"Time Remembered. Love always, Julie."

Now, more than anything, it was time to forget, or at least to try to.

One of the buyers at Bullock's, a friend of Julie's named Nancy Barker, was moving up to Los Angeles to take a job at the May Company, so they decided to rent a place together and split the bills. They found a little two-bedroom house in Hollywood, and Julie's dad rented a trailer and helped her move her stuff up to the big city.

Early the next Monday, Julie drove up Laurel Canyon, over the Hollywood Hills, and into the Valley to go to work at the new Bullock's in Sherman Oaks. The new store was everything she'd been told it would be—and then some. It was majestic—a luxurious temple to the gods of fashion and design—complete with goddesses. To present their clothing lines, management hired dozens of young models to stroll around the store and talk to the customers about the latest fashions.

The store was beautiful, but Julie's hours were just as grueling as before. And while the pay was a little better, it still wasn't enough to pay the bills. As the months rolled by, her bank account was getting smaller and smaller. Julie and Nancy moved into a little two-bedroom guest house in the Valley to save money, but before long, Nancy landed a high-paying job with Amway and moved into her own place. Now Julie was on her own.

One day, she was having a sandwich in the employee lunchroom with one of the models—a pretty brunette named Rebecca Jones—and mentioned that she needed to make more money.

"Well, why don't you go see Chris Petersen?" Rebecca asked. "He has a commercial production company over on Melrose Avenue in Hollywood. Maybe he'll hire you."

"Have you worked for him before?" Julie asked.

"Sure," she said. "He's great." Then she rummaged around in her purse, took out her address book, and wrote Petersen's name, phone number, and address on a napkin.

"Here," she said, sliding the napkin toward Julie. "Give him a call and tell him I recommended you."

"Okay," she said. Can-do.

Julie put in the call the next day. A nice lady answered the phone. "Why don't you drop by?" she said. "We can always use a little more help around here."

Julie got up early the next morning and drove over to the Petersen offices on Melrose. She parked on the street, went inside, and was greeted at the receptionist's desk by a very pretty blond who looked strangely familiar.

"I have an appointment with Mr. Petersen," Julie said. "I'm Julie Ann Johnson."

"Well hello, Julie. We talked on the phone yesterday. I'm Eve Brent. Chris is looking forward to meeting you."

"Eve Brent?" Julie asked. "From the Tarzan movies?"

"The one and only," Eve said with a wry smile. "This is my day job. Every actress needs one. Come on in and I'll introduce you to Chris."

Petersen was on the phone when they walked into his office. Talking fast to someone on the other end of the line, he looked up and motioned them in without missing a beat. "Okay, I'll have the rushes for you Tuesday," he said. "Yes. Come by the studio. I'll see you then." He hung up and looked at Eve quizzically.

"This is the girl I told you about," she said.

Petersen leaned back in his chair and looked Julie up and down. Middle-aged and bald, he was not a particularly attractive man, but he had a friendly face and kind eyes.

"Okay," he said, without asking Julie a single question. "When can she start?"

Eve looked at Julie and raised a perfectly plucked eyebrow.

"Start?" Julie repeated, not realizing that she'd already gotten the job, and without even knowing what the job was.

"Yes," Eve coaxed her. "When can you start? You'll be filling in for me on the switchboard and helping out around the office."

"Well . . ." Julie hesitated, not knowing quite what to say. "How much . . . ?"

"I'll pay a good switchboard operator $90 a week," Petersen said flatly.

"Ninety dollars a week?" Julie thought, the surprise in her eyes giving her away. "But I don't know anything about switchboards."

"Don't worry, she'll teach you," he said, waving them both out of his office.

"So when *can* you start?" Eve whispered as they left.

"Well, I need to give two weeks' notice," Julie said somewhat uncertainly.

"Okay," Eve said. "Two weeks it is. Work starts at nine and ends at five, Monday through Friday. See you in two weeks."

Julie left the office in a daze. She'd be getting paid a lot more money for a lot fewer hours, with two days off a week! Now she'd have to tell her boss she was leaving Bullock's.

Say good-bye to better sportswear for women, say hello to Hollywood!

Learning to operate the switchboard wasn't easy, but Eve was a good and patient teacher. It took Julie a few hours to get the hang of it, but by the end of the day, Julie was working the switchboard like a pro.

In her new job, there was something new to learn every day, and Julie approached it like going to college, which is what it was—a crash course in Hollywood. During her breaks from the switchboard, she watched the crews film commercials on the soundstage, learning the lingo and making mental notes on the intricacies of shooting on a tight schedule. There were jobs of all description behind the scenes and a union for every category of worker. But nearly all of those jobs were filled by men. The only place for women, it seemed, was in front of the camera.

So on a day off, she had some glossy black-and-white headshots taken and started taking acting classes after work. Her natural shyness worked against her, but she was having fun for the first time in years and meeting lots of interesting new people. It was 1962, and she was young and pretty, and now she was an aspiring actress in Hollywood!

Within a few months, Chris Petersen moved into new offices at the Fairbanks Building on Vine Street. Julie was now working the switchboard for two companies—Chris Petersen Productions and Jerry Fairbanks Studios.

Fairbanks, a handsome man with spectacles and a pencil mustache, was a producer of B-movies; but he'd won an Oscar in 1945, in the short-subject category, for a little film called *Who's Who in Animal Land*, a comedic tour of the animal kingdom. He got a star on the Hollywood Walk of Fame, but today he is all but forgotten. But to Julie, he was a star. He kept his Oscar in his office, and Julie saw it every time he called her in to run an errand. It was the first Oscar statuette she ever saw, the first Oscar she ever held in her own hands.

She was sitting at the receptionist's desk one day, answering the phones, when Eve Brent dropped by to see her.

"Yes, but your call is at 9:00 a.m.," she told the caller as Eve approached. "Can you make it, or do you have a conflict? Okay, I'll tell them."

Julie hung up and looked up at her supervisor.

"Did you get your pictures yet?" Eve asked.

Julie opened the lower drawer of her desk, retrieved the headshots she'd had taken, and showed them to Eve.

"Hey, they're good," Eve said, looking over the black-and-white glossies. "Did anybody ever tell you that you look a little bit like Doris Day?"

"No, not really," Julie said, blushing at the compliment. And it was quite a compliment. Not only was Doris Day a beautiful and talented singer, but she also was the biggest box office star, male or female, in the world that year—just as she had been in 1960 and would be again in 1963 and '64.

"Have you started your acting classes yet?" Eve asked.

"Yes, but . . ."

"Yes, but what?"

"They want me to act sexy," Julie pouted. "Like I'm nothing but boobs."

"I know the feeling," Eve said, looking down at her own ample bosom. "Just remember: you don't have to go to bed with any of them if you don't want to. Just decide what you want to do and do it." Then, after a thoughtful moment, she asked, "Which do you like better, comedy or drama?"

"Action," Julie said without hesitating. "I like action. I'm an athlete. I want to do things like Esther Williams did."

Esther Williams had been Julie's favorite star since she was a kid, when her dad took her to see all her new movies. Julie loved Esther Williams because she was not only beautiful but also a world-class athlete famous for her swimming and diving scenes.

As the twelfth actress to play Jane in the Tarzan franchise, Eve knew a little something about action films. "Then you just stick to your guns," she said, "and you'll find a niche."

One of the young production assistants poked her head around the corner. "Eve! You're wanted on the set!" she shouted.

Eve winked at Julie and hurried off to the set. Julie started to put her headshots back in the desk drawer but stopped. She spread the photos across her desk and looked at them, as if for the first time. "Hmmm," she thought out loud. There was a bit of a resemblance. How could she not have seen it before?

A few days later, Julie clipped a picture out of a movie magazine and took it to her hair dresser. "Like that," she told the stylist, pointing to the hairdo in the photo: bangs in front and long on the sides to frame her face, just like Doris Day in the picture.

After that, people started telling her she looked like Doris Day all the time.

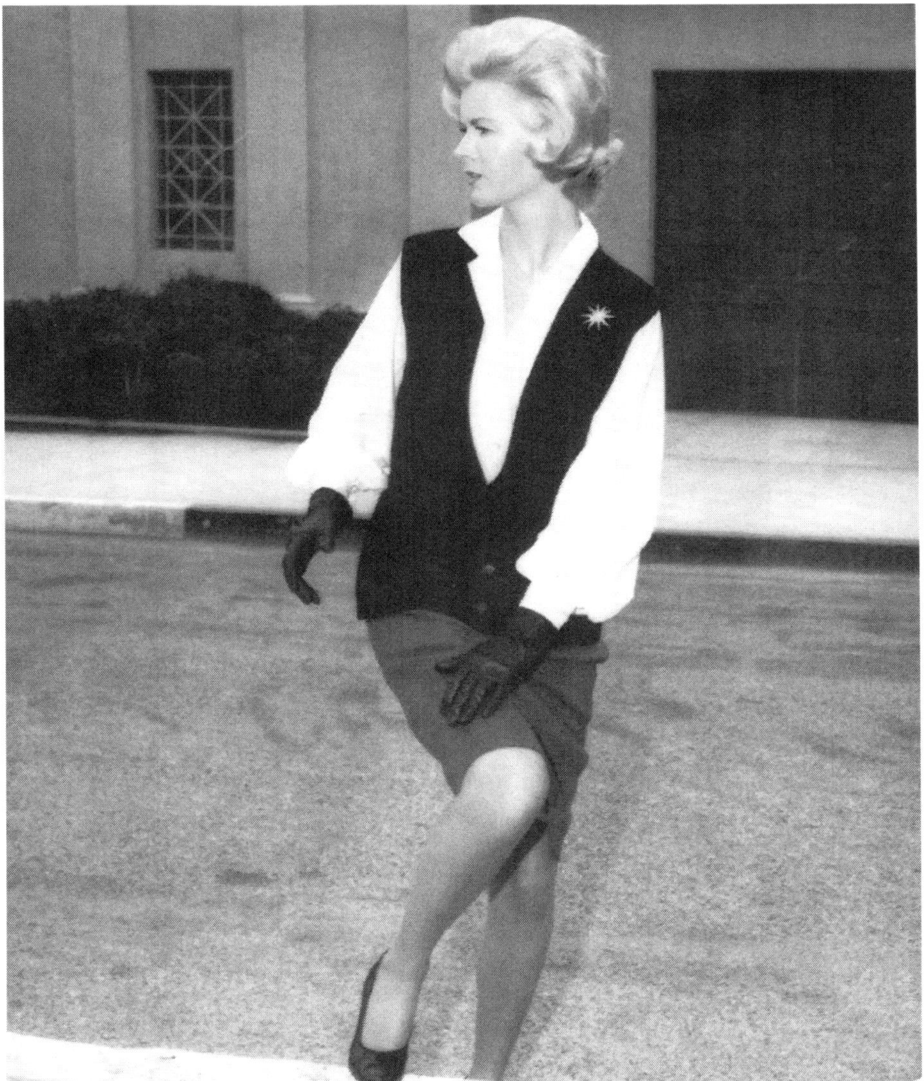

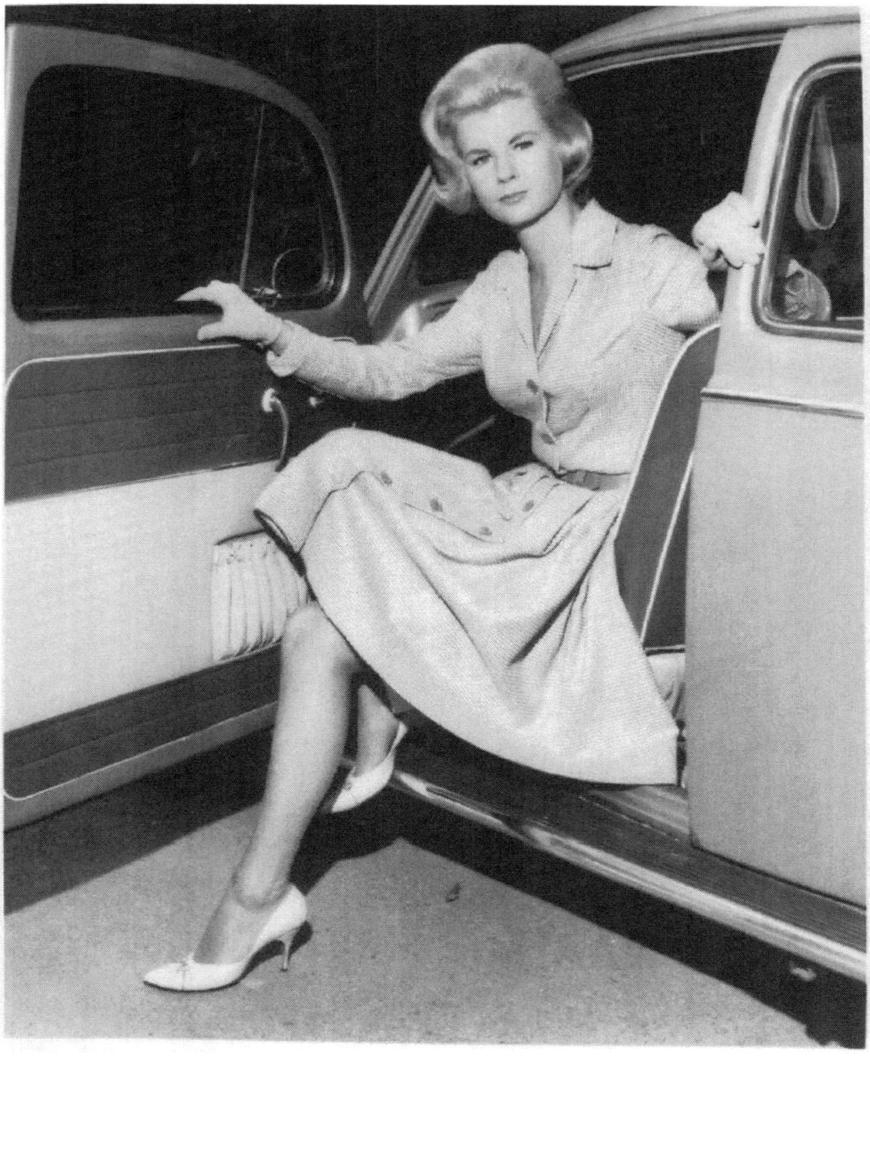

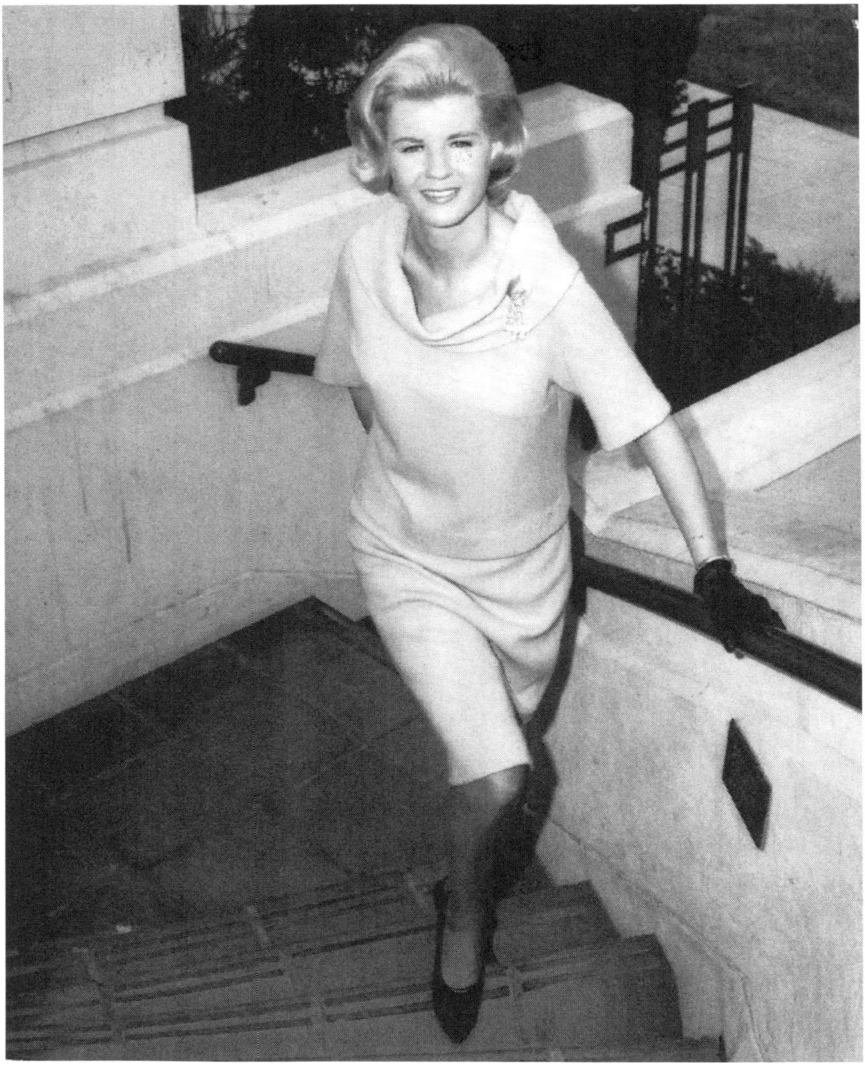

Chapter 24

Leslie Hoffman Takes a Stand

It was hot that August day in 1987 when stuntwoman Leslie Hoffman took the stand to testify at Julie's trial. The air-conditioning in the courtroom wasn't working, so the jurors fanned themselves with notebooks and magazines they'd brought from home. After Leslie was sworn in, Richard Grey started his questioning; but half the time, before she could answer, Spelling's attorney, William Koska would rise to his feet and make an objection. The judge overruled him most of the time, but Koska kept trying—over and over and over. It would have been comical if it hadn't been so hot.

"When you first entered into stunt work, were you aware of Julie Johnson's reputation?" Grey asked.

"Objection!" Koska said, rising from his chair. "Irrelevant. Immaterial."

Some of the jurors may have begun to wonder if those were the only words Koska had learned in law school.

"Overruled," the judge said.

"Yes," Leslie replied, a little nervous at first. "When you come into the business, you hear of various top people. You pick out mentors. When I came into the business, Julie Johnson and Jeannie Epper were the names that I heard."

Of all the many stuntwomen Julie had worked with during her twenty years in the business, only two stepped forward to testify on her behalf: Jeannie Coulter and Leslie Hoffman.

Stuntwomen are, without a doubt, among the bravest women in America, and yet even they can be intimidated into silence by the threat of blacklisting, but not Jeannie Coulter and not Leslie Hoffman.

Leslie came into the business in 1976. It was a good year to be a stuntwoman. *Charlie's Angels*, *The Bionic Woman*, and *Laverne & Shirley* all debuted that year, and *Wonder Woman* was still in its first season.

Even so, in 1976, stuntwomen were still second-class citizens in Hollywood, subject to discrimination, sexual harassment, and the indignity of seeing stuntmen putting on dresses and wigs and taking their jobs. But there was reason for hope. A year earlier, Kathleen Nolan had been the first woman ever elected president of the

Screen Actors Guild, and as SAG's president, she wanted to make some big changes. As president, she formed the Women's Committee and formed and chaired the guild's Stunt Committee. She asked the stunt community to come forth with their grievances, and stuntwomen had a lot of grievances. Julie, Jeannie Coulter, and Leslie Hoffman led the charge.

"We became very vocal," Leslie recalls. "When Julie, Jeannie, and I complained to Kathleen about discrimination and sexual harassment, that's when the trouble began."

All three stuntwomen were branded troublemakers, and in Hollywood, the only thing worse than making bad movies is making trouble. All three would soon be blacklisted.

Hollywood has a long history of blacklisting troublemakers and whistle-blowers. In the 1940s and '50s, hundreds of actors, writers, and directors who were suspected of being Communists or Communist sympathizers were blacklisted and driven out of the business.

And at the very same time that Julie, Jeannie, and Leslie were getting in trouble for making waves, a famous actor was landing in hot water for blowing the whistle on a corrupt studio boss. It happened in 1977, when Oscar-winning actor Cliff Robertson, famous for his portrayal of John F. Kennedy in *PT 109*, discovered that Columbia Pictures president David Begelman had forged his signature and stolen $10,000 from him. Robertson took his charges to the press, and after an investigation by the LAPD and the FBI, the Los Angeles district attorney's office filed felony grand theft charges against the studio boss. Begelman pleaded no contest and received a slap on the wrist—a $5,000 fine, three years probation, and community service.

The penalty would be much stiffer for Robertson however. Hollywood can forgive a crook, but it can never forgive a whistle-blower.

In 1980—two years after his conviction—Begelman was named president and CEO of MGM Studios; and Robertson, branded a troublemaker, was blacklisted. But Robertson had the last laugh. A famous book, *Indecent Exposure*, was written about the affair; and in the end, the general public came to see Robertson as the real-life hero that he was.

There would be no happy ending for Begelman. On August 7, 1995, he checked himself into the swank Century Plaza Hotel in Los Angeles, went up to his room, and shot himself in the head.

In 1981, while Robertson was struggling to save his career, Leslie Hoffman was elected to SAG's Hollywood board of directors—the first stuntwoman ever elected to that position. In 1982, she was named cochair of the SAG Stunt and Safety Committee, and in 1983 she became its chairperson. Leslie was now the leading voice for Hollywood's stuntwomen. She complained about stuntmen doubling for women and accused the stuntmen's groups of operating as hiring halls and illegally refusing to allow women to become members.

But there would be a price to pay. Her phone stopped ringing, and the job offers stopped coming in.

"When I was on the SAG board," she recalls, "I was absolutely blacklisted. I was blacklisted because I wasn't doing what the Stuntmen's Association wanted me to do. Two stuntmen told me that I'd better think about becoming an actress because I'm not going to work anymore as a stuntwoman."

Like Cliff Robertson, Leslie Hoffman was a hero who'd been blacklisted for speaking out. And her hero was Julie Johnson. So it had been an honor for her when she got to work for Julie on *Charlie's Angels*.

"Have you ever worked with Julie Johnson in the stunt field?" Grey asked.

Leslie looked over to the defense table to see if Koska was going to object. He didn't.

"Yes," she answered.

"On how many occasions did you work for Ms. Johnson?" Grey asked.

Leslie looked at Koska again and then answered, "I worked with her twice."

"Was that during the production of *Charlie's Angels*?"

"Yes," she said, "it was."

"Was she coordinating either of those episodes?"

"She was coordinating both episodes," Leslie replied.

One of those episodes, titled "Counterfeit Angels," was about three imposters posing as the Angels. There was a complicated chase scene in which one of the imposters, doubled by Julie, was hit by a car. It went off without a hitch.

In the other episode, called "Angel on High," the Angels uncover a plot to kill a famous stunt pilot. The stunts were great, and nobody got hurt.

"In the stunt business," Grey asked Leslie, "what is the importance of a person's reputation?"

"Objection!" Koska said, jumping to his feet. "Hearsay! Immaterial!"

"Overruled," the judge said.

"Reputation is everything," she answered. "The cliché used in the stunt business is that you're only as good as your last stunt."

"And what was Julie Johnson's reputation as a stunt coordinator?" Grey asked.

"Objection!" Koska interrupted. "Hearsay!"

"Overruled," the judge said wearily.

"She had a very good reputation," Leslie replied. "She was very caring, very careful, and made sure that stunt people were properly placed and padded. She functioned the way a stunt coordinator should function."

"Have you heard of any changes to Julie Johnson's reputation since you first entered the business?" Grey asked.

"Objection!" Koska said. "Vague and ambiguous."

"Overruled," the judge said. "You may answer."

"It has changed," she replied. "Instead of being a top stuntwoman in the business, she is now a troublemaker."

"Did you encounter Ms. Johnson at any of the committee meetings at SAG where she came to address concerns on behalf of stunt people?" Grey asked.

"We were on the Women's Committee together from 1978 to '81," she replied.

"During that period," Grey continued, "were there any particular issues that Julie Johnson became identified with?"

"Objection!" Koska said, wearily rising to his feet. "Irrelevant. Hearsay."

"Overruled," the judge said, even more wearily. The heat was clearly getting to him.

"She complained to the committee about safety on the set," Leslie told the court. "Her concerns were about drugs on the set and that stuntmen were still doubling women."

"In your own personal experience, what's the most important obligation of a stunt coordinator?" Grey asked.

"I would say safety for the cast and crew," she answered.

"That's all I have," Grey said. "Thank you."

Now it was Koska's turn at cross-examination.

"Is Ms. Johnson a friend of yours?" he asked Leslie.

"Yes," she replied.

"A close personal friend?" he pressed.

"She is a friend of mine," she said.

"You were in two *Charlie's Angels*?"

"Yes."

"Did you see anyone under the influence of alcohol or drugs at that time?"

"No," she answered honestly.

"On any Spelling-Goldberg shows you ever worked on, did you ever see anyone under the influence of drugs or alcohol?" Koska asked.

"No."

"While you were working with Ms. Johnson and she was coordinating those two Angels shows," Koska asked, "did you notice anyone trying to rush her to finish a scene to the extent that safety was at jeopardy?"

"No. Not on those."

"Nothing further," he said and took his seat at the defense table.

Judge Savitch was sweating visibly in his hot, black robe. Speaking to the jury, he said, somewhat incongruously, "You won't have to sit here for seven to ten more years and be without the benefit of a brain. As a matter of fact, you won't have to sit here for ten or fifteen minutes more at all and be in this hot courtroom. We are going to adjourn until nine o'clock tomorrow."

Koska seemed pleased with himself as the jurors filed out of the courtroom into the jury room. He'd gotten one of the plaintiff's witnesses to testify that she'd never seen anyone using drugs on the set of *Charlie's Angels* or on any Spelling-Goldberg show for that matter.

But just because *she'd* never seen it, would the jury believe it didn't exist? The outcome of the case might well depend on the answer to that one question.

A few months after walking out of the courtroom that day, Leslie packed up her belongings and moved with her husband to a farm they'd bought in upstate New York. She wouldn't come back to Hollywood for five years, when a courageous and independent stunt coordinator named Dennis Madalone hired her as a regular stunt player on *Star Trek: Voyager* and *Star Trek: Deep Space 9*.

"Dennis hired me and pressed others to hire me," Leslie recalled. "I worked because of this one good man."

Today, disabled by her many knock-down years as a stuntwoman, Leslie is one of the leading voices in Hollywood for the rights of disabled workers.

Some people, it seems, just never give up.

Leslie Hoffman

Chapter 25

A Career Is Launched

Julie was sitting at the receptionist's desk one day when a new client—a good-looking young man in a cheap suit—came in and asked to see Mr. Fairbanks.

"I have a ten o'clock appointment," he told Julie.

He gave her his name, and Julie called her boss's office.

"He'll be right out," she said, hanging up the receiver.

The young man turned away to take a seat and then looked back at Julie.

"You know, you'd be a great double for Doris Day," he said.

"Really?" Julie said, blushing at the compliment. Then, sheepishly, she asked, "What's a double?"

The young man laughed. "You know, the ones who do the action. They double for the actors on the dangerous stuff—the stunts."

"Stunts, eh?" Julie said. "That sounds interesting. They have women who do stunts too?"

"Yeah, sure," he said. "Plenty of 'em."

"Well, I *am* an athlete," she said.

"Well, you'd be a perfect stunt double for Doris Day."

It wasn't the first time she'd been told she looked a lot like Doris Day. In the past few months, she'd heard it at least a dozen times. People were always coming up to her and telling her that. One time, a young girl, mistaking her for the famous actress, even asked for her autograph.

The resemblance *was* striking. They had the same profile and the same bright eyes, the same high cheeks and the same sexy smile. And now, with her new hairstyle, Julie could have passed as Ms. Day's younger sister. But this was the first time that anyone told her that she could be her stunt double.

The young man then asked Julie a seemingly insignificant, but fateful, question.

"Are you with Teddy's?"

"Teddy's?" she asked, not knowing what he meant.

"Yeah," he said, "Teddy O'Toole's. It's the answering service for stunt people. You sign up with them and they call you for auditions."

"No, I'm not," she answered. "Do you have the number?"

"No," he said. "It's in the book." The phone book. Back then, there was only one big fat one for all of Los Angeles.

"I'll look it up," Julie smiled and scribbled down the name.

Jerry Fairbanks came out of his office and greeted the young client.

"Thanks!" she called after him as he walked away with her boss.

"What'd she thank you for?" Julie heard Jerry whisper.

"I'll tell you later," he replied, and they went into Jerry's office and closed the door.

Julie didn't know it then, but a door had just opened for her.

She called Teddy's the next day and made an appointment.

Teddy's was actually more than an answering service for stunt people; it was more of a referral service, a hiring hall. Producers would call in and ask for a certain "type"—man or woman, tall or short, young or old—with experience to match the job, and Teddy would send out several of her clients who matched the description for the audition.

"So I went to see Teddy," Julie recalls, "and she interviewed me and she said, 'Yeah, you'll be great,' and she put me on her answering service."

She was on her way.

Julie was working the switchboard a few days later when Eve stopped by for a chat.

"I hear you signed up with Teddy O'Toole's," she said. "You want to be a stuntwoman?"

"Well, you know, it sounds like it might be fun," Julie stammered, a little nervous to be talking about a different line of work with Eve.

"Well, I hear there's an audition across the street tomorrow," Eve said. "They're looking for a girl to jump over an ironing board. I'll recommend you, if you like."

"Really?" Julie said.

"Yeah. Here's the address and the name of the casting director," Eve said, slipping Julie a piece of paper. "It's at nine o'clock. Be sure to take your headshots. I'll fill in for you on the switchboard."

Julie looked at the name and address she'd written down and then looked up at her pretty friend. "Thanks, Eve. I owe you one."

The next day, Julie parked in the Fairbanks Building and walked across Vine Street to the offices where the audition was being held. Julie was fifteen minutes early, but there were already three young actresses, portfolios in hand, sitting in the waiting room.

"Is this where the audition . . . ," Julie started to say.

They all looked up and nodded in unison. Julie took a seat and waited to be called.

The casting director, a neatly dressed woman in her mid-forties, poked her head around the door and called in one of the young women. The actress, a tall blonde, went in and came out a few minutes later. Then the casting director called in another girl, and then a few minutes later, another.

Finally, it was Julie's turn. "Julie Ann Johnson?" the casting director said.

"Yes," Julie said. She got up and started to follow her into her office, but tripped over the carpet and nearly fell on her face.

"Tripping is not a good sign for what I'm casting," the woman said sternly. "Eve Brent recommended you. She says you're athletic. Is that right?"

"Yes, ma'am."

"We're casting a commercial for Magic Spray Sizing. Do you think you could jump over an ironing board?"

"Yes, ma'am," she said without hesitating.

"Anybody ever tell you you look like Doris Day?"

"Yes, ma'am," Julie replied, blushing. "I've been getting that a lot lately."

"Okay, then. Be here tomorrow morning at ten o'clock ready to jump for the director."

"Okay," Julie said and turned to leave.

"It would help if you left me a picture," the casting director said.

"Oh, yes, ma'am," she said, handing her a headshot.

"And stop calling me ma'am!"

Julie left and hurried back across the street to the Fairbanks Building, where Eve was dutifully filling in for her on the switchboard.

"How'd the audition go?" Eve asked.

"I flubbed it," Julie replied. "I tripped and nearly fell, and she said, 'Tripping is not a good sign for what I'm casting.'"

"Eww. That's not good."

"And I kept calling her ma'am too, and she said, 'Stop calling me ma'am!'"

"Eww. Not good either."

"But she told me to come back tomorrow at ten."

"What? You got a callback? On your first audition? That's fantastic!"

After work that evening, Julie drove straight home to her little bungalow in the Hollywood Hills. The phone was ringing as she opened the door.

"Hello?"

"Hello, beautiful." It was her dad.

"Oh, hi, Dad! Guess what. I have an audition for a TV commercial tomorrow!"

"A TV commercial?"

"Yeah. I have to jump over an ironing board."

"An ironing board? How do they want you to do it?"

"I have no idea," she said. "Dad, should I vault over it like a pommel horse or jump over it like a hurdle?"

"Well, do it both ways for them," he said.

"Yes," she said. "You're right. I have all night to practice."

"Wow!" he said. "My little girl's going to be on TV!"

"Well, I haven't gotten it yet."

"Oh, I'm sure you will," he said. "Who are they going to find better to jump over an ironing board?"

They both laughed, and she told him she'd call him tomorrow to let him know how it went.

"Okay," he said. "Good night, beautiful."

"Good night, Dad."

She hung up and then went into the kitchen, took her ironing board out of the broom closet, turned on the back porch light, and went out to the backyard to practice.

She jumped over it from a running start and from a standstill, with two hands on the board, swinging her legs over, and like a high hurdle, with one leg stretched out front and the other trailing behind. She jumped it every way she could think of except pole vaulting, and she would have jumped it like that if she'd had a pole.

She practiced for hours, sometimes she fell, but usually she didn't. When she made twenty jumps in a row without a miss, she figured she had it down.

She went to bed that night and dreamt of sheep jumping over ironing boards.

Julie awoke the next morning feeling refreshed. She showered and dressed and headed into Hollywood for her callback, arriving fifteen minutes early. She'd been in the production game less than a year, but she was a careful observer and knew that nobody ever got yelled at or fired for being fifteen minutes early.

Julie took a seat, and within a few minutes, three other girls—none of whom had been there the day before—joined her in the waiting room. They were all tall and pretty—models and aspiring actresses, Julie guessed. They all looked fit, but none of them looked very athletic. At ten o'clock, the casting director called one of the girls into the inner office. After a few minutes, there was a loud crash behind the closed door, like somebody had knocked over a water cooler. The girl sitting next to Julie snickered.

A few moments later, the first girl came out limping. Julie hoped she was all right. The snickering girl kept on snickering. The snickering girl was called in next, and after a few minutes, there was another loud crash. When she came back out, her mascara was running. She wasn't snickering any more.

When it was Julie's turn, she went in and saw the casting director standing next to the ironing board, and a middle-aged man with gray hair sitting in a chair against the wall.

"Julie, this is the director," the casting director said.

Julie went over and gave him a firm handshake, only to learn in later auditions that this was not the protocol.

"Julie, do you want to take a shot at it?" the casting director asked.

"Okay," Julie said. She approached the ironing board and put her hands on it to test its steadiness. Then she backed up three steps, took a deep breath, and ran toward it. Planting both hands firmly on the board, she swung her legs over it and landed gracefully on the other side.

The director wrote something in a notebook on his lap. "Could you do it for us again?" he asked, not looking up from his scribbling.

"Okay," Julie said. She backed up, ran at the board, and vaulted over it, sticking the landing again.

The director wrote something in his notebook and asked her to do it one more time.

"Okay," Julie said, and she did it again with the same result.

"Thank you," the director said. "We'll let you know."

Julie walked back across Vine Street to the Petersen offices. Eve was anxiously waiting for her there.

"Well, how'd it go?" she asked, clasping her hands excitedly.

"Okay, I guess," Julie said. "There were three other girls."

"When will you find out?"

"No idea," Julie shrugged. "They said they'd let me know."

A few days later, Julie was at her desk talking to a production assistant, making arrangements for a new Chris Petersen commercial.

"This is the list of props we're going to need by Friday," she told the PA.

The phone rang and Julie picked it up. "Yes, this is Julie Johnson," she told the caller.

The production assistant watched as Julie talked on the phone.

"Yes . . . Yes," Julie said. "Really?"

The PA could see Julie's eyes widen as a big grin spread across her face.

"I don't have an agent," Julie said into the phone. "Yes . . . Yes . . . Okay . . . I'll be there . . . Thank you."

Julie hung up and just sat there, grinning goofily.

"Who was that?" the PA finally asked.

"The casting director for that Magic Spray Sizing commercial I told you about," Julie said. "She wanted to know who my agent is. I got the job!"

"Really?" the PA said excitedly, and they both got up and hugged, bouncing up and down together.

Three days later, Julie was on a sound stage in Hollywood shooting the spray-on starch commercial. They'd done her hair and makeup and put her in tight pants and a T-shirt; and as the camera rolled, she vaulted over the ironing board, just as she'd done at the callback, landing gracefully and with a big smile.

"That's a take!" the director shouted.

And just like that, Julie was a stuntwoman. It was her first paid stunt.

That weekend, Julie drove down to La Habra to see her mom and stepfather, Stan. She'd been so busy she hadn't seen them much since they'd returned from South America. Her mother had gotten a job as a nurse's aide at St. Jude Medical

Center, and Stan had gone to work for a company that made tool and die. To Julie's delight, her mother was sober; she hadn't had a drink since coming back from Venezuela. Her mom was happy and beautiful, and there was a sparkle in her eyes that Julie'd feared had been drowned by all those gallons of gin.

Julie told them her big news, and they were so happy for her. Stan even gave her the $200 she'd need to join the Screen Actors Guild, which was a lot of money for Julie back then—two weeks' pay.

The next Monday, she went down to SAG's office on Sunset Boulevard to join up.

One of the greatest days of any actor's life is the day he or she becomes a member of the Screen Actors Guild. Everyone who joins remembers that day—the day they got their SAG card. And so it was with Julie. She went to the membership department and showed the lady there the letter she'd gotten from the company that had hired her for the Magic Spray commercial.

SAG is an "open shop," meaning that anyone can work once in its jurisdiction without being a member, but after that, you have to join up if you want to keep working.

Julie gave the lady her $200, which covered the registration fee and the first year's dues; and a few minutes later, the lady came back and handed Julie a SAG card with her name on it. She was now a member of the Screen Actors Guild!

"When you get your first SAG card, it's like a dream," Julie recalls. "I think every actor who gets their first SAG card is in awe. I know I was."

Back at work that day, she called Teddy O'Toole and told her that she was now a proud SAG member. After that, Teddy started sending her out on auditions two or three times a week.

"And just about every audition I'd go on, I'd get!" Julie recalls with a laugh, realizing now, all these years later, how remarkably lucky she'd been.

Work and auditions, work and auditions. It was a hectic pace, but it was exciting, and every day brought a new challenge. In October, Teddy sent her on an audition for the *The Beverly Hillbillies*, and she got it, doubling in a scene for actress Nancy Kulp. The job was pretty simple, rowing a boat. But the location was cold and damp—the middle of Long Beach Harbor. The pay was good, and now she had another credit—her first as a stunt double.

After two hours of paddling around in the harbor, Julie changed out of her costume and raced back to Hollywood to start another long day at the Petersen Company.

She was tired when she returned home that night to her little bungalow in the Hollywood Hills. She put a TV dinner in the oven, set up a TV tray, and turned on the television. Fiddling with the TV tray, she heard the jingle before she saw the picture, "You can't run away from ironing day . . ."

Looking up, Julie saw herself jumping gracefully over an ironing board and landing with a big smile. "I'm on TV!" she cried out loud.

She called her dad and told him, and then she called her mom and told her.

A few weeks later, she got her first residuals check, and after that, the checks started pouring in like rain through a leaky roof. The ad ran constantly, and nearly every time it ran, someone would call and say, "Hey, Julie! I saw you on TV!"

Over the next year, she'd receive more than $16,000 in residuals from that one commercial, which was a small fortune in those days. And for Julie, it wasn't so small.

"I'd never seen that kind of money before," she laughs. "And from one job!"

It was three times more than she made in a year at the Petersen Company—and for only one day's work!

Balancing her day job with all the auditions she was going on was becoming increasingly more difficult; but her immediate supervisor, Al Belkin, was a nice guy and he always made sure that one of the assistants covered for her. Clearly, though, she couldn't keep this up indefinitely.

One Friday that November, Julie had an audition over at General Service Studios in Hollywood. It was a beautiful Southern California day. She took an early lunch break and headed over there in her blue Corvair. Turning on the car radio, she heard the shocking news: President Kennedy had been shot in Dallas.

Arriving at the studio, she pulled up to the gate and gave the guard her name.

"Have you heard?" he asked.

Julie nodded, knowing what he meant without asking. He waved her through, and she found a parking spot. As usual, she was fifteen minutes early, but this time she didn't go right in as was her custom. She sat for a while listening to the radio, each new update worse than the last. Finally, she turned off the radio and went inside, where people were standing round a television set watching Walter Cronkite deliver the terrible news.

"From Dallas, Texas, the flash, apparently official: President Kennedy died at 1:00 p.m. Central Standard Time, 2:00 Eastern Standard Time . . ."

The audition was cancelled. Julie headed back to work and found the place nearly deserted. "Where is everybody?" she asked one of the assistants.

"In Al Belkin's office," he said. He'd obviously been crying.

Julie went into her boss's office, where half a dozen people were watching an old black-and-white TV. Several of the women were in tears. Julie stood there numbly for a while and was startled when the phone on Al's desk rang. He answered it.

"Yeah . . . yeah," he said. "Okay."

Belkin hung up and then stood at his desk.

"All right, everybody," he said. "We're done for the day. Everybody go home."

No one moved, as if frozen in time. Then Belkin summed up how everyone felt.

"This is a sad day for our country," he said solemnly.

Julie drove home with tears in her eyes. The streets were empty. Everything seemed empty.

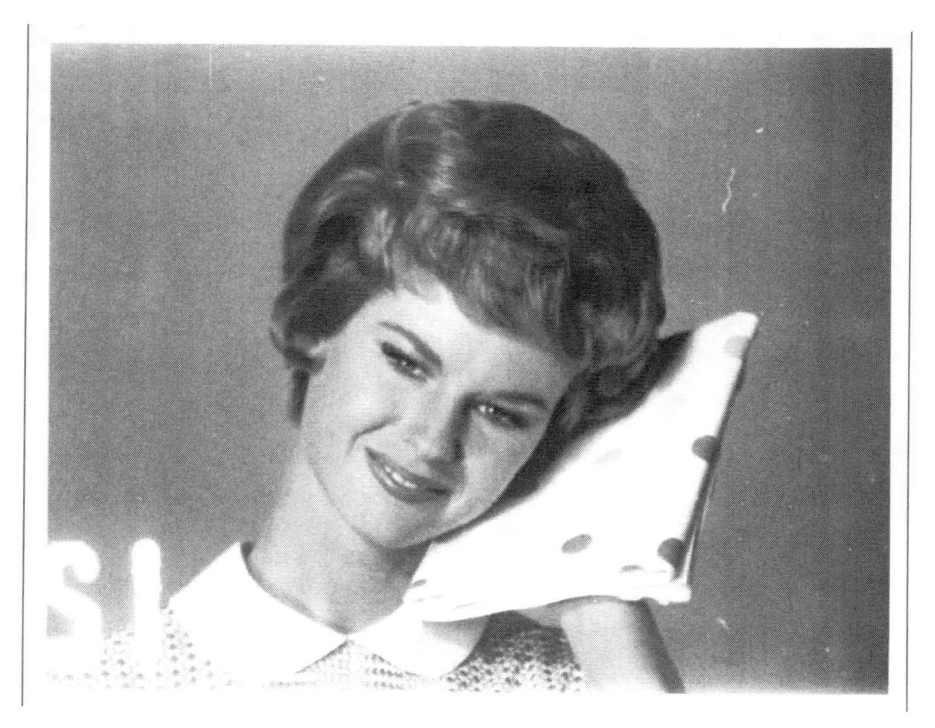

First, Magic Spray Sizing

RUNNING AWAY FROM IRONING DAY (MAGIC SPRAY).

Over the Ironing Board

Chapter 26

Ronnie Rondell Takes the Stand

A lot of little boys want to be cowboys when they grow up, but a lot of cowboys want to be like Ronnie Rondell when *they* grow up. Not so tall but ruggedly handsome, Ronnie was a man's man—the patriarch of a stunt dynasty. He'd worked on over one hundred films, including *The Blues Brothers, Smokey and the Bandit,* and *Close Encounters of the Third Kind*; and when Julie was coordinating *Charlie's Angels*, he was her boss—the supervising stunt coordinator on all of Aaron Spelling's shows.

Ronnie took the witness stand on August 13, 1987, and his testimony would prove crucial to Julie's case. He'd been the first on the scene to come to Julie's aid when Bobby Bass nearly killed her that day out at Indian Dunes. He'd been the one who looked into Julie's complaint that Bobby had been high on coke that day, and after she complained, he was the one who told her she was fired.

A movie projector had been set up in the courtroom the day he testified, and after Ronnie was sworn in, Richard Grey screened the footage of Julie and Jeannie Coulter bailing out of the station wagon. The jury watched in silence as Jeannie fell out of the car and hit the ground like a rag doll, knocked unconscious in a cloud of dust. The camera set-up was so bad that Julie wasn't even in the shot. If she had been, the jury would have seen her knocked out too and then going into convulsions, flopping around on the dirt runway like a dying fish. Then they would have seen Ronnie Rondell rushing to her side and throwing himself on top of her to keep her from further injuring herself.

When the lights came back up, Grey began questioning Rondell about the days immediately following the accident.

"Julie asked you to stop by her home and talk with her privately about this incident a day or two later, isn't that correct?" Grey asked.

"Yes," Rondell answered.

"And did you do that?"

"Yes, I did."

"Before you talked to Julie, did you have any reason to suspect that unlawful drug use in any way contributed to the hazards that we saw on the videotape?"

"Absolutely not!" Rondell stated emphatically—perhaps too emphatically.

His categorical denial may have reminded some of the jurors of Captain Renault's feigned outrage in *Casablanca*, when he tells Rick, "I'm shocked! Shocked to find that gambling is going on in here!"

"Did Julie ask you to come to her house and speak with her about the situation?" Grey asked.

"Yes. She wanted to talk to me, and I wanted to see how she was doing," Ronnie said. "I drove over the next day."

"How did she appear to you, visibly, when you visited with her at her home?"

"She appeared pretty good," he answered. "In pretty good spirits. She had a very sore neck, and as I recall, she had some headaches."

Julie, sitting at the plaintiff's table, scribbled furiously on a notepad. "I was wearing a neck brace and was sore <u>all</u> over," she wrote, underlining the word "all." She pushed the note toward her attorney, but he dismissed it with a glance, as if to say, "You'll get your chance when you testify." Besides, Grey knew from long experience that juries don't like it when plaintiffs or defendants scribble notes to their lawyers while witnesses are testifying. It's distracting, and it makes them look desperate and demanding.

"How much time did you spend talking with her that day?" Grey asked.

"I imagine I was there a half hour," he answered. "Maybe forty-five minutes."

"And what did you talk about?"

"Well, you know . . . 'Nice house. How are you feeling? How is your neck? How is it coming? Do you feel okay?' Things like that."

"Was there anything of a sensitive nature that she discussed with you?"

"Yes," Ronnie said.

"Tell us what was said."

"Julie told me that she had heard from one of the other people something about Mr. Bass leaving the honeywagon and saying he had done the last of the coke, as I recall. And I said, 'Well, Julie, do you think Bobby was doing drugs that day?' And she said, 'Yes, I think so.' And I told her that I would look into it."

"Was she angry?" Grey asked.

"She was upset about it," Ronnie replied.

"What did she say, or do, that indicated that to you?"

"Well," Ronnie hesitated, "I think she was tense, as I recall. And she didn't know for a fact that he had been doing drugs. She heard it secondhand. I told her that there was no place for that. So, yes, she was upset. But I mean, she wasn't crazy with it or anything."

"Was she speaking in a soft-spoken manner?" Grey asked.

"Well, yes. I don't think she was yelling."

"Was she speaking slowly and deliberately or formally?" Grey asked.

"Objection!" Koska said. "Irrelevant! Immaterial!"

"Overruled," the judge said.

"I don't recall her specific, exact mannerisms," Ronnie said.

"Isn't it a fact," Grey pounced, "that she was very, very angry, and that she told you that she was very, very angry about what had happened?"

"Objection!" Koska said, rising from his chair. "Argumentative! No foundation!"

"Overruled," the judge declared.

"As I stated, she was upset about that, but I don't believe she was very, very upset, and she wasn't yelling, as I recall."

"Was there anything that she said, sir, that indicated to you that she was upset, as you have described it here today?"

"I don't know how to answer that question," Ronnie replied, genuinely confused. "I don't know what you want to hear."

"Well," Grey said, "did she say, for instance, 'I put my life on the line on this stunt! I could have been killed!'"

And that, in fact, is exactly what she said.

"I don't recall that exact phrasing, no," he replied.

Grey was getting worked up now, and his voice was getting louder and more accusatory with each question.

"Did she say to you, for instance, 'Not only did I do the stunt, but you didn't even capture me on film! The camera was on the wrong side of the car!'"

And that, in fact, is exactly what she said.

"I don't recall that at all," Ronnie answered.

"Did she say to you, 'This drug situation has gotten out of hand and something has to be done about it!'"

The jury could sense that Grey was trying to pull the truth out of the witness, but the judge wanted him to tone it down a notch.

"Mr. Grey," the judge scolded, "you don't have to raise your voice when you ask the question. Just ask the question."

"Very well, Your Honor."

Ronnie answered the question without Grey having to ask it again.

"I don't believe she said anything about a drug situation that had gotten out of hand," he said, although that is exactly what she said.

"Do you recall anything else of significance that was said during your conversation with her that you haven't already mentioned here in court?" Grey asked.

"Nothing other than that after Julie made the statement about Mr. Bass, I told her that I would look into it."

"Did you say something to the effect, 'I'll take care of it,'" Grey asked, knowing that that's exactly what Ronnie had told her.

"I don't recall specifically what I said," he answered.

"In substance, then, was Ms. Johnson asking you to look into this as a problem that she saw at work?"

"Well, it seemed to me," Ronnie answered, "that she had heard something secondhand, and she was concerned about it and wanted me to look into it."

"Didn't she also tell you that she was concerned that the car was traveling at a much higher rate of speed than it should have been during filming?" Grey asked, knowing again that that's exactly what she had told Ronnie.

"I don't recall that that was mentioned," he replied.

"Didn't she talk to you about the car picking up speed instead of slacking off, hitting the accelerator instead of the brake, or something to that effect?"

"She may have."

"How did the conversation wind up, then, before you left Julie's house?" Grey asked.

"Other than I hoped she was feeling better, and as I previously said, that I would look into it."

"And did you, in fact, look into it?"

"Yes, I did," Ronnie answered.

"What did you do about it?"

"Well, because Mr. Harrison was on the set, he was the first person I contacted," Ronnie replied. "I asked him if he had any knowledge of drug use on the set, specifically about Mr. Bass. He said no, he did not."

This, of course, was like asking Butch Cassidy and the Sundance Kid to investigate a train robbery. As Jeannie Coulter had sworn in her deposition—and as the jury would later learn—she'd personally witnessed Rondell, the man heading up the investigation, and Roy Harrison, the first person he'd turned to, to get to the bottom of things, snorting cocaine together.

Rondell testified that he then asked Bobby Bass if he'd taken cocaine that day.

"I went directly to Mr. Bass," Ronnie continued, "and told him what Julie's suspicions were, and Mr. Bass flatly denied it."

"When was that?" Grey asked.

"It was shortly after. I don't recall exactly when."

"The same day that you met with Julie?"

"I doubt it was the same day," Ronnie replied.

"Where did you see Mr. Bass?"

"I don't recall."

Grey could see the jury taking notes and decided he'd milked this line of questioning for about as much as he could get. Now he wanted to address the code of silence in the stunt community and the culture of covering up for each other's drug problems.

Tragically, it was a culture that contributed to the death of Rondell's own son, Reid Rondell, who, high on coke, had been killed two and a half years earlier in a helicopter crash while filming a stunt for *Airwolf*.

"In your experience in the stunt community," Grey asked, "is there a kind of taboo about talking about drug-related matters that impact on the work?"

"Objection!" Koska bellowed, rising from his chair. "Hearsay! Speculation!"

"I'll overrule it," the judge declared.

"Would you state that again?" Ronnie asked.

"Is discussion of drug-related activities on the set a touchy subject?" Grey asked.

"I don't think people are afraid to talk about something like that," Ronnie answered, "but I don't think, for the overall good of the stunt community, that you would want to go to the newspaper with something like that."

Which was, more or less, just what Julie had done by bringing this lawsuit.

Then Grey asked him point-blank, "Have you ever seen anyone taking illegal drugs on the set of Spelling-Goldberg productions?"

"Are you talking about the stunt team?" Ronnie asked evasively.

"Yes," Grey said. "Stunt people during production on the set."

"Absolutely not," Ronnie said defiantly.

"Other than confronting Mr. Bass and hearing his denial, did you do anything else as a follow-up to the concerns that Julie Johnson expressed to you?" Grey asked.

"No, I did not," Ronnie answered.

"Did you pass those concerns along to anybody else at Spelling-Goldberg?"

"No, I did not."

"Were you satisfied, after talking to Bobby Bass and Roy Harrison, that the matter should be closed?" Grey asked.

"Yes," he said. "I was."

And that was it. Case closed. Investigation over. Two women had almost been killed because Bobby Bass had been high on coke, and yet, Rondell didn't think it necessary to do anything more about it. Which was too bad for Heidi von Beltz, who, a year later, would be left a quadriplegic because Bobby Bass had been high on coke again while stunt coordinating *Cannonball Run*. Any stunt coordinator in his right mind—and not high on cocaine—would have insisted that Heidi be provided with seat belts for her stunt. But Bobby Bass hadn't been in his right mind; he'd been high on coke. And if Ronnie Rondell had really cared—if he'd really looked into Julie's complaint instead of dismissing it after simply interviewing his alleged drug buddies about it, Bobby might have been fired. And if word had gotten out, he might not have been hired as the stunt coordinator on *Cannonball Run*. If Ronnie had done a proper investigation, Heidi might be walking around today or riding a bike or jogging or climbing stairs or standing in line at the bank or combing her hair or brushing her teeth—none of which she can do today.

Action has consequences, and so does inaction.

"That's all I have," Grey told the judge and returned to his seat at the plaintiff's table.

Koska would get his turn at cross-examination, but there was nothing that he could do to restore Rondell's credibility as a witness. Jurors would later say that they were convinced that Julie and Jeannie Coulter had been injured that day out at Indian Dunes because Bobby Bass had been high on cocaine—and, by implication, that

Ronnie Rondell had failed in his responsibilities to conduct a proper investigation of Julie's complaint.

In his cross-examination of Rondell, Koska would try to convince the jury that Julie had not been fired because she'd complained about drugs and safety. In the end, however, the jury would conclude not only that she'd been fired for speaking out but that she'd been branded a troublemaker and blacklisted throughout the industry as well.

Chapter 27

The Cattle Call

Julie was sitting at her desk at the Petersen Company one day, reading the *Hollywood Reporter*, when a headline caught her eye. It said, "Uni Seeks New Faces."

"Well, I have a new face," she thought and read on. The article said that Universal Pictures was holding open auditions for aspiring actresses. In the business it was known as a cattle call. Julie jotted down the time and place of the audition and quickly made arrangements for someone to take her place on the switchboard.

On the appointed day, Julie drove over the Cahuenga Pass into the Valley and onto the Universal lot. She gave her name at the guard gate and was waved through. She parked her car and walked to a sound stage with a big sign out front that said, Open Audition. It was two o'clock, and for the first time in her career, she was late.

Inside, a hundred young women were standing in line, scribbling their names on sign-in sheets and talking to casting directors. Julie got in line, signed up, and waited to be called. And waited. And waited. And waited.

As the hours passed, fewer and fewer girls were left waiting to be called. By five o'clock, Julie was the last one there. Finally, a young man in a black suit and red tie approached her. "You must be Julie Ann Johnson," he said.

"Yes," she said. "That's me."

"You're the last one on our list," he said, looking down at the list of a hundred names and ninety-nine checkmarks.

"Say," he said, looking up from the list. "Did anyone ever tell you that you look like Doris Day?"

"Yeah, I get that all the time," Julie said. "But you're the first one today!"

They both laughed at that, and then he introduced himself.

"My name's Steven," he said. "I'm an assistant casting director here at Universal. Let's go into my office."

She followed him into a small office with a tiny desk cluttered with stacks of résumés and 8 x 10 glossies. She handed him hers.

"Have a seat," he said, looking over her résumé.

"I see you're an athlete," he said, "and that you do stunts."

"Yeah, I've done a couple," she said.

"Fantastic," he said. "Ya know, you're the last girl we saw today, but the first one with stunts on her résumé. Everybody wants to be a movie star. Nobody wants to do the dirty work. I should have you meet Abby Singer. Wait here a sec."

Steven got up from his desk and hurried out of the office. A few minutes later, he returned with a man in his midforties with big cheeks and a high forehead.

"Julie," Steven said, "I'd like you to meet Abby Singer. Abby, this is Julie Johnson."

Julie reached out and gave Abby a firm handshake.

"Abby's a production manager at Universal," Steven continued. "Or should I say, *the* production manager at Universal."

"Steven tells me you're a stuntwoman," Abby said. "Have we seen you in anything?"

"Well, I jumped over an ironing board for Magic Spray Sizing," Julie said.

"That was you?" Steven said with genuine surprise. "I've seen that ad a hundred times."

Julie nodded, embarrassed by her notoriety.

Abby asked her a few questions about herself, and she gave him short answers. She told him that she born to be an athlete, that her father was a coach, and that her grandfather was a Hall of Fame baseball player.

"What's his name?" Abby asked, intrigued.

"Sam Crawford," she said. "He played on the Detroit Tigers with Ty Cobb."

"Really," Abby said, impressed. "And what about you? Do you want to be an actress or a stuntwoman?"

"A stuntwoman," Julie said without hesitating.

"Okay," Abby said. "Come with me. You too, Steven."

They walked across the soundstage to another office. Abby knocked on the door and then pushed it open without waiting for anyone to say, "Come in." A dozen men were sitting around a long table looking at headshots and résumés. Everyone looked up as they entered the room.

"Gentlemen," Abby said, "I'd like to introduce you to Julie Johnson. She's an athlete, and she does stunts. Let's see if we can find her some work."

And they did, lots of it. They'd call her for an audition, and she'd get the job, mostly *nondescript* work on TV shows and low-budget movies. She was the girl hanging onto the back of a speeding hotrod, the girl who got knocked down in the street, the girl falling down stairs, the girl hit by a car.

It wasn't long before Al Belkin, her supervisor at the Petersen Company, called her into his office.

"Julie?" he said with an arched eyebrow.

"I know. I know. I've got to pick one or the other," she said. "I either have to stay here or go out into the world."

She loved working there. The pay was good and she liked the people. But in the end, it was an easy call. It was time to go out into the world; it was time to try her hand at stunts full-time.

She gave her two weeks' notice and hugged everyone when she left. It was especially tough saying good-bye to Eve Brent, who'd done so much for her, but they both knew that this was the right thing to do.

Over the next two years, the stunt work was steady and her résumé was growing. There was something new and adventurous to do every day. She couldn't have asked for a more exciting career. After-hours was different though. She dated a little, but not much. She still hadn't gotten over Eddie and hadn't met anyone remotely like him. Eddie was patient and earnest and tender. Eddie was all heart; the men in Hollywood were all hands. Stuntmen were too rough and actors were too soft. She didn't go out with married men, and she didn't sleep around to advance her career. She wasn't that kind of girl. And besides, she knew that if women could sleep their way to the top, there'd be more women at the top; and in those days, there weren't any women at the top or anywhere near it.

In 1964, Teddy's sent her on an audition for a new show called *The Man from U.N.C.L.E.*, which starred Robert Vaughn and David McCallum as secret agents who battled evil for an international spy agency. Julie got the job, and it turned out to be a great gig—she ended up working on a dozen episodes over the next two years, doubling for many of the show's female guest stars.

On one of those episodes, she was called out to the MGM back lot in Culver City to shoot a scene on a man-made lake. Her job was to pilot a speedboat while two stuntmen, playing bad guys, chased her in another speedboat.

The two boats were doing figure 8s in the lake when suddenly, the chase boat accidentally hit the dock, throwing the two stuntmen into water. The pilotless chase boat, still going at full speed, was roaring around the lake in tight circles. Julie saw what was happening and turned her boat around to head it off. But before she could get there, it ran over one of the stuntmen, Freddy Waugh. Its propeller ripped a deep, foot-long gash from his shoulder to his spine. Julie managed to catch up with the driverless boat and nudged it away from the men as crewmembers in another boat dove in and pulled Freddy out of the water. Freddy was hurt real bad.

Darrell Hallenbeck, the director, thought that Freddy had been killed for sure.

"Oh my god!" he recalled on seeing Freddie lay bleeding on the dock. "He's chopped to pieces! His back was open from his tailbone to his shoulders—just laid open, exposing his spine. It was the worst thing I ever saw in my life."

An ambulance arrived and Freddy was rushed to the hospital. Miraculously, he survived and, after a few months and several surgeries, was back on the job.

For Julie, it was a wake-up call to the realities of the stunt business.

"That was the first time I'd seen an accident on the set," she recalls. "It was an eye-opener. I realized that you can really get hurt doin' this stuff."

Julie worked regularly throughout all of 1966, including doubling for Stephanie Powers on several episodes of *The Girl from U.N.C.L.E.*

Later that winter, Teddy's sent her on an audition at 20th Century Fox. She drove to the lot on Pico Boulevard, gave the guard her name, and was waved through the gate. Waiting to interview her was Francisco "Chico" Day, the legendary assistant director; he'd worked with Cecile B. DeMille on *The Ten Commandments* and was one of the few Hispanics working in Hollywood. In fact, he'd been the first, and for many years the only, Mexican-American member of the Directors Guild of America.

Julie took a seat in the waiting room, and a few minutes later, Patty Elder walked in. Blonde and firmly built, Patty was a stuntwoman who'd started in the business at about the same time as Julie. On this day, they were both up for the same job.

They small-talked for a while, and then Chico came out of his office. Chico was a wiry little man with a big nose and a tuft of black hair that seemed to be blowing in all directions at once. Julie knew she had the job as soon as he spoke.

"We're casting the new Doris Day film," he said. "It's called *Caprice*."

People had been telling her that she looked like Doris Day for years now. And they were almost the same height, which in the stunt business is even more important than looks. Doris Day was 5'6" and Julie was 5'6 1/2" and Patty Elder was a good three inches shorter. And sure enough, Julie got the job.

Caprice was a comedic spy spoof starring Doris Day and Richard Harris on the trail of a secret formula that can "change the world"—a hair spray that can keep ladies' hair dry even in the rain!

A few days after their first meeting, Chico called Julie and asked her to meet him on the Fox lot in Culver City. When she got there, he gave her the low-down.

"We're gonna go up to Mammoth and you're just gonna hang from a rope ladder under a helicopter about forty feet in the air," he told her.

"Okay," Julie said. It sounded exciting. And she'd never been to Mammoth Mountain, a popular California ski resort in the Eastern Sierra Nevada Range.

The company flew her up to the Mammoth Lakes Airport in a little twin-engine prop plane, and after landing, she took a cab to the lodge where the crew was staying.

Early the next morning, Chico called her room and told her that he'd have a van waiting outside to take her to the location.

Freddy Waugh was in the front seat with the driver when the van pulled up.

"Hey, Freddy! How ya' doin'?" Julie called out.

"Can't complain," Freddy said and gave her a friendly wink.

Julie got into the back of the van, and they headed up to the mountain location. It took them half an hour on winding, icy roads to get there, and they never once talked about the accident that nearly took Freddy's life. It was the stuntmen's code of silence.

It was cold and windy on the mountain when they got to the location, and there were several feet of fresh snow on the ground. Julie went into one of the dressing room trailers and a costumer fitted her in full ski gear and boots and handed her a pair of skis. Stepping back outside, Julie trudged across the snow to the helicopter, where Freddie was talking to the second assistant director, known in the business as the second AD.

The second AD was explaining the shot: Freddie would come in, dangling from the chopper on a twenty-foot rope ladder, and pick Julie up. The helicopter would hover forty feet off the ground, fly around for a few minutes, and they'd get their shot. Then everyone would go back to the lodge and drink hot cocoa by the fire. It was going to be a piece of cake.

But Freddy wanted a test run first.

"Just take us up a little ways and we'll hang for a minute to test the gear," Freddy told the pilot. "Twenty feet, okay?"

The pilot looked at the second AD, who nodded.

"Okay," the pilot said. "Got it."

The safety gear that day consisted of a harness that Freddy was wearing that he would attach to the rope ladder to keep him and Julie from falling. That would be their lifeline. Julie, doubling for Doris Day, wouldn't have a harness; she'd have to hang on to Freddy for dear life. Wearing skis would make the whole scene all the more difficult.

Julie had never been on skis on snow before, but she had shot a ski scene for a sitcom the year before. In that sketch, Juliet Prowse, playing a whacky housewife, was vacuuming her house on skis and then had to ski down the back steps. Julie doubled for her skiing down the steps. It was like wearing a giant pair of scissors, but she nailed it.

No skiing would be required for this scene on the freezing mountaintop, but it would be tricky nonetheless. With both skis on, Julie wouldn't be able to fit her leg through the bottom rung of the rope ladder when the chopper swooped in to pick her up. So she'd have to leave one ski off, and when the chopper came in, crew members on the ground would attach the ski to her boot and the chopper would take off.

This would have worked fine except for the snowstorm whipped up by the helicopter's rotor blades. Even so, in these near-white-out conditions, she pulled it off; and with Freddy holding on to her, she gave the pilot the good-to-go sign. Then, caught in a gust of wind that came roaring up the mountainside, he took off straight up. The acceleration and the weight of the skis and boots pulled down on her as the chopper continued to climb. It was brutally cold and the rungs of the ladder were slippery—like horizontal icicles.

She was slipping. The chopper rose quickly to fifty feet, then sixty, seventy, eighty. They kept rising and rising, into the clear sky, pushed higher and higher by a powerful updraft.

The wind was blowing hard over the mountaintop, and with the downdraft of the prop wash, it was like being hit by a tornado from the side and by a hurricane from above.

"The wind took us up a hundred feet," Julie recalls, "and I started slipping. Between the wind and the weight of the outfit and the boots and the skis, Freddy just couldn't hold me."

Julie held on as best she could, but she could feel herself slipping out of his grip. If she fell, she'd be killed for sure. Freddy clutched at the nape of her coat to get a better grip, but her coat started coming off over her head. Realizing that she was about to fall, Julie let go with one hand and waved wildly to the pilot, yelling "Down! Down! Down!"

The pilot, finally seeing that they were in trouble, pressed forward hard on the controls and put the chopper into a steep nose dive. Then, at the last moment, he leveled it off and sat them down gently on the ground, whipping up another huge cloud of fresh snow.

Crew members ran to them to see if they were all right.

"I couldn't have held her much longer," Freddy told them in a calm voice. "We've got to harness her hip to my hip and harness her other side to the ladder so that it's like a little chair for her to sit in."

The crew hooked her up as Freddie said, and after tugging on the rigging real hard to make sure it was secure, Julie gave the second AD the thumbs-up.

"Okay!" he shouted. "Let's get this on film before we lose the light!"

Then, with cameras rolling, they did the whole thing all over again, with Julie and Freddy suspended below the helicopter. This time, though, the chopper didn't just go up forty feet, or even one hundred feet, as it had in the test run. *Whoosh!* It went straight up—four hundred feet!

"It was a beautiful view," Julie recalls with a laugh, "but I thought, 'Oh my god, what am I doing up here?'"

It was cold, but she wasn't slipping this time, and quickly relaxed into it. The mountains and lakes below were so tranquil—like a postcard that stretched as far as the eye could see. The chopper made several passes in front of the camera, and then the second AD shouted to the pilot over his radio, "Okay! That's a print! Bring 'em down!"

Later that afternoon, Julie sat next to the fireplace at the lodge, sipping hot cocoa and reflecting on the day's events. It had been the first time she'd nearly been killed doing a stunt—but it wouldn't be the last.

She left Mammoth the next day, and when she got home, Teddy's called and said Chico Day wanted to talk to her. She hung up and called Chico at his office on the Fox lot.

"We got some more stuff for you to do," he told her. "You'll be doubling Ms. Day again. We'll be shooting your scene at a house in the Hollywood Hills on Friday."

"Okay," Julie said.

He gave her the address and call time, and she jotted it down.

"By the way," Chico said. "You did a good job up on the mountain. Freddy told me what happened. He said you were terrific—four hundred feet up in the air and not a frightened bone in your whole body."

"Thanks," Julie said.

"See you Friday then," he said.

Julie found the address on Doheny Drive. It wasn't hard—it was the house with half a dozen large equipment trucks and trailers parked out front and several off-duty LAPD motorcycle cops providing security. Julie parked and went inside. The place was bustling with workers setting up lights and running cables to a generator out on the street. Chico was talking to one of the camera guys out on a huge redwood deck overlooking all of Hollywood.

"Hey, Julie!" Chico said, greeting her with a big smile. "Let's get you in costume."

He took her back outside and into one of the dressing trailers parked on the street.

"This is Julie Johnson," he told the costumer. "She'll be doubling for Ms. Day."

As Julie was being fitted, Chico explained the stunt, which involved hanging from beneath the deck they'd just been standing on and dropping down onto the steep hillside below.

"Think you can do that?" he asked.

"Yes, sir," she said.

"Great. You'll be working with Richard Harris on this one. At the end of the scene, he'll drive around and pick you up in a convertible.

Richard Harris! The star of *Camelot*! In a convertible!

"Okay, then," Chico said. "Get your wig on, and I'll come get you when camera and sound are ready."

Chico left and the hairdressers started fitting her for the wig. A few minutes later, there was a knock at the dressing room door. It was Chico. Peeking his head around the door, he told Julie, "Ms. Day wants to see you."

"Doris Day wants to see *me*?" she asked, a bit taken aback.

"Yeah," Chico said. "She's waiting outside."

Julie straightened her wig, took a deep breath, and went out to meet the star of the show. Going down the steps, she saw Doris Day walking toward her. Julie had never been starstruck, but this time she was.

"It was kind of surreal," she recalls. "It was like, 'Oh my god, I'm standing in front of Doris Day!'"

Doris stopped in her tracks, placed her hands on her hips, and looked Julie up and down. "Well, she's kind of skinny, isn't she?" she asked skeptically.

"Oh, don't worry about that, Ms. Day," Chico said nervously. "We're going to pad her up and fill her out under the dress."

"Well, okay," Doris said. "That'll do."

Chico took Julie back into the trailer and had the costumers pad her up to make her a better match for the star. When they were through, Julie could have almost passed as her twin.

"I filled out the dress a little tighter, and you couldn't tell the difference," she laughs. "You could come in so close with the camera and you couldn't believe what a good match it was."

A few minutes later, Chico came back to the trailer and took Julie to meet the director, Frank Tashlin.

Tashlin, a good-looking man with short-cropped gray hair, was talking to the cameraman when Chico and Julie walked into the house.

"Put the camera here and light it from behind," he told the cameraman, who set about doing it.

"Excuse me, Frank," Chico said. "This is Julie Johnson. She'll be doubling for Ms. Day today."

Tashlin turned and did a double-take when he saw Julie standing there in full costume and wig. "Jesus!" he said. "Where'd you get this girl? She's a dead-ringer for Doris!"

"Yeah, ain't she?" Chico said, proud of his discovery.

"We should have used her last year for *The Glass Bottom Boat*," said Tashlin, who'd directed Doris Day in that film as well.

"Frank, do you have time to show her the job?" Chico asked.

"Yeah, sure," the director said, still amazed by how much Julie looked like the film's star. "Come over here, Julie," he said. "It's Julie, right?"

"Yes, sir," she said as he took her by the arm and walked her over to two pieces of masking tape that that had been put on the hardwood floor in the shape of an X.

"This is your mark," he said. "When I say 'action,' you take off and run for the railing on the deck over there. Okay?"

"Yes, sir," she said.

"Come with me," he said and led her to the railing.

As they walked across the deck, Julie could see, through the cracks in the flooring, electricians pulling cables and setting up lights underneath the deck.

"Now, once you get over here," he said, slapping the rail with the palm of his hand, "you hop over and then climb down as far as you can go. Okay? But be careful. It's a pretty long fall from up here."

"Got it," she said, looking over the rail to the brush and rocks on the hillside twenty feet below.

"Good, now come with me." Tashlin took her out the back down and down around the house to the underside of the cantilevered deck they'd just been standing on. It was supported by massive wooden beams and steel girders.

"The next shot will be down here," he said. "You'll be hanging from the underside of the deck. The carpenters have placed a few metal crossbeams here,

here, and here," he said, pointing them out to her. "You'll swing hand over hand on these crossbeams, like monkey bars. Got it?"

"Got it," Julie said.

"Then, from up there, the bad guys will pour a big bucket of water on you through the cracks in the floorboards. And when you get hit by the water, you'll fall a few feet to the hillside right here."

He pointed out the landing spot, which had been cleared of rocks and brush.

"I'll make sure the water's warm, okay?" he said with a laugh.

"Okay, sir," she replied. "Thanks."

"Then, after you fall, you'll scramble down the hill to the road down there. See it?"

She nodded.

"Then, in the final take," he said, "Richard Harris will drive up in a convertible with the top down, and you'll jump over the door into the front passenger seat, and he'll drive off. That's it. Got it?"

"Got it," she said confidently.

"Good girl," he said, patting her on the back.

Julie went back in the trailer and waited to be called. An hour later, there was a knock on the door. It was Chico. "It's show time!" he said, a big grin on his face.

He led her back into the house and took her to her mark. The room was bathed in silence and electric light.

"Are you ready?" Chico asked her.

Julie nodded.

"She's ready!" Chico said in a loud voice and then stepped away.

"All right," the director said. "Roll cameras!"

The camera loader clapped the clapperboard. It sounded like a pistol starting a race.

"Action!" shouted the director.

Julie, in full costume and wig, raced across the deck, scampered over the railing, and disappeared over the side.

"That's a print!" Tashlin shouted.

Making movies is like making love—a lot of buildup and then a few minutes of action. An hour later, the cameras and lights had been repositioned under the deck, and it was time to shoot the next scene.

Somebody brought a ladder and held it as Julie climbed up and grabbed hold of the monkey bars that had been put up under the decking.

"Quiet on the set!" someone yelled.

"Roll cameras!" the director shouted, and once again, the camera loader clapped the clapperboard. "And . . . action!"

Julie swung back and forth on the monkey bars for a few seconds, and then two prop men up above poured a huge bucket of water onto her through the floorboards of the deck. As the director had promised, the water was warm.

Completely drenched, Julie fell, on cue, to the hillside a few feet below.

The force of the water, however, knocked one of her shoes off; and when she fell, she landed hard. She picked up the shoe and, with cameras rolling, scrambled down the rocky hillside in nylons and only one shoe on. Running downhill, her bare foot was gouged by bits of glass, small rocks, and stickers. At the bottom of the hill, she limped to the road; and when Richard Harris drove up in the convertible, she jumped into the car and they raced away.

"That's a take!" the director shouted, to the applause of the crew.

In the film, Julie can be seen, doubling for Doris Day, limping down the hill and leaping, one shoe in hand, into the convertible and driving off with Richard Harris. It worked even better than planned.

Fortunately for Julie, it was the last shot of the day. Back in the dressing room trailer, a medic looked at her foot. It was bleeding, and she could barely walk. "You got to go to the studio hospital," the medic said, "and they'll clean that up for you."

Julie drove to the Fox lot on Pico and went to the studio hospital, where a nurse cleaned up her foot and wrapped it in a bandage. She'd had some bumps and bruises as a stuntwoman, but this was the first time she'd been sent to the hospital—but it wouldn't be the last.

Even though she'd been injured, Julie hit all her marks, and the director and the film's star both loved her work.

"My films abound in difficult stunts," Tashlin wrote in a letter of recommendation, "and through the years, I have worked with many capable stunt people, but never anyone more cable and willing than Julie Ann Johnson. Doubling for Ms. Doris Day in *Caprice*, Julie gave me what I wanted and more."

Doris Day was even more effusive. "You did some marvelous work, Julie," she wrote in a letter to Julie. "I would dearly love working with you again, and if the opportunity presents itself, you can rest assured we will call you pronto!"

And Julie would work for her again and pronto—the very next year on her hit TV series, *The Doris Day Show*.

First Theatrical Headshot

"Caprice" doubling for Doris Day, 20th Century Fox

Chapter 28

Aaron Spelling Takes the Stand

"Call your next witness," the judge told Julie's attorney.

"Plaintiff calls Aaron Spelling," Richard Grey said in a loud voice.

Spelling, wearing a dark business suit and tie, strode through the courtroom and took the witness stand and smiled at the jurors, as if to an adoring audience, his short-cropped hair even whiter than his teeth.

The clerk swore him in, and Grey started out by asking him about his background—how he came to be the most famous television producer in the world.

Spelling gave him the short version.

"I came out here from Texas as an actor," he said in a raspy, cigarette-tinged voice. "I was an actor, writer, director, and producer. I was an executive producer at Four Stars for years and then formed my own company with Danny Thomas and then my own organization." The long version was more poignant.

He grew up in a small frame house on the wrong side of the tracks in Dallas, the fourth son of Jewish immigrants. As a child, skinny and frail, he was tormented by bullies, who picked on him mercilessly, subjecting him to anti-Semitic taunts and beatings on his way home from school.

"I grew up thinking 'Jew boy' was one word," he wrote in his memoirs.

He had a nervous breakdown when he was eight and spent a year in bed recuperating, reading books. He'd later say that those days were the dawn of his love of great storytellers. Lying there in bed, reading about great men and great adventures—and nursing his hatred of bullies—he vowed that one day he would be rich and powerful and that nobody would ever bully him again. One day, he would be the bully.

His family was poor and crowded into a tiny house. "I still have nightmares about it," he later recalled. "Wall-to-wall people, one bathroom."

Confined to bed in that little house, he dreamed of one day living in the biggest house in town. And one day he would. On the day he testified at Julie's trial, he was working on plans to build the biggest house in Los Angeles. And after his death in

2006, when the palace he'd built in Holmby Hills was put up for sale, it was listed for $150 million—the most expensive house in America.

Spelling told the court about some of the shows he'd produced—shows that all the jurors were familiar with. He'd already had hits with *Charlie's Angels, The Love Boat, Fantasy Island, Starsky and Hutch,* and many others, including *Hotel* and *Dynasty,* which were still on the air. But on this day, as he prepared to answer more of this lawyer's questions, some of his biggest hits were yet to come, including *Melrose Place* and *Beverly Hills, 90210.*

"Are you acquainted with Julie Ann Johnson?" Grey asked.

"Yes, I am," he replied. He'd met her on the set and at cast parties.

"Did anyone ever talk to you about the quality of her work?" Grey asked.

"She was a very good stuntwoman," Spelling replied truthfully.

"When she became a stunt coordinator, were you aware of that move?"

"Yes," he said. "I was."

"Did you have any involvement in hiring her as the stunt coordinator?"

"Indirectly, I did," Spelling replied. "They asked my approval of it."

"And you gave it?"

"I was thrilled that they were going to take a chance on a woman," he said.

"Why?" Grey asked. "Was that unique at that particular period of time?"

"To the best of my knowledge," Spelling said, "at that time, there were no women stunt coordinators in television. Maybe there was one I didn't know about, but at that time, there were, if any, very, very few. So basically, I thought it was terrific."

"So at that time, stunt coordinating was pretty much a male-dominated field?"

"Yes," Spelling answered. "At that time."

Excellent! He'd just confirmed that stunt-coordinating was a males-only club, and the jury would soon learn how he'd fired its only woman member.

"Were you aware of the decision to terminate Julie Johnson's employment on *Charlie's Angels*?" Grey asked.

"To my knowledge," Spelling answered, "Ms. Johnson was never terminated. She finished the season."

In Hollywood-speak, having someone call you on the phone and tell you that someone else will be doing your job was not being fired. It's just a matter of not having your employment renewed. But for many—if not all—of the jurors, this kind of Tinsel Town double-talk was a distinction without a difference. Many of them had been fired at one time or another, and they knew what it felt like, and they knew it when they saw it. Spelling could call it something else if he wanted to, but it only made him lose credibility in the eyes of the jury.

"Let me rephrase it then," Grey said, acceding to Spelling's desire to split hairs. "Were you aware of the decision that she not be brought back for the next season?"

Spelling looked at Grey, then at the jury, and then coolly lied.

"Yes," he answered confidently. "We were meeting in my office and the producers told me that they would like to make a change. Our ratings in the fourth season were not as good as the first three years, and we got word from the network that they were moving the show from nine o'clock on a weeknight to eight o'clock on Sunday nights, which necessitated format changes. On Sunday nights at eight, we couldn't do the kind of show we'd been doing—it was more of a family hour. And although *Charlie's Angels* was never a violent show, we had to make sure there was no violence on the show."

That was his explanation. The move to the earlier timeslot on Sunday nights required *Charlie's Angels* to be a different kind of show, one with "no violence." So naturally, a different show would mean different stunts, and different stunts would mean a different stunt coordinator. And that, he said, is why Julie's contract was not renewed.

But it was all a lie.

In fact, *Charlie's Angels* was one of the most violent shows on television, and anyone in America with a TV set knew it. Over the course of five seasons, there were hundreds of murders, beatings, hijackings, shootings, stabbings, strangulations, and kidnappings. In its 110 episodes, there were 107 character deaths: 33 in the first season, 19 in the second, 26 in the third, and 18 in the fourth. In the first season alone, a reporter is murdered, a model is murdered, a beautiful stock car racer is murdered, a nudie magazine centerfold is murdered, four U.S. Army Intelligence officers are murdered, the owner of a winery is murdered, a cruise ship crewmember is murdered, and a child who witnesses a murder picks up the murder weapon and shoots Jaclyn Smith's character in the head.

And despite what Spelling told the jurors—that in the fifth season "we had to make sure there was no violence on the show"—the show remained as violent as ever. In fact, there was violence on every episode: shootings and kidnappings, suicides and murders. A model is strangled, an actress is shot in the stomach with a bow and arrow, a man is shot and killed on the street, a cabdriver is burned alive. All told, there were 11 character deaths in the 16 episodes of the fifth and final season.

There had been no "format changes." It was the same, tired old show that had lost its main star—Farrah Fawcett—and then its audience.

ABC unceremoniously cancelled it halfway through of the fifth season, right in the middle of a storyline in which Jaclyn Smith's character is lying in a hospital bed, her head wrapped in bandages, teetering between life and death after she'd been shot, once again, in the head.

There would be no resolution, no conclusion, and it would be the lowest-rated season of the show's run.

So who did Spelling replace to make these nonexistent format changes? Did he fire the producers or the writers? The directors or the actors? No. He fired the stunt coordinator, the only female stunt coordinator he'd ever employed, the only person on the show who dared complain about safety and drugs on the set.

The lie sounded reasonable—so much so that Julie's lawyer even missed it. He let it pass and moved on to his next question.

"Was anybody given the task of informing Julie Johnson of the decision not to renew her as stunt coordinator for the fifth season?" Grey asked.

"I'm sure the head of production probably did it or the unit manager," Spelling replied.

He'd fired so many people he just couldn't recall.

Actually, it was Ronnie Rondell, the stunt supervisor on all of Spelling's shows, the man who Julie had complained to about Bobby Bass's cocaine use, the man who Jeannie Coulter swore she saw snorting coke with Roy Harrison.

"After the decision was made," Grey asked, "did you receive any contact of any kind from Julie Johnson requesting to see you?"

"Yes, I did," Spelling replied.

A few days after she was fired, Julie wrote Spelling a heartfelt note asking for a meeting so that she could ask him why she had been let go and to thank him personally for having given her the opportunity to coordinate. Spelling just blew her off.

"Her letter came to my secretary, who brought it to my desk," Spelling said imperially. "I asked Norm Henry, the vice president of production, to please answer Ms. Johnson, because I wasn't involved in that strata of production. And I assume he did. It was his responsibility and his job to do so."

Everyone on the jury who'd ever been fired probably knew a boss like Spelling—one who delegated the dirty work to someone else and then wouldn't even talk to the person he'd fired.

Grey then turned to the issues of safety and drugs on the set.

"Mr. Spelling," Grey asked, "during the period 1978 to 1980, was there any kind of policy established at Spelling-Goldberg Productions to make sure that the stunt work, or filming in general, was done safely?"

"I really can't answer that," he replied, to the surprise of many of the jurors, some of whom scribbled his vague answer in their notebooks.

"We put out our policy about safety . . . We do many other things at the company . . . and we expect them to be implemented," he sputtered.

In fact, the company had virtually no safety policy at all. As one of Spelling's underlings would later testify, the company's stunt safety policy consisted of only nine words: "No stunt should be done that is not safe."

Even that policy, however, was routinely violated. The jury would later hear testimony that stunt scenes were routinely shot, over Julie's repeated objections, with inadequate safety equipment and unsafe cars. And when serious accidents did occur, they weren't reported to the Occupational Safety and Health Administration, as was required by federal law.

When Julie and Jeannie Coulter were injured and sent to the hospital that day in 1979 out by Magic Mountain, a report of the accident was filed with the company, but the company failed to file a report of the accident with OSHA, whose guidelines specifically require the "reporting of . . . multiple hospitalization incidents to OSHA."

Grey pressed on, grilling Spelling about his company's drug policy.

"Then let me ask you this," Grey said. "Do you know if the company had any kind of policy about illegal drug use on the set?"

"Not only the company," Spelling answered grandly, "but my personal policy was very strong on that. And everyone knew it."

Well, not everyone. As Jeannie Coulter stated in her deposition, just about everyone on *Charlie's Angels* but her and Julie were sniffing cocaine, including the "directors, stunt coordinators, production people, production manager, the stuntmen, the actresses, and the electricians."

Pressed for the names of people she'd heard were using coke on the set, Jeannie named one of the show's stars and the show's unit production manager, Kim Manners. She also swore that she'd personally witnessed Roy Harrison and Ronnie Rondell sniffing coke.

"It was very simple," Spelling continued. "Anyone caught using drugs on the set would be summarily dismissed, whether they were an actor or member of the crew."

In fact, no one was ever caught; no one was ever dismissed, summarily or otherwise.

There was no drug testing, no anonymous tip hotline, no real investigation of complaints about drug abuse on the set, nothing to enforce Spelling's nonexistent drug policy. In fact, the company's real policy was the same as the stuntmen's code of silence: "Keep your mouth shut and you might work." And the only person who violated that policy was Julie.

During his cross-examination, Koska asked Spelling if he blacklisted Julie after she was let go as the show's stunt coordinator.

"Of course not," Spelling huffed.

"Did you tell anyone, with any production company, not to hire Ms. Johnson?"

"No," he said emphatically.

The jury, however, didn't buy any of it.

The jury, Spelling's lawyer wrote in their appeal, "inferred the blacklisting of plaintiff in the entertainment industry by the defendant, other stuntmen's organizations and production companies."

And they were certainly right about that.

Besides being one of the most powerful men in Hollywood, Aaron Spelling was also one of the most vindictive. Spelling expected loyalty from his employees, and if they left or were fired, he'd try to make sure they never worked in Hollywood again.

Larry Mollin was one of Spelling's top writers in the 1990s, writing and producing 128 hours of *Beverly Hills, 90210* for Spelling at the Fox Network. But when Mollin left the show, Spelling tried to have him blackballed in the industry.

"This happened to lots of writers," Mollin recalls. "After I left the show, a Fox executive told a friend of mine he could not hire me because he did not want to piss off Aaron Spelling. I'd seen him do it with other people. He would go out of his way to prevent you from working. He went out of his way to harm people."

The jury didn't believe Spelling's answer about drugs either.

The jury, his attorneys later observed, determined "that drugs were pervasive in the entertainment industry and that it should send a message to the entertainment industry to rid itself of drugs."

And the entertainment industry was soaked in cocaine in those days. As *TV Guide* noted in a 1981 headline: "It's Snowing in Hollywood Every Day."

And on *Charlie's Angels*, it was snowing hard.

Chapter 29

Good-bye, Sam

In 1967, Julie doubled for actress Celeste Yarnall, who played Ensign Chekov's love interest on "The Apple" episode of the original *Star Trek* series. Julie's all-American good looks—and matching hair and wardrobe—made her almost indistinguishable from the bewitchingly beautiful actress.

That same year, she doubled for the much older Portia Nelson in the original film version of *Doctor Dolittle*. In a memorable scene, Nelson opens a cupboard and out flies a flock of doves. Startled, she falls over backward down a flight of stairs. Nelson, of course, didn't do the stair fall. That was Julie.

Later that year, Julie got a call from Abby Singer, the man who'd given Julie her start at Universal. Doris Day was doing a sitcom for CBS, he told her, so naturally he thought of her for the stunts.

Abby flew her up to San Francisco to shoot the "trailer"—the opening scene that would be seen at the beginning of each episode as the titles roll. Doubling for Doris Day, Julie can be seen in long shots at the start of each show, running up and down the hills of the City by the Bay, jumping on and off cable cars—a skill she'd honed hopping on and off packed, moving buses as a child in Mexico City.

The rest of the show was shot in Los Angeles, so over the next five years, whenever there was a stunt involving the star—a pratfall or some other form of physical comedy—Julie would be called in to do it.

The year 1967 was a great year to be young. That summer—the Summer of Love—saw a spiritual awakening in young people all across the country—a stirring fueled, in part, by drugs. Julie never tuned in, turned on, or dropped out, but she had a powerful sense of right and wrong and a strong social conscience. She'd been in the business long enough to know that stuntwomen were second-class citizens, so she and a few friends decided to do something about it: they formed the Stuntwomen's Association of Motion Pictures. Initially, their goals were modest: more jobs, better pay and safer working conditions. But they laid the groundwork for more "radical" notions to come—equal pay and an end to sexual harassment and discrimination. The times, they were a changin'.

The year 1968 would prove to be a very bad year for the country, and a very sad year for Julie. The war in Vietnam was raging, seemingly without end; and that year, Martin Luther King and Bobby Kennedy would both be assassinated within months of each other.

In April, Julie went over to see her grandpa Sam, who was living in a little duplex on Hudson Avenue, south of Sunset. Sam had just turned eighty-eight, but he was in pretty good shape. She took him to a local park, and they tossed a baseball around—just like the old days when she was a kid. A friend came along and snapped a few photos of them together. They would be the last photos ever taken of the legendary ball player.

A month later, on May 26, Julie got a call from her mom. Sam was in the hospital. It was serious. Could she pick her up in Fullerton and take her to see him?

Julie got in her old Corvair and raced down to Fullerton. It was a Sunday, so there wasn't much traffic on Interstate 5. Her mom was ready when Julie got there, and they drove back up to Hollywood.

"I hope he doesn't suffer," Virginia told her daughter. "I hope it's quick."

They drove the rest of the way in silence.

When they got to Hollywood Community Hospital, a nurse directed them to Sam's room. He was in a coma, hooked up to oxygen, with IVs dripping fluids into his arms. Julie was shocked. Her mom expressed no emotion. They pulled up chairs on each side of his bed and held his hands. After a while, a doctor came in to see the patient. Sam, he told them, had suffered a stroke. One second he was fine, and the next he collapsed on the floor at home. His wife Mary called an ambulance, and he was rushed to the hospital.

"How serious is it?" Virginia asked.

"It's hard to say," the doctor replied, "but given his age . . ."

They stayed a few more hours, and at eight o'clock, a nurse came and told them that visiting hours were over. Julie drove her mom back to Fullerton, kissed her good night, and drove back home to the San Fernando Valley and her little house on Van Noord.

Julie had a job the next day—a stair fall for an episode of *Marcus Welby, M.D.* It went fine, but her mind kept going back to her grandpa and those happy days out at Pearblossom with her dad.

Two weeks after Sam had his stroke, Julie's mom called her again to come get her.

"Sam's dying," her mother told her on the phone. "The hospital just called. Can you come get me?"

"Yes," Julie said. "I'm leaving right now."

It was Saturday, June 15—her mother's sixty-first birthday.

They made it to the hospital just in time. Sam was still in a coma, only now he had pneumonia. The doctors had him hooked up to a suctioning machine, which made a horrible gurgling sound every time he breathed. It sounded like death.

Once again, Julie and her mom took up positions on both sides of the bed and held his hands. They sat there for two hours without saying anything, and then, suddenly, the horrible gurgling stopped. He'd stopped breathing, and just like that, he was dead.

Virginia got up out of her chair and kissed her father on the forehead. Then Julie did the same.

By this time, nurses and doctors had come running into the room, alerted by beeping monitors that his heart had stopped.

Virginia took Julie by the hand and led her from the hospital room. There was nothing left to do or say. Julie was in shock. She'd never seen someone die before.

For Virginia, it was the worst birthday of her life. She adored her father, but she didn't say more than a few words during the long drive back to Fullerton, nothing about her memories of her father or of her travels around the country with him when she was a child and he was a famous baseball player. And she didn't cry.

"She was never a crier," Julie said. "She always said, 'Suffer in silence.'"

And that's what she did.

"She never really showed a lot of emotion," Julie said. "As a child, I always tried to make her laugh. She was always so sad. Anyway, I took her home, and then I had to get back to work the next day."

Sam had bought burial plots for the entire family out at Rose Hills Cemetery in Whittier, but his second wife Mary had different ideas. She'd bought two plots—one on top of the other—at a cemetery out in Inglewood. And that's where she buried him, and a few years later, that's where she would be buried—right on top of him, far away from his family. She finally had him where she wanted him all along: right under her thumb—literally.

Celeste Yamall, Star Trek

Julie doubling Celeste Yarnall on "Star Trek"

Chapter 30

Jeannie Coulter Takes the Stand

Jeannie Coulter sat alone on a hard wooden bench in the courthouse hallway, waiting to be called to testify in Julie's case. It had been five months since she'd given her deposition, and Aaron Spelling's lawyers were inside the courtroom at that very moment trying to get Judge Savitch to throw it all out. It was Friday, August 14, 1987.

In her deposition, Jeannie had sworn under oath that she'd seen Julie discriminated against because of her gender, that she'd witnessed Ronnie Rondell and Roy "Snuffy" Harrison snorting cocaine together in a van on the way to a location shoot for a TV movie called *Diary of a Teenage Hitchhiker*, and that Harrison later sexually harassed her and then blacklisted her in the industry after she refused to have sex with him.

Obviously, Harrison had hit on the wrong girl. Pretty and petite—and square as a saltine cracker—Jeannie was married to a cop and never tried illegal drugs of any kind.

Her charges were explosive and could win the case for Julie if the judge allowed them into evidence. So naturally, Spelling's attorneys were going to try to exclude them.

"A motion has been made to exclude evidence at the trial elicited from Jeannie Coulter," Judge Savitch told the attorneys outside the presence of the jury. "I am going to deny the motion as it relates to the incident on *The Hitchhiker*. In the court's mind, the probative value clearly outweighs any undue prejudice."

The judge did, however, grant a defense motion to exclude any of her testimony about blacklisting. She would also not be allowed to testify about anything having to do with sex discrimination, since Julie's previous attorney, Monty Mason II, had "voluntarily" dismissed sex discrimination as a cause of action in her complaint.

Turning to Richard Grey, the judge warned him and his witness to steer clear of those subjects.

"I spoke with her a moment ago in the hallway, Your Honor," Grey said, "and I told her of the court's admonition that she not address the subject of blacklisting or the subject of sex discrimination."

Spelling attorney William Koska then made one last pitch to try to persuade the judge to limit another key portion of Jeannie's testimony.

"One other point," he told the judge, and Grey knew what was coming: Koska was going to try to get the judge to exclude Jeannie's testimony about witnessing Rondell snorting cocaine with Roy Harrison.

"I don't believe," Koska said, "that there is ever going to be any allegation, proof, or testimony that Mr. Rondell has some sort of cocaine addiction, or ever did."

There are turning points in every trial, and for Julie's, this was a big one. In legal dramas on TV, the key moment almost always comes at the end of the show when someone dramatically confesses from the witness stand. In real-life trials, however, turning points often come with a simple ruling by a judge, out of earshot of the jury. That would be the case in Julie's trial. If Jeannie wouldn't be allowed to testify about what she'd witnessed, the jury would never know that the man Julie had brought her complaint to about drug abuse on the set of *Charlie's Angels* had a drug problem himself—and then told her she was fired.

Grey held his breath awaiting the judge's ruling.

"I think the incident, as you have it in the deposition, has relevancy," the judge ruled.

And that was it; Jeannie would be allowed to testify about that.

"Let's call in the jury," the judge said.

The clerk brought the jury into the courtroom, and the judge instructed Grey to call his next witness.

"Plaintiff calls Jeannie Coulter," Grey said, and Jeannie was brought in from the hallway, took the stand, and was sworn in.

Grey walked Jeannie through her career as a stuntwoman, beginning in 1966 and ending the day in 1979 when she and Julie were nearly killed out at Indian Dunes. She described how she'd worked on numerous films, including *The Blues Brothers, A View to a Kill,* and *Jaws 2,* and on many of Spelling's TV shows.

"Can you give us some specific details about your involvement as a stunt person on *Charlie's Angels*?" Grey asked.

"I worked on the pilot and through all the years it was shot," Jeannie said. "I doubled for Kate Jackson, Farrah Fawcett, and Jaclyn Smith. I was basically Farrah's double."

"Can you give some examples of the different types of stunts you've been involved in?"

"Through the years," she replied, "I've done everything, such as fire work, car chases, car crashes, fights, high falls—everything."

"Is stunt work hazardous duty?" Grey asked.

"Very," she answered. "I've had five friends killed in the business. So yes, it is hazardous."

"Are you acquainted with Julie Johnson?" he asked.

"Yes, I am," she said.

"Did you know of Julie Johnson before you met her personally?"

"Yes, I did," she said. "I heard about Julie when I started out in the business. She was talked about around town as an excellent stuntwoman, and I worked with her and observed her working and wanted to be just like her."

"Did you work with her on *Charlie's Angels*?" Grey asked.

"Yes," she said. "Julie and I worked on *Charlie's Angels* together for a few years. She doubled Kate Jackson before she became a stunt coordinator."

"Can you give us your best approximation of how many times you and Ms. Johnson worked together on the show?" Grey asked.

"I guess around two hundred days," Jeannie answered. "Could be more because she was coordinating, and I wasn't working *with* her, I was working *for* her."

"Ms. Coulter, did you work with Julie Johnson in January 1979 on a stunt that involved the two of you jumping out of a moving vehicle on a dirt airstrip?"

"Yes."

"Do you have a clear recollection of the filming of that stunt?" Grey asked.

"Very clear," she replied.

"How was that stunt rehearsed, if you remember?"

"Well, we shot an opening scene while the car is driving from miles away, and we're speeding on this runway," she recalled. "And then we prepare for the big stunt, which was us jumping out of the car. We rehearsed it maybe three or four times."

"And what would the rehearsals involve?"

"We ran the car down the runway about four times to get our speed," she said. "At that point, I was opening my door and looking out to the dirt flying past me to kind of judge the car's speed. The driver was telling me how fast he was going, and I was looking down to see how fast the dirt was coming up."

"During the rehearsal, who else was in the car with you?" Grey asked.

"Julie Johnson was doubling Farrah Fawcett. I was doubling Cheryl Ladd. Howard Curtis was there doubling an actor, and Bobby Bass was doubling another actor."

"And who was driving the vehicle during the rehearsal?"

"Bobby Bass was driving it," she said.

"Had you and Mr. Bass—and by 'you' I mean collectively you and Julie Johnson—agreed upon a maximum safe speed within which that stunt scene was going to be filmed?" Grey asked.

"Absolutely."

"And what speed was that?"

"Well, when we started out, we were going fifteen miles per hour and Bobby was supposed to level it out to under ten miles an hour," she said. "In fact, I emphatically said, 'It's going too fast!' I said, 'It has to be under ten miles an hour.' And that's exactly how I said it to him."

Julie looked at the jurors and saw several of them scribble something in their notepads. Richard Grey noticed it too.

"That was during rehearsal?" he continued.

"Yes."

"Did you have any difficulty communicating with Mr. Bass during the rehearsals that day?"

"Yes, I did," she said. "He wasn't listening to me when I told him it was too fast for me to jump out of the car."

"Was there anything else visibly wrong with Mr. Bass at the time of the rehearsal?" Grey asked.

"Objection!" Koska said, rising from his chair. "Hearsay! Speculation!"

"Overruled," the judge said.

Jeannie looked at Grey to see if it was all right to answer his question. He nodded.

"Bobby was kind of in a daze," she said. "I don't know what the problem was, but he just wasn't reacting to what I was saying to him. He was just kind of not there."

Koska leapt to his feet again. "Move to strike the response as nonresponsive and calling for a conclusion," he declared.

"Denied," the judge ruled again.

"Let's pick up from the point where you get into the car and start the actual filming," Grey said. "Where were you and Julie positioned in the car?"

"I was on the right side in the backseat," she said, "and Julie was on the left side behind the driver."

"And aside from doubling for an actor, did Mr. Curtis have any other function to fulfill in the performance of that stunt?"

"Yes, he did," she answered. "Howard was to tell us when to jump so that we both would jump at the same time."

"So tell us what happened when it came time to jump," Grey said.

When the car got to its mark, Jeannie recalled, she and Julie opened the doors and Howard Curtis told them to jump, but Bobby didn't slow the car down—he hit the gas.

"Bobby was going so fast," she said, "that the weight of the open door made me kind of go out backward so that the momentum of the speed threw me down. I couldn't get out of the car the proper way, and I hit the ground rolling."

"After you jumped out of the vehicle, what happened?" Grey asked.

"I thought I was going to die, and I was disoriented," she answered. "I got up and was running. Cheryl Ladd grabbed me and held me, because I didn't know what I was doing. I had a concussion, and I turned around and I saw Julie over on the ground, and she was in convulsions. She was lying facedown in the dirt. So I just . . . I couldn't believe it. I thought she was really badly injured."

"After that, what happened?"

"We were taken to the hospital in the backseat of a station wagon," Jeannie replied.

"Were there any paramedics at the scene of the accident?"

"No."

"Did you receive any kind of medical emergency treatment at the scene?"

"No," she said, and several jurors jotted that down in their notebooks.

"On the ride to the hospital, did you form any opinion as to why you and Ms. Johnson wound up in the station wagon on the way to the hospital that day?"

"Yes, I did," she answered. "Bobby Bass did not do what he was supposed to do. He was like in a daze, and he just didn't perform, and that's the reason we were hurt."

"And did you come to any opinion about the speed of the car when you opened the door and exited the vehicle?" Grey asked.

"Yes," she said. "He was going much too fast. He was going like three times the speed we were supposed to go. When they said, 'Action!' he just floored it."

"That wasn't the way it was rehearsed, was it?"

"No," she said. "Not at all."

"Can you compare what you've just described with the way the stunt was planned and intended to work?" Grey asked.

"If we would have had been going below ten miles an hour," she said, "the weight of the doors wouldn't have come back and pushed so hard on us and we could have gotten out easier. The faster you go, the wind and the momentum closes the door on you."

"And how had you planned on landing on the ground if the stunt had been done properly?"

"Well, I wanted to get out of the car and go straight into a shoulder roll. But I couldn't get out of the car properly because the door whipped me back and threw me to the ground. I didn't have time to tuck and roll."

"In your opinion, was there anything wrong with the way that stunt was carried out?"

"Yes," she said. "He was supposed to be going a certain speed that we rehearsed, and he didn't do it, and that's why we got hurt."

"How serious was the risk that you and Ms. Johnson were exposed to because the vehicle was traveling faster than it had been planned in rehearsal?"

"Objection!" Koska said. "Speculation."

"Overruled," the judge said.

"We could have been killed," she answered.

Grey let her answer hang in the air for a moment and then walked back to the plaintiff's table and pretended to look through some papers. After shuffling them around for a while, he returned to the witness box and resumed his questioning.

"What type of treatment did you receive at the hospital that day?" he asked.

"A doctor looked at me and said I had a mild concussion," she answered.

"How long were you at the hospital?"

"Not a long time," she said. "Maybe two hours."

"What time did you get back to the set?"

"We got back in time for lunch."

"And why did you return to the set?" he asked.

"They had to get one last shot, and Julie and I had to do it because we were the doubles and we were the only ones there."

"How were you feeling after you returned from the hospital?" Grey asked.

"I had a headache," she said, wincing at the thought of it. "I mean, when you jump out of a car going twenty-five miles an hour, you just hurt all over."

"Did you have lunch when you returned from the hospital?" Grey asked.

"Yes. They had a catering service that fed us on the set," she answered. "We stood in line and waited to be served."

Grey then asked her if Bobby Bass was in line for lunch that day as well.

"Yes. He was in the line a few feet ahead of us. Like where Julie is sitting," she said, pointing to Julie at the plaintiff's table. "About that distance."

Then the judge spoke up. "That is what? Ten feet or something like that?"

"Yes, sir," Jeannie answered, a little startled to be questioned by the judge directly.

"Did something unusual happen while you were standing in the lunch line behind Bobby Bass?" Grey asked.

"Yes," she replied. "He just kind of ignored us. He just looked around like we weren't even there."

Grey pressed her for more details. This was going to be useful when he questioned Bobby Bass on Monday.

"His eyes were real glassy," she said, "and he just was . . ."

"Move to strike," Koska said, interrupting her. "No foundation."

"Overruled," the judge said.

"Go ahead," Grey told her, "and describe how he appeared to you that day."

"Gosh, he was just in a daze," she recalled. "He wasn't normal. He wasn't himself. He was just in a daze. He wasn't there. He didn't even come over to ask how we were, and that wasn't like him."

"Did you have direct eye contact with Mr. Bass?" Grey asked.

"No," she replied. "He looked at us, but it was just like a blank stare, like when somebody looks right past you and doesn't see you are there."

"Did he approach you and talk to you and Julie in the lunch line?"

"No."

"Did he sit and have lunch with you and Julie?"

"No."

"Did you see Mr. Bass attempt to do any more stunt work later that day?"

"Yes," she replied. "After lunch, Bobby had to spin a car."

"What do you know about Mr. Bass's prior skills and experience in spinning cars?"

"Excellent," she answered.

"How did he do on that particular occasion?" Grey asked.

"He could not spin the car," she said. "In fact, Ronnie Rondell had to go out and spin the car for him. Bobby just could not do it. He took it down the dirt runway, but he could not spin the car. He just kind of went straight. He wasn't doing it at all."

"How many times did he try to do it?" Grey asked.

"Probably five times," she answered.

Grey asked her what it takes to get a car to spin.

"Well," she said, "you get the car up to a certain speed, turn the wheel, pull the emergency brake, and the back end of the car should come around."

"Is that a particularly difficult thing for a driver to do who is trained in precision driving work?" Grey asked.

"No, sir," Jeannie laughed knowingly. "Not at all. Especially in dirt."

Then Grey moved in for the kill.

"Did you talk to Julie Johnson about information that she had heard concerning Bobby Bass before the accident?" he asked. "Just answer yes or no."

Grey was referring to Julie's having overheard someone say that "Bobby got the last of the coke this morning!" Grey knew he couldn't ask Jeannie to repeat what Julie had said she'd heard, as that would be hearsay, but he wanted to get it on the record that Julie had told her something about Bobby that day.

"Yes, sir," Jeannie replied.

"Based upon that information," Grey continued, "did you come to be concerned about any additional problem that may have contributed to the accident that we haven't already discussed in your testimony?"

"Objection!" Koska said. "Hearsay! Speculation! Conclusion!"

"Sustained," the judge said, finally upholding one of Koska's objections.

Grey would try it a slightly different way.

"Based upon your observation of the way Mr. Bass appeared to you both during the filming of the stunt and later when you saw him again in the lunch line, did you have any concerns about the state of his sobriety at the time he was driving that car?"

"Objection!" Koska said. "Calls for a conclusion! Hearsay!"

"Overruled," the judge said.

"Yes," Jeannie answered. "Absolutely."

"What was the nature of those concerns, Ms. Coulter?" Grey asked.

"Objection!" Koska tried again. "Speculation! Conclusion! No foundation!"

"Overruled," the judge said.

"My concern," Jeannie said, "was that Bobby was driving a car that we were jumping out of and that he'd taken something to alter his timing and his job, which endangered everyone's life."

"Did you discuss those concerns with Julie Johnson sometime the same day after the accident?"

"Yes, I did," she said.

"Have you ever worked on a Spelling-Goldberg production during the period 1978 to 1980 where you have observed any persons in the stunt field employed by that company taking any illegal drugs on the set or near the set during a workday?"

"Objection!" Koska shouted, jumping to his feet. "Irrelevant! Immaterial!"

The judge looked down his glasses at Grey. "The way the question is couched, the objection is sustained."

Grey would try again.

"Have you ever observed any activity at or near a Spelling-Goldberg set that caused you concern that hazardous substances might be being used by people associated with the stunt work that you were performing."

"Absolutely, yes," Jeannie answered.

"Now, let me focus your attention on a movie for television that you worked on called *Diary of a Teenage Hitchhiker*," Grey said. "Did you observe such activity while you were working on that particular production?"

"Yes, sir," she replied.

"Would you please describe for us what you observed in that connection?"

"Objection!" Koska said in the most disgusted tone he could muster. "Immaterial! Evidence Code Section 352."

Well, at least this objection was something new for the jury.

Section 352 of the California Evidence Code allows a judge to exclude testimony if its probative value would be substantially outweighed by the probability that it would create an undue prejudice in the mind of the jury. Judge Savitch, however, didn't think that it would. "Overruled," he said.

Jeannie looked at the judge to see if it would be okay for her to answer. He nodded, as if to say, "Go ahead."

"Ronnie Rondell, Roy Harrison, and I were in a van," she said. "I was in the backseat, and we were going to drive to another location. Ronnie was the second unit director. Roy was the stunt coordinator. Before they started the car, Roy took out a little tiny bottle with a black top that had some white stuff in it. Roy put some of it on his finger and put it up to his nose and put another finger over his nostril and snuffed it into his nose. Then he gave it to Ronnie Rondell, who did the same thing."

Several jurors started scribbling notes.

"Did anyone offer it to you?" Grey asked.

"No, sir," Jeannie replied.

"Did you observe anything else on that occasion that caused you concern about doing the job?"

"I'm sorry," Jeannie said, a bit miffed. "Wasn't that enough?"

Several members of the jury laughed out loud and then scribbled in their notebooks.

"Do you know if Spelling-Goldberg Productions had any kind of policy to control the use of dangerous or hazardous substances on the set?" Grey asked.

"No," she answered. "There was none that I know of."

"Were there any procedures that you were aware of for reporting somebody that was under the influence of drugs or alcohol to the point where they couldn't safely perform their stunt work?"

"No."

"Had Mr. Rondell ever told you that it was Mr. Spelling's policy that if somebody was caught under the influence on the set that they would be immediately terminated?"

"No."

Grey took a deep breath and looked at the jurors. From their expressions, he could see that they'd gotten his points: that Spelling-Goldberg was lax about safety and drugs.

Now it was time to shift gears. Sex discrimination wasn't a part of this case—thanks to Monty Mason II—but Grey wanted to bloody Spelling's nose with it nonetheless.

"Have you ever been a stunt coordinator?" he asked, preparing to establish her bona fides for the jury.

"Yes, sir, I have," she said. "On *The Young and the Restless, Airport 77,* and on various one-day jobs where I had to coordinate the stunt I did myself."

"On a practical level, what is the difference between working as a stunt player and as a stunt coordinator?" he asked.

"A coordinator," she said, "is responsible for budgeting the show, setting up the stunts, telling the different departments what they need to know, telling all the stunt people what to do and how it should be done. You have to know the camera angles—what the camera is going to see when you set up your stunt. You have to know what apparatus you need to be safe. It's a big responsibility, and the major concern is for safety. And of course, you have to get an action scene that looks fabulous—that looks like it killed everybody, yet everybody is safe and sound. It takes a lot of preparation and a lot of years of doing stunts."

"And you have done that type of work yourself?" he asked.

"Yes, sir."

"And how often have you done it?"

"Over the years," she said, "maybe fifty . . . sixty days."

"And you have worked under the supervision of other stunt coordinators?"

"Yes, sir."

"Can you identify some of these notable stunt coordinators that you have worked for?"

"Hal Needham, Ronnie Rondell, Dar Robinson," she replied, naming some of the best in the business.

"You worked on *Charlie's Angels* in episodes where Julie Johnson was the coordinator, is that correct?" he asked.

"Yes, sir, I did," she said. "Many times."

"And were her duties as stunt coordinator similar to the duties that you've described here today?"

"Yes."

"Did she possess the attributes that you have just mentioned?"

"Yes," she said. "Julie was prepared. She made sure that she notified everybody of the things that were necessary. She called talented people in to work for her. She was very alert on the set and stood right by the camera all the time. She was very concerned about what was happening and the safety of everybody on the set. There was no difference between Julie doing her job and the other stunt coordinators I have worked for."

"Where would you rank Ms. Johnson in comparison to some of the other notable stunt coordinators—*male* stunt coordinators—that you mentioned?" Grey asked.

"Equally at the top," she replied.

"You've described some of Julie Johnson's strengths as a stunt coordinator," Grey stated. "Can you tell us anything of her weaknesses as a stunt coordinator?"

Several jurors leaned forward in the jury box, waiting to hear what she had to say.

"She was a woman," Jeannie said flatly.

"What do you mean by that?" Grey asked.

"Objection!" Koska said. "Calls for a conclusion."

"Overruled," the judge said.

"In our business, it's basically run by men," Jeannie said, "and when a woman comes in, especially in the stunt field, it's like you're not supposed to be there."

Koska jumped to his feet. "Move to strike the latter part as speculation and a conclusion on the part of the witness."

"Denied," the judge ruled.

Grey asked Jeannie to give a few examples to illustrate how Julie had been treated differently than male coordinators on *Charlie's Angels*.

"One day," she testified, "we were on location and I had to do a stunt where I had to climb up on a six-foot ladder and bulldog a man."

"What is bulldog?" Grey interrupted.

"Fly through the air and hit him," she explained. "And we had to fall down into a trench, and it was quite a distance. Julie insisted to the director that I should have a pad to cushion my fall. But he was in a hurry, and after they argued a while, he finally told her, 'Okay, you've told me what you want. Now go over there and sit down. We're going to shoot this.' He would have never talked like that to a man."

Koska leapt to his feet again. "Move to strike the last portion of the witness's statement—'He would have never talked like that to a man.' Speculation."

The judge sustained the motion and instructed the jurors to disregard that portion of her testimony. But can a jury ever really disregard what they hear from a witness? Especially when it's true?

Grey then tried to draw testimony from Jeannie showing how Julie had been blacklisted in the industry, even though the judge had told him to steer clear of that topic.

"Ms. Coulter," he asked, "did you ever become affiliated with any professional societies or organizations of stunt persons?"

"Yes, I did," she answered.

"For what purpose?" he asked.

"To be in a group of women that were known as some of the top stuntwomen in the business," she replied.

"What organization did you join in that regard?"

"The Society of Professional Stuntwomen."

"When did you join?"

"1978," she answered.

"And who were the primary leaders of the group?"

"Julie Johnson and Jeannie Epper," she replied.

"What types of activities did the group become involved in on behalf of its members?"

"We tried to help women in the stunt field," she said.

"Do you recall hosting a meeting of that organization at your own home in April of 1982?" Grey asked, alluding to the day Jeannie Epper told Julie that none of them would ever work again if Julie didn't drop her lawsuit.

"Yes, sir, I do," she said.

As Jeannie had sworn in her deposition, Epper had walked into her dining room and delivered a message to Julie and the five other stuntwomen assembled there. "I've got something to say," Epper told the women. "Julie, I've been sent here to tell you that if you don't stop making waves and drop this lawsuit, none of us are going to work in this business." And on that day, Julie's blacklisting had begun.

"Was there something about this particular meeting in April of '82," Grey asked, "that distinguishes it from the many others that you have attended?"

Koska knew what Grey was up to; Grey was going to try to get testimony about Julie's blacklisting into the record—something that the judge had specifically ruled he would not allow.

"Objection!" Koska said, rising from his chair. "Calls for a conclusion. Speculation on the part of the witness."

The judge knew what Grey was up to as well.

"Sustained," he said.

"Was there any controversy at that meeting in April 1982 involving Julie Johnson and Jeannie Epper that you now recall?" Grey asked.

"Objection!" Koska blurted out. "Hearsay! Calls for speculation."

"Sustained," the judge ruled again.

"What happened at the end of that meeting?" Grey tried again.

"Jeannie Epper stood up . . . ," Coulter said, but was interrupted by Koska.

"Objection! Calls for speculation. Irrelevant. Hearsay. Immaterial." His objections were coming so fast now that he didn't even bother to sit down.

"Sustained," the judge ruled.

"At the end of that meeting," Grey kept trying, "was Julie Johnson still in the group?"

"Objection!" Koska said. "Irrelevant. Immaterial. Hearsay."

"Sustained."

Grey continued to press ahead, trying to get what had happened at Jeannie Coulter's house that day into the court record. Clearly, Koska and the judge weren't going to allow Jeannie to say that Julie had been blacklisted that day, so he tried to slip as much of her answer into his questions as possible.

"Did what happened at that meeting," Grey pressed ahead, "indicate to you that Julie Johnson was suffering any adverse consequences in her career as a result of bringing a lawsuit? *This* lawsuit?"

"Objection!" Koska said, citing all the same reasons.

"Sustained," the judge agreed.

"How long have you known Jeannie Epper?" Grey asked.

"Objection," Koska said. "Irrelevant. Immaterial." He was objecting to every question Grey asked now.

"Overruled," the judge said.

"Probably fifteen years, at least," she answered.

"Is Jeannie Epper a member of a large family of stunt players within the industry?" Grey asked.

"Objection," Koska said, still standing at the defense table. "Irrelevant. Immaterial."

"Sustained," the judge ruled.

"Do you know who succeeded Julie Johnson to her position as stunt coordinator of *Charlie's Angels?*" Grey asked.

"Gary Epper, Jeannie Epper's brother," she answered before Koska could object.

"Objection! Immaterial! Move to strike!"

"Sustained," the judge said. "The jury will disregard the witness's last statement."

Grey's questions and Koska's repeated objections had definitely piqued the jury's interest. As a rule, jurors take their responsibilities very seriously. But jurors are people, too; and like most people, when something is being hidden from them, they want to know what it is.

"Was there anything that happened during the meeting at your house," Grey continued, "that you attributed as having had a very negative effect on Julie Johnson's career in the stunt industry?"

There. He'd said it as plainly as he could without violating the judge's order.

"Objection!" Koska said. "Leading. Hearsay. Conclusion. Vague and ambiguous."

And it certainly was leading, although it certainly wasn't hearsay. It did require her to draw a conclusion, and it was only vague and ambiguous because the judge wouldn't allow the direct truth to be told.

"Sustained," the judge ruled.

"Has Julie Johnson continued her professional association with other stuntwomen?" Grey asked, still trying to let the jury know that Julie had dropped out of the Society of Professional Stuntwomen after Jeannie Epper delivered the warning that day in Jeannie Coulter's dining room.

"Objection!" Irrelevant. Immaterial. Speculation."

"Sustained."

"What information do you have personally," Grey asked, "about the opportunities that have been available to Julie Johnson since her employment was terminated by Spelling-Goldberg Productions . . ."

"Objection!" Koska interrupted.

". . . to obtain further employment in the stunt field of the entertainment industry?" Grey continued.

"Objection! Calls for a conclusion. Speculation. Hearsay."

"Sustained," the judge said.

"This morning," Grey pressed on, "you described Julie Johnson's reputation in the stunt industry when you first entered the business. Have you detected any changes in that reputation from that time until today?"

Koska objected again, but this time the judge overruled it.

"It totally went the other way," Jeannie said, finally getting to answer a question.

"What do you mean by that?" Grey asked.

"Negative," she said. "Totally negative."

"Do you know approximately when Julie Johnson ceased to be employed by Spelling-Goldberg Productions?"

"I believe it was 1980," she said.

"Have you ever worked with her again on any other stunt work?"

"No."

"Objection," Koska said, still on his feet. "Irrelevant. Immaterial."

"Overruled," the judge said. "She can answer that question, and the answer is *no*."

"Do you know how frequently Julie Johnson worked before she was terminated by Spelling-Goldberg Productions?" Grey asked.

"Objection to the question," Koska said. "No foundation."

"Overruled," the judge declared.

"Julie worked all the time," Jeannie answered. "She was an excellent stuntwoman."

"I would move to strike that as nonresponsive, Your Honor," Koska said.

"Granted," the judge said. "The part that the jury is to disregard is that she was an excellent stuntwoman. That part is stricken."

Even so, the jury had heard it and knew that she had been an excellent stuntwoman.

"When you say that Julie worked all the time," Grey continued, "how far back do those observations go before the time she was terminated?"

"Julie worked as long as I knew her name," Jeannie answered. "When I came into the business, Julie was working as a stuntwoman. She was very well known."

"And after *Charlie's Angels*, did you ever work with her again?" Grey asked.

"Objection!" Koska said. "Vague and ambiguous."

"Overruled," the judge said. And then turning to Jeannie, he asked, "Did you work with her after that?"

"No, sir, I haven't."

"Did you ever see her working with anybody else in the stunt field since that time?" Grey asked.

"No, sir," Jeannie replied.

"How well do you know Julie Johnson?" Grey asked.

"I've just worked with her for years," she answered. "I don't socialize with her or anything. I just worked with her. That's it."

"And did you see any change in Ms. Johnson's personality in the times that you encountered her after her termination?" Grey asked.

"Objection!" Koska said, still standing. "Leading, suggestive and argumentative."

"Overruled."

"Yes, I definitely did," Jeannie answered.

"Would you describe the changes that you observed following her termination?" Grey asked.

"Same objection," Koska said.

"Overruled."

"I believe she was heartbroken because she wasn't working," Jeannie said.

And it was true. She was heartbroken. And nearly broke as well.

Grey looked at the jury and then at Jeannie in the witness box. She'd been a great witness—his star witness. Through her, he'd been able to present every major aspect of the case to the jury: that Julie had been a top-notch stunt coordinator, that Julie had been discriminated against because she was a woman, that she'd been terminated after complaining about drug abuse on the set of *Charlie's Angels*, and that after she was terminated, she'd been blacklisted, even though the word never came up at trial.

Now it was time for Grey to wrap it up.

"Have you been placed under any pressure to come here today to testify?" he asked.

"No, sir," she answered.

Then, taking one last stab at painting Hollywood as a town where people live in fear of being branded troublemakers, he asked, "Have you personally been in any way worried or apprehensive about the consequences of your coming into court to testify?"

"Yes, sir," she answered before Koska could object.

"Objection, Your Honor!" Koska said. "Irrelevant. Argumentative. Move to strike the answer."

"The answer is stricken," the judge said, "and the objection is sustained. The jury is instructed to disregard the witness's last statement."

The jury might disregard it, but they couldn't un-hear it.

"That's all the questions that I have, Your Honor," Grey said and took his seat at the plaintiff's table.

Julie looked at her attorney with tears in her eyes. She knew then that she had a good shot at winning her case.

Koska took his turn at cross-examination, but he couldn't shake Jeannie from the testimony she'd given that day. There would be no un-ringing of the bell. The damage had been done.

Jeannie Coulter with lion friend

Chapter 31

Life Goes On

Stunt work is like combat, you don't get hurt or killed every time you go out; but the more often you do it, the more likely you are to get hurt—or killed.

Not long after Sam died, Julie was nearly trampled by a team of horses while doing a stunt for Rod Serling's *Night Gallery*. Later that year, she was nearly killed while doubling for Eleanor Parker in a horror film called *Eye of the Cat*. The stunt called for Julie to be pushed in a wheelchair down a steep street in San Francisco. Cables had been attached to the wheelchair to keep it from running into the cross-traffic, but they neglected to strap Julie into the chair. When the crew yanked on the cables to stop the chair's headlong rush down the street, Julie was launched from the chair over the hood of a car going through the intersection. She wasn't seriously hurt, so they did it again—this time with a seat belt.

In 1969, Julie sustained a serious injury on the TV show *Mannix*. It was lucky no one was killed. The stunt called for two motorcycles—a stuntman and woman on each bike—to race toward an oncoming car and, then at the last moment, to peel away, just avoiding a head-on collision. Julie was on the back of one of the bikes, and after the motorcycles zoomed past the car, they were supposed to swerve back to the middle of the road and then race off. But the bikes got too close and collided at high speed.

"The bikes crashed and we all went flying up in the air. I came down and landed hard on my ribcage on one of the motorcycles," she recalls with a wince. "It was excruciatingly painful. I had to crawl to the bathroom the next morning."

Somehow, she made it to her doctor's office.

"You again," Dr. Terwilliger said.

"Good morning to you too, Doctor," she said sarcastically.

"Let me see," he said, looking at her patient file. "The last time you were here, it was a car hit. This time . . ."

"A motorcycle wreck," she said sheepishly.

"Where does it hurt?"

"My ribs," she said.

"Okay. Let's have a look."

Julie raised her shirt, revealing darkly bruised ribs.

"We'd better get an x-ray of that," he said. "And this cut," he said, pointing to a gash on her sternum, "we'd better give you a tetanus booster too."

"Do I have to?" Julie said plaintively.

Julie was fearless on the job. She wasn't afraid of heights or fire or falling or horses or fast cars. But she was scared of needles. She absolutely hated shots; she had ever since she was a kid.

"Yes," the doctor said, calling his nurse into the examining room. "Patty, Julie here needs an x-ray and a tetanus booster."

The nurse took Julie to the x-ray room, and Julie held still while the x-rays were taken. It was painful just lying flat on the table.

A few minutes later, Julie was back in the examining room when Dr. Terwilliger walked in looking at her x-rays.

"You have a cracked floating rib," he said, not looking up from the film. "Not much we can do for that. Just use hot and cold compresses, and get plenty of rest."

"But I have an audition tomorrow," she said. "Can I . . . ?"

Julie stopped midsentence when the nurse walked in carrying a huge needle. It looked like something you'd use to pump up a flat football.

The nurse had Julie roll up her sleeve and swabbed her arm with alcohol.

"You need bed rest," the doctor said. "I know you're tough, but you're not impervious to pain, are you?"

The nurse raised the needle and squirted out a small stream of fluid. Julie turned her face away from the instrument of torture as far as she could. Then, in one quick motion, the nurse pinched up a piece of Julie's skin and inserted the needle.

"AAHHHHH!" Julie howled.

The doctor had his answer.

A few weeks later, Julie was back at work, her still-sore ribs wrapped in cloth bandages. Later that winter—the winter of 1969—she flew up to Calgary, Canada, to shoot *Little Big Man*, where she got kicked in the head by a horse and was knocked unconscious. She felt fine a few days later, and when she got back home, she decided not to tell Dr. Terwilliger about that one.

The 1970s began with a bang for Julie—or at least, with the sound of shattering glass. In 1970, she performed one of the most memorable stunts ever performed by a Hollywood stuntwoman. Almost everyone who ever saw *Play Misty for Me* remembers it.

It began with a call to Teddy's from the Malpaso Company—Clint Eastwood's production company. Eastwood was looking for a stuntwoman to double for Jessica Walter, the movie's seductive but psychotic villainess, in the film's big finale. Julie had done several stunts for Jessica in the past, including a stair fall at Universal, and the actress had recommended her to Eastwood.

"I was a good double for her," Julie recalls. "We were the same height and build. You put the right wig and clothes on me and you couldn't tell us apart."

Malpaso flew Julie up to Carmel, the seaside artists' colony on the Monterrey Peninsula, where the film was shooting. She spent the night at a Holiday Inn, and in the morning, a van took her to the location—a private home high on a cliff overlooking the blue Pacific. Jessica was at the house when Julie arrived and introduced her to Clint. He was so young, so handsome, and so tall. Eastwood was already a famous movie star, but he was an unproven director. *Play Misty for Me* was to be his directorial debut. And what a debut it would be.

The film, a classic tale of stalker-suspense, stars Eastwood as a disc jockey at a jazz station in Big Sur who attracts the amorous attention of a demented fan. After an ill-advised affair, she sets out to destroy his life. When he tries to break it off, she cuts her wrists in his bathroom. Later, she stabs his housekeeper, kidnaps his girlfriend, stabs a policeman, and attempts to kill him with a pair of scissors. The violent final scene ends with Eastwood punching her in the face, knocking her through a sliding glass door and off the balcony to her death on the rocky shore far below.

Enter Julie Johnson.

"Clint showed me how he wanted to do the stunt," Julie recalled. "He blocked it out—choreographed it from the time she takes the first stab at him with the scissors."

"As soon as she stabs at me," he told Julie, "I'll block her wrist. Then you step in. I'll spin you around, and then here comes the punch. Got it?"

"Got it," Julie said.

They rehearsed the scene in slow motion a couple of times and then did it twice in real time with cameras rolling.

The first take was fine. Eastwood gives Julie a "movie punch" to the face—missing her, but swinging close enough so that on camera it looks like the real thing. Julie is knocked through the sliding glass door—which is fitted with special breakaway glass—and is hurled backward across the balcony, over the railing, and falls onto a pile of mattresses stacked on top of boxes twelve feet below. The landing area was tight, perched on a narrow ledge precariously close to the edge of a hundred-foot fall to the sea below.

"Cut!" Eastwood yelled, and then ran to the balcony and looked over to see if Julie was okay. She was. Looking up from the mattresses, she gave him the thumbs-up sign.

"Great," he said, smiling at her below. "Let's do it again."

The shot was fine; but a good director, if he has the sun and an extra piece of breakaway glass, will almost always want to shoot it again and then use the better of the two shots. And Eastwood was a good director—and he had an extra piece of breakaway glass. The prop crew had made two sliding glass doors fitted with the stuff, and they immediately began installing it. They had it ready in no time.

Julie came back up, and they did it again. Only this time she did it a little faster.

"Action!" Eastwood yelled then swung Julie around, "punched" her in the face, and knocked her flying through the glass door again. This time though, Julie went backward through the glass harder, and went over the railing faster. At the last moment, she grabbed the railing to slow herself down. If she hadn't, she could have missed the mattresses and overshot the landing spot and fallen one hundred feet to her death.

"It was a very tight area," she recalled.

As it was, she'd hit her left leg on the edge of the deck when she was falling over backward and ended up with a huge bruise. But she was okay, and naturally, that was the shot Eastwood would use in the movie.

"Clint Eastwood was very, very friendly, very professional, very kind, and very considerate," Julie recalls. "He wanted to make sure I was comfortable and did everything he could to make sure that the stunt was safe. He's one of the good guys."

Julie would work with Eastwood again on *Dirty Harry* and, a few years later, on *Magnum Force*. Both were ND—nondescript—jobs involving melee scenes. Both went off without a hitch.

In 1971, she was hired to double for Lynda Day George on the original *Mission Impossible* TV series and, later that year, began a six-year run as Susan St. James's stunt double on *McMillan & Wife*, doubling for her in car chases, falls, and even a tightrope walk. "I was her main double," Julie remembers. "I did a lot of shows—more than half a dozen episodes a season. I was on call."

Still, there was time for other work.

In 1972, Julie landed her first jobs as a stunt coordinator. The first was for a TV movie called *Women in Chains*, starring Ida Lupino as a parole officer who goes undercover to investigate brutality in a women's prison.

"I designed a fight scene in prison for Ida Lupino," Julie recalled.

It went off smoothly, looked great, and nobody got hurt.

A few months later, she got a call from her old mentor, Abby Singer, over at Universal. Martin Ritt, he told her, was prepping a movie there called *Pete 'n' Tillie*, a bittersweet comedy starring Carol Burnett, Walter Matthau, and Geraldine Page. Ritt, he told her, needed someone to design a fight scene for him and maybe double for Carol Burnett, the great comedienne.

"Naturally," Abby told Julie, "I thought of you. Do you want to come meet him?"

"Sure," Julie said and made arrangements to meet with the famous director, whose credits included *Hud, Hombre*, and *The Spy Who Came in from the Cold*, and who would later direct such classic films as *Sounder, The Front*, and *Norma Rae*.

The next day, Julie drove onto the Universal lot and was directed to Ritt's office.

Ritt explained that he wanted to stage a comedic fight scene between Burnett and Page, but of course, didn't want either actress getting hurt.

"Do you think you could design a scene like that for me?" he asked.

"Sure," Julie said confidently.

Ritt gave her the general outline, and Julie told him she'd get back to him with some ideas so that the actresses could do the scene safely and without stunt doubles.

A few days later, Julie got back to Ritt and told him her plan.

"Terrific!" he said, and he would shoot it just the way she'd drawn it up.

The day of the shoot on the Universal back lot was bright and warm. Julie went to hair and makeup and got into a wig and print dress just in case she had to step in for Burnett. As it turned out, she wouldn't have to.

Julie was introduced to the actresses and then choreographed the scene for them. There would be three cameras—one for the wide shots of the fight and two for the medium close-ups of Page and Burnett.

"We blocked it, and I showed them what to do," Julie recalled.

The knock-down, drag-out scene—involving a wooden rake, a garbage can, and a high-pressure hose—ends with Burnett pulling Page's wig off and waving it triumphantly in front of her horrified friend. Running nearly two minutes on-screen, it's the funniest scene in the movie, and the expressions on the actresses' faces during the melee are priceless.

The film received mixed reviews, but critics and audiences loved the fight scene. Film critic Charles Champlin, writing in the *Los Angeles Times*, called the fight scene "wondrous." To this day, it remains one of the funniest girl-on-girl fight scenes in movie history and helped win Page an Oscar nomination.

The Academy Awards is easily the most anticipated event in the movie business each year, but the most joyous are the cast and crew screenings that each film gets before its release to the general public. It's a time when friends and colleagues, who may not have seen each other for months, are reunited to see the film they'd worked so hard on. And unlike the Oscars, no one goes home a loser.

The cast and crew screening for *Pete 'n' Tillie* was held at a small theater on the Universal lot.

There are plenty of laughs in the film, and a few tears as well, but the biggest laughs on the night of the cast and crew screening were saved for the fight scene. The cast and crew literally howled when Burnett stuck the hose up Page's skirt and roared again when Burnett pulled off Page's wig. By their reaction, the look on her face was the funniest thing they'd ever seen.

Martin Ritt, the director, was happy too.

"Julie did a fine job," recalled Phil Bowles, the film's first assistant director. "It was a hilarious spot in the film, and Martin Ritt was quite pleased."

"Julie Johnson worked for me on *Pete 'n' Tillie* at Universal in 1972," Ritt recalled, "when she designed for my approval a fight between Carol Burnett and Geraldine Page. Her work was quite satisfactory."

"Quite" indeed. It was the funniest part of the movie, which is saying a lot for a comedy starring Carol Burnett and Walter Matthau.

"*Pete 'n' Tillie* was a big credit for me," Julie recalls.

It put her on the map as a coordinator and would put her on the path to coordinating stunts for one of the biggest hits of the 1970s—*Charlie's Angels.*

Chapter 32

Bobby Bass Takes the Stand

Bobby Bass entered the courtroom and took a seat behind the defendant's table. Julie hadn't seen him in eight years. He looked the same, only more nervous and fidgety than she remembered. He had a lot to be nervous and fidgety about.

The judge excused the jury and then spoke to Bass.

"Mr. Bass?"

"Yes," Bass said, standing up quickly.

"Would you please step forward?"

The court clerk showed him to the witness stand.

"Please raise your right hand," the clerk told him. "Do you solemnly swear that the testimony you may give in the cause now pending before this court shall be the truth, the whole truth, and nothing but the truth, so help you God?"

"Yes, I do," Bass said.

It was the first of many lies Bass would tell over the next two days.

After Bass was sworn in, Judge Savitch took the unusual step of reading him his rights against self-incrimination.

"During the last few days," the judge told him, "there have been some statements about you and testimony about you, sir. That may mean that you might want to invoke the constitutional privilege against self-incrimination, which is guaranteed by the Fifth Amendment and by the California constitution.

"A witness is entitled to claim the privilege once he is sworn. It may be that you might be chargeable with various crimes arising out of the events that you might testify to.

"There has been testimony here about your possession of controlled substances—possibly cocaine. And you may be asked specific questions about that. You may be asked, for example, whether or not you were under the influence of cocaine while performing a particular stunt. And if you say *yes*, of course, that may tend to incriminate you in the event there is some kind of a criminal prosecution for a felony."

Bass was not worried about that. It would be impossible to charge him with possessing cocaine seven years earlier without any proof other than his own admission. And since he had no intention of telling the truth, there would be no such admission—not so much because he was worried about possible criminal repercussions, but because of the certainty that he would never work in Hollywood again if he admitted under oath in a court of law that he had been high on cocaine while performing a stunt in which two stuntwomen had been seriously injured. He knew that the industry tolerated cocaine use, but that it would not tolerate anyone who *admitted* using cocaine. Using drugs on the job use was not a fire-able offense, but admitting to using drugs on the job was.

Admitting to using cocaine in a court of law would also put an end to his more important work, his top secret work, his work as a covert CIA operative.

No one in the court that day knew anything about that however.

The judge took a long hard look at the stocky man with the buzz haircut sitting in the witness box. Bass had stopped fidgeting but was sweating and looked more nervous now than ever. The courtroom was so quiet Julie could almost hear him gulp.

"I want you to know that you have this right," the judge told him again. "Do you wish to consult an attorney?"

"No, sir," Bobby answered firmly.

"So do you have anything you wish to state in connection with this privilege against self-incrimination?" the judge asked.

"Yes," Bass said.

Julie could sense everyone in the courtroom leaning forward at once, even though she already had a pretty good idea what Bass was going to say next.

"I would like to wave my right and continue on," Bass said, and everyone leaned back in their chairs.

It was the only thing he could say. For while "taking the Fifth" is not considered an admission of guilt in *court*, it certainly is considered an admission of guilt almost everywhere else and would have gotten him blackballed in Hollywood just as quickly as if he'd admitted he was high on coke when he nearly killed Julie and Jeannie Coulter. His CIA handlers probably wouldn't be too happy about it either.

Satisfied that Bass understood his rights, the judge adjourned the court.

The next day, Bass was sworn in again. Only this time it was in front of the jurors—although they would not get to see a replay of Bass being advised of his constitutional right against self-incrimination.

And as before, he swore to tell the truth, the whole truth, and nothing but the truth.

And as before, he lied.

Every weekday, in every courtroom in every city and small town across America, someone is lying under oath. Someone is saying, "You did it!" and someone else is saying. "No, I didn't!" One of them is lying. It happens all the time.

Perjury is one of the most serious felonies that goes unpunished most often in America. When verdicts are rendered, witnesses who testified falsely for the losing side are almost never brought up on perjury charges. And so it was with Bobby Bass.

This wasn't the first time he'd lied on the witness stand, nor was it the first time he'd played a central role in a lawsuit brought by a stuntwoman he'd nearly killed while high on coke. A year earlier, in this very same courthouse, he'd been a key witness in a civil trial involving a horrific stunt car crash on the set of *Cannonball Run* that had left stuntwoman Heidi von Beltz a quadriplegic for life. Bass was the film's stunt coordinator; Heidi was his fiancée.

Heidi sued the film's director, Hal Needham, for negligence; and when the case came to trial in 1986, Bass testified that the stunt car that he'd placed her in was safe, even though he knew it wasn't. In fact, it was a deathtrap. It had no seat belts, bald tires, defective steering, and a malfunctioning clutch. Even the speedometer didn't work. When they tried to get the car running on the morning of the stunt, another car had to push it to get it started. Needham had a mechanic work on it for a while, and Bobby Bass then took it out for a trial run. Bobby said it was fine, but it wasn't—and it still didn't have seat belts or a working speedometer.

When it came time to film the stunt, the car's driver, Jimmy Nickerson, still didn't think it was ready. He wanted more repairs, but was told that the parts from Los Angeles hadn't arrived and that he'd have to "make do." Testimony would later be presented that Nickerson was high on drugs that day.

Tragically, the car, which was supposed to weave between a line of oncoming cars, crashed head-on into the first car in the line, hurling Heidi against the windshield and breaking her neck.

Still, Bobby Bass testified that he and Needham thought the car was safe.

The jury didn't believe him and awarded her $4.5 million.

"He knew the car didn't have seat belts," recalled David Sabih, Heidi's trial attorney, "but Needham didn't want to stop. He wanted to save money. It would have taken an hour or two to put them in. All the other cars had seat belts. Bobby whitewashed it for Hal Needham."

A year later, Bobby would do the same for Aaron Spelling.

Julie's attorney started his line of questioning by asking Bass about his background. The stuntman seemed nervous, fidgeting in the witness stand throughout his entire testimony. Julie wondered if he was on coke now too.

"How long have you been a professional stuntman?" Grey asked.

"I have been working part-time since 1963 and full-time since 1966," he replied.

Bobby's résumé as a stuntman was impressive. He'd doubled for many of Hollywood's top stars, from John Wayne to Sylvester Stallone and Burt Reynolds. He'd worked on more than forty films, including *The Green Berets, Close Encounters of the Third Kind*, *The Blues Brothers*, *Independence Day*, *Predator*, *Batman & Robin*, *The Bodyguard*, *Smokey and the Bandit*, and *Scarface*. He coordinated many others, including *Lethal Weapon*, *Thelma and Louise*, *Hooper*, and *Rocky V*, to name a few. He even worked occasionally as a bit actor, landing small roles on films and TV shows, including the original *Star Trek* series, in which he usually played a security guard or Klingon warrior who got killed off early on in each episode.

"Can you give us some examples of the experiences you've had doing stunt work?" Grey asked.

"First, I worked as a nondescript stuntman," he answered. "We would do fights, falls, water, working fire, high falls, car work, and motorcycle work. I hold the world record for rocket car stunts."

"Would it be fair to say that driving has become your specialty, Mr. Bass?"

"I would say that it is one of my specialties. Yes, sir."

"What are some of the others?" Grey asked.

"I would say teaching martial arts and doing martial arts fights," he answered. "Any type of fighting, working with the actors personally."

Bobby was one of the nicest and coolest guys in Hollywood, but he was also one of the toughest. A third-degree black belt in judo, he taught martial arts and weapons handling to Mel Gibson, Michael Douglas, Danny Glover, and O. J. Simpson. Needless to say, he could have kicked any of their butts.

Grey didn't ask, but Bass's real specialty was black ops, clandestine operations. Few people in Hollywood knew it; but Bobby Bass, a former Green Beret, was a genuine secret agent who ran covert operations for Air America, the CIA's airline that many believe ran drugs to fund its operations.

"He ran ops in South America for Air America," said Ronnie Rondell, one of Bobby's best friends. "He ran ops when he was a stuntman and would have to go away for a month at a time."

"He was part of that whole deal," said stuntman Dick Ziker, who even today is reluctant to talk about his old friend's secret life. "I'm not at liberty to say much."

Ziker did, however, recall the time he was walking down a street in London and happened to see Bobby walking toward him. Ziker started to speak to him, but Bobby waved him off.

"He gave me the eye, saying 'No, no, no,' and kept walking," Ziker said with a laugh.

Another time, Ziker recalled, Bobby called him and started speaking in code. The next time he saw him, Ziker asked what that was all about. "Sorry," Bobby explained, "they were tapping my phone calls."

"His military personnel file is still classified top secret," said stuntman Pete Turner, who, like Bass, had been a member of the army's elite special forces. "He gave me my first job in the business."

Bobby was also one of the most heavily armed men in Hollywood.

"He'd open his stunt bag and he'd have a dozen nice firearms in there," Turner said with a laugh. "He never went anywhere without a small arsenal."

Bass was also one of the most beloved stuntmen in the business.

"He was one of the best friends any man could have," Ziker said.

"He was a great guy," Rondell agreed. "You would want him as your best friend."

"He was the original real deal," Turner said. "He smoked weed with Steve McQueen!"

Bobby, however, was not universally loved.

Shortly after his fiancée was paralyzed for life on *Cannonball Run*, he dumped her and married actress Bo Derek's mother, who was a hairdresser for Ann Margaret.

"He abandoned her days after the accident," recalled David Sabih, Heidi's former attorney. "He could have at least abandoned her a little later."

But whether Bobby Bass was a nice guy or not wasn't the issue that day as he sat in the witness box at Julie's trial. At issue was whether or not he was high on coke the day he nearly killed her and Jeannie Coulter and whether he had a history of recklessly endangering stuntwomen.

"Is it important," Grey asked him, "for a passenger in a stunt vehicle to have a seat belt as well as the driver?"

"I would have to say that this would depend on what stunt was being performed," Bass answered.

"Let's assume a stunt where driver and passenger are weaving in and out of oncoming traffic," Grey said. "Would a seat belt be essential for the passenger under those circumstances?"

"Objection!" Koska said, jumping to his feet. "No foundation. Immaterial."

"Where are we going with this?" the judge asked Grey.

"Approach the bench, Your Honor?" Grey asked.

"Yes," the judge replied, waving the lawyers to the bench.

"Your Honor," Grey told the judge out of earshot of the jurors, "this witness was the coordinator of a stunt in which his fiancée, Heidi von Beltz, was the passenger in a vehicle on *Cannonball Run*. She had no seat belt. There was testimony at her trial that the driver of that vehicle was under the influence of drugs. She came out of that collision a quadriplegic. I want to ask this witness whether the lack of a seat belt for the passenger is a safety-related problem. Further, we have witnesses who have placed Ms. von Beltz at the scene of Julie Johnson's accident as a spectator when Bobby Bass was driving."

"It has nothing to do with this case," the judge said. "How does testimony about whether a passenger should have a seat belt relate to the incidents here? I don't see the connection."

"We have a serious allegation here," Grey explained, "that Mr. Bass was negligent or under the influence of drugs while he was driving Julie Johnson."

"That may be true," said the judge, unmoved by Grey's argument. "Ask that question and how it relates to safety generally. It seems to me that this other incident doesn't apply to this case. And I think the probative value is really far outweighed by the undue prejudice. It's inflammatory, so I'm going to sustain the objection."

And that was it. The jury would never get to hear what Bobby Bass had done to Heidi von Beltz.

Returning to the plaintiff's table, Grey looked at some notes and then resumed his questioning of Bass.

"Were you involved in the performance of a stunt in about January 1979 on *Charlie's Angels* as the driver of a vehicle from which Julie Johnson and Jeannie Coulter were to jump from a moving vehicle?" he asked.

"Yes, that's correct," Bass replied.

"Do you have a clear recollection of that stunt?"

"Yes," Bass said.

"First of all, where was the stunt filmed?" Grey asked.

"It was done on a dirt runway in the Indian Dunes area of Valencia," Bass said.

Rustic and remote, and yet only thirty miles north of Los Angeles, Indian Dunes had long been a popular locale for Hollywood film shoots. Over the years, dozens of movies and TV shows have been shot there, including *The Color Purple, Escape from New York, The Two Jakes, China Beach, Black Sheep Squadron*, and many others.

But Indian Dunes also has a tragic history.

The first film-related fatality there occurred in 1924, when Dick Kerwoo, a thirty-two-year-old daredevil, fell from an airplane while wing-walking during a silent movie shoot.

Then, in 1982, just three years after Julie and Jeannie Coulter came so close to being killed out at Indian Dunes while filming *Charlie's Angels*, actor Vic Morrow and two children—seven-year-old Myca Dinh Lee and six-year-old Renee Chen—were killed there when a miss-timed special effects blast brought a low-flying helicopter crashing down on top of them during filming of *Twilight Zone: The Movie*.

It was the worst movie accident of all time; and at the end of the ensuing trial, which was also held in this very same courthouse, director John Landis and four others charged with involuntary manslaughter were acquitted—just three months before Bobby Bass took the witness stand in Julie's case.

"And what were you being asked to do on *Charlie's Angels* that day at Indian Dunes?" Grey asked.

"There were two stunts that I was to perform," Bass answered. "One was to drive while the girls jumped from the car. The other was a 180-degree spin around on the dirt runway."

As it turned out, he didn't—or couldn't—do either one of them right.

"Who was there that day on behalf of Spelling-Goldberg?" Grey asked.

"I remember seeing Kim Manners, who was the production manager," Bass said. "I remember Blair Gilbert, the first assistant director, and Roy Harrison and Ronnie Rondell."

Tragically, Rondell's twenty-two-year-old son, stuntman Reid Rondell, was burned to death in almost the same location in 1985 when the helicopter he was riding in during filming of the TV show *Airwolf* crashed and burst into flames. The Los Angeles County Coroner determined that he'd snorted cocaine shortly before the fatal crash.

"Do you know what the plot involved when the two ladies were going to jump from the vehicle you were driving?" Grey asked.

"Just basically that these two girls had been apprehended—two of the Angels," Bass said. "There was a gentleman sitting between them in the backseat, and they were going to elbow the man and open the doors and jump out."

"Did you rehearse the stunt?"

"Yes," Bass said. "We did."

"Who was involved in the rehearsal?"

"Julie Johnson and Jeannie Coulter were in the backseat," he said. "Howard Curtis was sitting next to me—he had the walkie-talkie—and myself."

"Was there anybody outside the car participating in the rehearsal process?"

"I recall Roy Harrison was standing around nearby but . . ."

"What was he doing, if you recall?" Grey asked.

"He was just watching what we were doing."

"What did you do when you were rehearsing?" Grey asked.

"We were shown the area where we were to drive and approximately the point where the girls were to jump from the vehicle," Bass explained. "I started the car up, put it in second gear, and slowly, very slowly, proceeded in the direction that they were going to do the actual filming."

"What were you trying to do during the rehearsal process?"

"We were trying to find a speed that the girls felt comfortable jumping out of the car."

"Did you talk about that with them during the rehearsals?" Grey asked.

"Yes, we did," he answered. "We did four practice runs. I remember when we started out on the first run, I put it in second gear. Julie Ann was sitting behind me, and so I drove very slowly in second gear all the way down to the end of the run. Then she said, 'Let's do it again.' There was no other conversation during that whole period of time."

In fact, Julie had repeatedly told Bass during the rehearsals as he raced down the runway to make sure that he slowed down at a prearranged mark just before the jump spot. Each time, he brushed her off. "I got it," he'd say. "I got it. I got it." And each time he said it, it was more vacant and distant than the last.

"As the driver," Grey asked, "did you feel responsible for the safety of Julie Johnson and Jeannie Coulter that day?"

"I felt that since I was the wheelman—the person who was brought in specifically to do the driving—that I would do my best to give the girls what they wanted to perform the stunt."

Grey then walked to the jury box and, with his back to the jurors, asked Bass the question that would be the key to the whole case.

"Mr. Bass," he said, "before you started working on that stunt that morning, had you taken any drug or other substance that would have impaired your ability to safely perform your responsibility to those ladies?"

"No," Bass said flatly.

Grey turned and looked at the jurors for a long moment to let his lie sink in.

"Is there anything else that was said or done during the rehearsal to get ready for the stunt?" he asked.

"Well, I recall that we practiced going back and forth four times, and I left it to Julie to tell me what speed to obtain," he claimed. "There was never a number. We never decided on fifteen or thirteen or twelve miles an hour at all. It was up to Julie to say, 'Faster, faster, hold it right there,' and I would maintain the speed that she felt comfortable."

"Is that the way you were going to do the stunt?" Grey asked. "That Julie was going to tell you, 'Faster, faster, hold it right there, and I'll jump according to that'?"

"Yes. That's correct."

"No reference to the speedometer, Mr. Bass?"

"None whatsoever."

"No consensus between the three of you as to what could constitute a maximum safe speed for that stunt?"

"There was never a number that was determined," Bass insisted.

In fact, as Jeannie testified, they'd agreed to jump at ten miles an hour, but when the car hit its mark and they were hanging out of the open doors, instead of slowing down as they'd agreed, Bobbie inexplicably floored it. Unable to get back inside the car, she said it was going close to thirty miles an hour when they fell out of the car.

"Isn't it true, Mr. Bass, that what you were trying to do was to get up to a maximum speed that was a relatively low speed—fifteen miles per hour or less—and then back off from that speed before the women were to safely jump?"

"No," Bass said. "That would not be the correct way to do the stunt."

In fact, that was the only way to do the stunt safely.

"Do you recall the speed on the speedometer that you were actually traveling when Julie Johnson said, 'Okay, that's a good speed'?"

"No," Bass said, finally telling the truth. "I did not look at the speedometer."

It was a damaging admission. He'd just confessed that he'd never even looked at the speedometer for a stunt that depended entirely on his driving the car at a safe speed.

Grey continued his verbal offensive.

"After the last rehearsal run, was there a break?" Grey asked.

"There was a short break," Bass said, "maybe fifteen or twenty minutes."

"Did anyone leave the car for any reason during the break?" Grey asked, knowing full well that Bass had gone to the honeywagon to get "the last of the coke."

"I don't recall that," Bass lied again. "I think we were ready to go. Camera was set, so I don't recall anybody going away from the car."

"Do you know where the honeywagon was in relation to where the car was stopped before the filming started?" Grey asked.

"Yes," Bass replied. "It was on the south side of the runway. I know that for sure."

Grey took a long, hard look at Bass and then began peppering him with questions about his use of cocaine that day.

"Did you take any substance during the time between the rehearsal and the time that you started driving that vehicle that impaired your ability to safely carry out your stunt driving responsibilities?"

"Objection!" Koska shouted, leaping out of his chair. "Irrelevant! Immaterial!"

"Overruled," the judge said emphatically.

"No," Bass lied.

"Isn't it a fact, sir," Grey continued, "that there was a break of ten or fifteen minutes and everybody got out of the car, walked around, used the restrooms, and came back after that break was over?"

"I don't recall that," Bass lied.

"Isn't it a fact, sir, that you parted company with those women during the break period and went off on your own at that time?"

"I don't recall that," Bass lied again.

"Isn't it true, Mr. Bass, that during that break, you went and found and took cocaine and had that in your system at the time you drove the car on the film, sir?"

"Objection!" Koska said. "Irrelevant. Hearsay. Immaterial."

Clearly, it was not irrelevant or immaterial. And it was certainly not hearsay. Grey was asking Bass about something the he had personally done—not something that he'd heard that someone else had done.

"Overruled," the judge said.

"No," Bass lied again.

If he was angry, he didn't show it. Bobby Bass was one of the coolest guys in Hollywood. He'd smoked pot with Steve McQueen, after all, so he wasn't about to lose his cool under questioning by some pipsqueak lawyer.

Grey told the judge that this might be a good time to take the morning recess. The judge agreed. He needed a break too. Saying "overruled" all day can get exhausting.

Chapter 33

The Comfort of Angels

In May of 1976, the cast and crew of *Charlie's Angels* were filming the sixth episode of the show's first season when a minor accident on the set changed the course of Julie's life.

"It had something to do with a taxicab pulling away from the curb," recalled Ronnie Rondell, "and Farrah Fawcett was running after the cab and the bumper snagged her and knocked her down."

Farrah was okay, but the producers were furious; their breakout star could have been seriously injured. So they fired the show's stunt coordinator, Ron Stein, and one of the show's stuntwomen, Donna Garrett.

Dick Ziker, who'd coordinated the show's pilot, was called back to coordinate, and he brought in Julie to replace Garrett.

Julie had been busy, but now she was working almost every day. She'd been doing a lot of movies, like *Magnum Force*, *Earthquake*, and *Blazing Saddles*, but there'd be little time for making movies now.

In *Blazing Saddles*, she wrestled a stuntman atop a cigarette machine in the film's finale, when the actors start a wild pie fight in the Warner Bros. commissary. She didn't get hurt in that scene, but she ended up in the hospital—along with quite a few other stunt performers—on *Earthquake*, which starred Charlton Heston and Ava Gardner as a man and wife caught up in the drama of a huge earthquake that flattens Los Angeles.

"A lot of people got hurt on that show—a *lot* of people—a half a dozen or more," Julie recalls. "Some of them were really bad injuries—broken bones and head injuries."

In the film's finale, Heston's character is killed while trying to rescue his wife and more than seventy others trapped inside a flooded and crumbling underground parking structure. Julie, doubling for Ava Gardner, nearly broke both of her legs.

The scene was shot one night on the back lot at Universal Pictures, where there's a giant man-made lake that was to be emptied into one of the studio's parking garages to simulate a flood caused by a burst dam.

"They brought all this dirty lake water through this tunnel into the garage where they all get drowned," Julie recalled. "They kept bringing more and more water through this tunnel, and we're all swept away."

The survivors climb a ladder to escape the flood, but halfway up, someone steps on Ava Gardner's hand. Standing in for Gardner, Julie falls fifteen feet into the raging water below. But the water isn't deep enough.

"They called for me to jump too soon," she laughs about it now. "From up there, I couldn't see that the water was only a couple of feet deep. There wasn't enough water down there, but the second unit director's yellin' at me, 'Come on! Come on!' So I let go, and when I went down, there was a curb down there and my knees hit the curb because there wasn't enough water to buffer me. I wasn't expecting that."

Swept away by the raging torrent, Julie kept her head abovewater even though her knees were killing her. Once the cameras stopped rolling, stuntmen downstream fished her out of the water. Back on dry land, Julie took her first steps and nearly crumpled to the ground in pain.

"Oh god!" she thought. "Did I break my knees?"

Julie found a nurse and asked for some ice to put on her swollen knees.

"Is this our last shot?" she asked the nurse.

"I don't know," she replied, "but you go to your dressing room. I'll get you some ice."

It was after midnight and freezing cold as Julie sat shivering in her dressing room, a robe thrown on over her wet clothes, two large bags of ice on her knees, waiting to see if she was going to be called back to the set for another shot. There was no heater, and Julie's breath billowed out like cigarette smoke in the cold, damp air of the trailer.

Then there was a knock at the door.

"Come in," Julie called out in as strong a voice as she could muster.

An assistant director poked his head inside. "Ms. Gardner wants to see you," he said.

"What?" she said.

"Can you make it down to her dressing room?" he asked.

"Yeah," Julie said, not really sure if she could or not.

Julie left her ice bags behind and hobbled down to Ava's dressing room and knocked on the door. It was easy to find; it was the one with a big star on the door and Ava Gardner's name neatly stenciled on it.

Opening the door, Gardner looked down at Julie, who looked like a wet kitten.

"Get in here!" she said to Julie and held the door open for her as she struggled up the steps. Ava had been in the water too, and she too was in a robe with wet hair. But she didn't look like a wet kitten. She looked like a wet goddess.

"I hear you got hurt," she said, motioning Julie to a chair. It was warm inside the trailer, but Julie was still shivering.

"Well, my knees are hurt a little bit," she said. "I hit a curb or something on the bottom. There wasn't enough water."

"I'm so sorry," Ava told her, with real sympathy in her voice.

"I'll be okay," Julie said, hoping that she would.

Gardner took out a flask and poured a jigger of amber fluid into a little glass.

"Here," Gardner said, handing it to Julie. "You need a little brandy."

"Well, I'm still on the clock," Julie said, taking the glass but not sure whether she should take a drink.

"Oh no," Gardner laughed. "We're through for the night."

"In that case . . . ," Julie said and took a sip of the best brandy she'd ever tasted.

"Well, you were great out there tonight," Ava told her, "but I'm sure sorry you got hurt."

"I'll be fine," Julie assured her. "That's what they pay me for."

Julie finished her brandy, and then the assistant director knocked on the dressing room door and shouted, "You're released Johnson!"

Julie thanked Ava for the drink and for her concern and then went back to her cold trailer to collect her things. She left the set and drove straight to North Hollywood Hospital. On the way there, she thought about Ava Gardner. Julie wasn't awestruck by movie stars; she never had been. But she was deeply moved by Ava's kindness.

By the time Julie got to the hospital, she could barely walk. Someone brought her a pair of crutches, and she limped into the emergency room.

"So there I was," Julie chuckled, "smelling of swamp water and brandy, with mud all over my face and arms, and everything's eschew, and I walk in there wondering, 'What are they going to think?'"

"I just got off work at Universal," she told the admissions nurse. "That's why I look like this. And if I smell of brandy, it's not because I'm drunk or anything. They gave me some brandy to warm me up."

She said "they" instead of "Ava Gardner" because she had never, ever been a name-dropper.

The nurse smiled noncommittally, took her name and insurance card, and told her to have a seat with the others in the waiting room: people with bloody noses, hacking coughs, and all manner of ailments. Julie looked, by far, worse off than anyone else there.

Before long, she was called in for an x-ray, and after it was done, a doctor came into the examination room.

"There's nothing cracked or broken," he told her, looking at the x-ray film. "You just bruised your knees really good."

Julie told him, too, that she wasn't drunk, and he put his hand on her shoulder.

"I know," he said. "Just go home and put some ice on your knees."

Julie limped out of the hospital and, when she got home, took a hot shower to wash away the smell of that horrid swamp water. It was so bad she had to wash her hair twice.

By comparison, *Charlie's Angels* would be a piece of cake.

Julie had been hired on the show to double for Kate Jackson, but she'd end up doubling for Farrah and Cheryl Ladd too. The work was steady, and Julie settled into a routine—if being shot out of a cannon every day can ever be said to be routine.

June 26, 1976, was a Sunday, and Julie had the day off. Her father was coming to see her, but he was running late. He'd dropped off his wife Margo and stepdaughter Tina at the airport—they were flying to Boston—and he'd stopped for lunch in Hollywood before coming up to visit Julie in Van Nuys. He was supposed to be at Julie's place by one o'clock, so when it got to be a quarter to two, Julie started worrying.

"Well, okay," she thought. "Where is he?"

At two o'clock the phone rang. It was an LAPD sergeant calling.

"Is this Julie?" the sergeant asked.

"Yes," she said.

"Who are you to Arthur L. Johnson?" he asked.

"I'm his daughter," she replied. Something, she knew, was terribly wrong.

"Ma'am, I regret to inform you that he is dead."

It was the worst phone call of her life.

"I lost it," Julie recalled many years later.

She slumped to the floor and nearly dropped the phone.

"What?" she said, although she'd heard every word he said.

"Ma'am, I'm sorry to . . ."

"Where is he?" she interrupted. "What happened?" She was nearly hysterical now.

Julie's dad, the one man in her life she could always count on, had parked his car and walked up to have lunch at a coffee shop on Hollywood Boulevard. It's where he always ate when he came down from Three Rivers, the rustic little town he lived in near the back entrance of Sequoia National Park. But this time was different. This time, after lunch, as he walked back to his car, he collapsed in the middle of the street. Several people rushed to help him. Someone called the police, and an ambulance arrived in no time. One of the responding officers found Julie's phone number written on a piece of paper in his pocket and radioed headquarters with the information. Someone there called Julie.

The cause of death hadn't been determined yet, the sergeant told her, but it was an apparent heart attack. He'd been taken to Hollywood Community Hospital. Julie thanked the officer—although it's not the kind of news anyone is ever thankful to receive—and hung up. Composing herself, she called her mother and told her the news.

"Are you okay?" her mother asked.

"Well, not really," Julie replied.

"Can you drive?"

"Yes. I guess so," she said.

"All right," her mother said. "Come get me."

Julie drove down to Fullerton and picked up her mom, and they drove together back up to Hollywood. Sunday traffic was light, and they got there just after four o'clock. Art had only been dead a few hours. A nurse ushered them into a small room off the emergency room and seated them on a comfortable old couch.

"How many grieving people had sat right here?" Julie wondered of the battered, old tear-soaked couch. Julie cried, but Virginia didn't. Julie had never seen her mother cry.

A few minutes later, two policemen came in.

"Are you Julie?" one of the officers asked.

"Yes," she said, standing up.

The policeman handed Julie her father's wallet. She flipped it open and saw his driver's license.

"Is this your father?" the policeman asked.

Julie nodded.

"We need someone to identify the body," he said.

His choice of words—"the body"—was heartless. A few hours earlier he'd been her father. Now he was "the body."

"I'm his ex-wife," Virginia stepped up. "I'll go in and identify him."

It was a small act of thoughtfulness, but on this day—the saddest day of Julie's life—it was the kindest thing her mother had ever done.

Virginia left with the officers, and Julie sat back down on the tear-soaked couch, her father's wallet cradled in her hands like a dead bird.

Virginia returned a few minutes later and, without a word, led Julie out of the hospital. Outside, it was a beautiful spring day. The sun was shining, birds were singing, dogs were barking, people were going about their business, but her father was dead. Whoever said that "April is the cruelest month" didn't know what they were talking about.

Somebody had to call Margo and tell her that her husband was dead. But Margo was still in the air, on her way to Boston. Julie and her mother drove to Julie's place in the Valley, and Julie made the call. Margo hadn't arrived yet, but her son-in-law Joe was there.

"Don't worry, Julie," he told her. "I'll take care of everything."

And he did. He took care of everything: the mortuary, the cremation, the memorial service at a little cemetery in Exeter, up near where her dad had lived in the foothills of the Sierra Nevada.

For Julie, those days were a blur of tears and remembrance. She saw her father for the last time, dressed in his finest Sunday suit, lying in state at the mortuary. Then there was the long drive up north, the heartfelt Christian Science funeral service in the shadow of the great mountains, and then the long drive back home. And she took comfort knowing that her father had made his long journey home, too, and that he'd still be looking after her from up there.

A few days later, she went back to work.

"It was good being busy," she sighs, thinking back on those sad days.

She would throw herself into her work, and her work would become her life—until that awful day in January 1979 when Bobby Bass, high on coke, nearly killed her, and her life began to fall apart.

"Earthquake" Julie doubling Eva Gardner, Universal Pictures

Chapter 34

The Return of Bobby Bass

After the morning break, Richard Grey resumed questioning Bobby Bass about that day at Indian Dunes.

"What happened after Ms. Johnson exited the car?" Grey asked. "What is the next thing you remember?"

"I remember seeing her really whacked to the ground," he said. "She got thumped pretty good, so we stopped and went back. I believe that she and Jeannie Coulter were taken in one of the company cars to be checked out, to see if they would be okay."

"And then during the lunch break, did you run into them in the lunch line?"

"They had come back from the hospital," Bass said, "and we were all concerned to see if they would be okay. We have a very close community in the stunt business, so we went over to ask them if they were okay and all."

Of course, it wasn't true. He hadn't gone to talk to them; he just stood there in the chow line glowering at them. They both thought it was the strangest thing.

"So you went over to speak to Ms. Johnson and Ms. Coulter during the lunch hour?" Grey asked.

"If I recall, I was already in line with some of the stunt people, and when they came back from the hospital, we just went over to them right away and asked them how they were and all. And Julie said she got a pretty good rap, on her shoulder and her head, I think, and we were concerned that she would be all right."

"So you were standing in line, and they came up behind you in the line. Is that the way it was?" Grey pressed on, letting Bass dig his hole deeper and deeper.

"Yes," Bass said. "We were in the line. We hadn't started to eat yet."

"When you say 'we,' who was 'we'?" Grey asked.

"It would be the stunt people," Bass replied. "Like Howard Curtis and Roy Harrison."

"Did anyone accompany you when you went over to see Julie and see how she was?"

"I know that I made the effort," Bass said. "I think Roy Harrison was with me in line, and he went over with me."

"Please, Mr. Bass, don't speculate or imagine what would have happened," Grey snapped at him. "If you remember, tell us. Do you remember anyone else, other than yourself, who joined you when you went to speak with Ms. Johnson about how she was?"

"Objection!" Koska said, rising to his feet. "Argumentative! Asked and answered!"

"Objection overruled," the judge said.

"I remember that I went over there to see how they were," Bass insisted.

"How much time did you spend with them after you went over to see them?" Grey asked.

"Oh, I would say probably just a few minutes. We just got in line with them and walked through, and we sat down at the table altogether."

That, no doubt, is what most people would have done after they'd nearly killed someone on location. But that's not what Bobby Bass did. And Grey wanted to keep rubbing his nose in it—to show the jury that this man would lie about almost anything. But the judge had heard enough.

"Counsel," he said to the attorneys. "Come to the bench with the reporter, please."

The lawyers approached the bench, and out of earshot of the jury, Judge Savitch gave Grey a tongue-lashing.

"I have given you wide latitude with these questions," he told Grey. "I think we have come far enough. I understand your purpose, but I think we are going very far afield when you keep going back over the same subjects, such as this standing in line—repeatedly!"

"Your Honor," Grey spoke up, "the credibility of any witness is always at issue. We have a direct credibility dispute over this incident, and we have allegations that this gentleman was under drug influence . . ."

"I'm going to cut you off if you keep on doing this," the judge said, cutting him off. "You keep going back and back and back to the same point. At least ten minutes of questioning on his being in line. Okay. I have given you some latitude, but it is far enough. I want you to understand that."

"Thank you, Your Honor," Grey replied, and the lawyers returned to their places.

"Mr. Bass, what did you talk about with Julie Johnson when you came up to her in the line?" Grey asked, seemingly ignoring what the judge had just said. But there was no objection from Koska, so he kept going.

"I asked her how she was and how she was feeling," he said.

"What did she say?"

"She said that she got rapped pretty good in the head and she was feeling fair," he answered, making up a conversation that never happened.

"How much time did you spend with her all together during the lunch period before you each went back to work?" Grey continued.

"Objection!" Koska asserted. "Immaterial."

"Overruled," the judge said, continuing to give Grey latitude despite what he'd said at the bench conference.

"Oh, I would say from the time we stood in line and the time that we all sat down together, maybe fifteen or twenty minutes," Bass said.

"Time enough to eat your lunch?" Grey asked.

"Yeah. Time enough to eat my lunch. I eat kind of fast," Bass replied, to the amusement of several of the jurors.

"Did you work again in the afternoon?" Grey asked, already knowing the answer.

"Yes, we did," Bass said.

"What type of filming were you doing in the afternoon, sir?"

"I was to perform a 180-spin around in the dirt," Bass replied.

"Did you have any difficulty accomplishing that on that particular day?" Grey asked.

"Yes," Bass answered.

"How many times did you try to do the 180-spin around in the dirt that afternoon?"

"Once," Bass said.

"Didn't you actually try to spin that vehicle four or five times and you just couldn't do it?" Grey asked, knowing that that was what had actually happened—and that there were plenty of witnesses.

"No," Bass replied.

"Isn't it true that Ronnie Rondell had to do it for you that day because you were not in condition to make that vehicle spin?" Grey asked, knowing that Rondell had, in fact, had to step in and do the stunt for Bass.

"No," Bass replied.

"Isn't it true, Mr. Bass, that at the time that you encountered Julie Johnson and Jeannie Coulter in the lunch line that you were so impaired from the use of cocaine that you couldn't even speak to them?" Grey asked, pressing home his chief accusation.

"Objection!" Koska said, rising to his feet. "Argumentative! Asked and answered!"

"Overruled," the judge decreed. "You can answer."

"No," Bass said.

"I have no other questions," Grey said and sat down next to Julie.

Koska then rose from his chair and began his cross-examination.

"Before this particular stunt, Mr. Bass, have you ever driven vehicles where persons jumped out of the car?"

"Yes."

"Anybody ever been injured in any of those incidents?" Koska asked.

"Objection," Grey said, not bothering to stand up. "Irrelevant."

"Sustained," the judge said.

"Now, during the actual performance of the stunt, Mr. Bass, whose directions, if any, were you following regarding the speed of the car?" Koska asked.

"Julie Johnson's," he said.

"Did you follow those directions?"

"Yes," Bass said, although in fact, when she told him to slow down before the jump, he sped up.

"What was the last thing you heard Ms. Johnson say?" Koska asked.

"I had it in second gear when she said, 'Okay, faster . . . a little faster . . . a little faster . . . hold it right there.' And I held that speed for quite a ways, and then they jumped at their mark."

"Mr. Bass, have you won any awards for vehicular stunts?"

"Yes. I won two awards," he said. "One was for the best vehicular stunt of 1976, and then I won the same year for best vehicular stunt in an action sequence. It was on a film called *To Live and Die in L.A.*"

"Are you aware of the problems involved if, in fact, someone tries to do stunt work under the influence of drugs?" Koska asked.

"Yes, I am."

"Did you ever do such a thing, sir?"

"No, sir."

"That is all, Your Honor," Koska said and sat down at the defense table.

Richard Grey then began his redirect examination of the witness.

"Mr. Bass, would you agree that it would be absolutely unforgivable for you or anyone else, for that matter, to drive a stunt car while under the influence of cocaine or any other substance that would impair your ability to drive safely?"

"Yes," Bass said coolly.

"Do you consider yourself to be extremely safety conscious?" Grey asked.

"Yes."

"As part of your safety precautions, would you always take steps to ensure that there were seat belts installed in vehicles whenever they were needed, whether for the driver or a passenger?"

Grey was trying to slip in, one last time, the fact that Bass had put Heidi von Beltz into a stunt car with no seat belts on *Cannonball Run* and that because of his tragic lapse of judgment, she'd been left a quadriplegic for life. But Koska wasn't going to let him get away with it.

"Objection!" Koska shouted, jumping to his feet. "Irrelevant. Immaterial."

"Sustained," the judge said.

"I have no further questions," Grey said.

"May the witness be excused?" the judge asked Koska.

"Yes, Your Honor," Koska replied.

"You may be excused," the judge said.

And with that, Bobby Bass walked out of the courtroom a free man. There was no one there to arrest him, and he was never charged with perjury.

CHAPTER 35

Snuffy

In 1987, stuntman Roy "Snuffy" Harrison would play a central role in Julie's case against Aaron Spelling; and twelve years later, he'd find himself at the center of one of the most sensational murder trials in Hollywood's history. In Julie's case, testimony would be heard that painted him as a cocaine abuser who blacklisted a stuntwoman who refused to have sex with him. Twelve years later, he'd emerge as one of the men actor Robert Blake allegedly tried to hire to kill his wife.

Harrison says he got his nickname the day he was born, August 9, 1935, when his father noticed a character in a comic strip named Snuffy Smith. The nickname stuck, and he carried it the rest of his life. It didn't have anything to do with the vast amounts of cocaine he allegedly sniffed. At least that's what he always said.

His first big break came in high school when he befriended Ronnie Rondell, the son of a well-known assistant director. Young Ronnie would go on to become one of Hollywood's greatest stuntmen and launch a dynasty of Hollywood stuntmen and women. And being a good friend, Ronnie took Snuffy along for the ride.

Harrison was a pretty good stuntman too, but nowhere near the caliber of his friend. They'd both worked on feature films and on most of the top TV shows, but Ronnie would go on to coordinate more than a dozen major motion pictures; the closest Snuffy ever got to coordinating movies was on a bunch of forgettable, low-budget, made-for-TV movies.

Harrison was on the *Charlie's Angels* set that day out at Indian Dunes when Bobby Bass's recklessness sent Julie and Jeannie Coulter to the hospital. Identified by Coulter as one of Hollywood's Cocaine Cowboys, Jeannie testified that she once witnessed Snuffy sniffing cocaine with their boss—and his mentor—Ronnie Rondell.

In her deposition, Coulter also swore that Harrison blackballed her in the industry after she refused to have sex with him.

It happened in 1980 on location in San Francisco while shooting an episode of Aaron Spelling's hit show *Vegas$*. Harrison, she said, was the show's stunt coordinator, and she'd been hired to do some stunts.

"We were shooting one evening," she testified, "and the stunt coordinator asked me to go to his room, and I said, 'No thanks, but thanks for the compliment.' The next day, he had another girl doubling the same girl I was doubling—the actress Michelle Phillips—and I said, 'I don't understand what this is.' And he said, 'Shut up and never mind,' and told me if I didn't like it, that I could go home and I'd never work again for Spelling-Goldberg, and he'd make sure I'd never work again or anywhere else if he could help it. And that's basically what happened to me. And I don't work anymore."

"What did you do after he told you this?" Spelling's lawyer asked during her deposition.

"I cried and I threw up," she said matter-of-factly.

After Bobby Bass testified in Julie's case, Roy Harrison was called to the witness stand. As the judge had done with Bass before him, Harrison was informed of his right to refuse to answer any questions that might incriminate him. Like Bass before him, Harrison waived his Fifth Amendment privilege.

Richard Grey started his questioning by asking Harrison about his background as a stuntman. Harrison said he'd been in the business for twelve years and had coordinated a dozen TV shows, including *The Love Boat* and *Fantasy Island*.

"Are you acquainted with Julie Johnson?" Grey asked.

"Yes, sir."

"How long have you known her?"

"Twelve years, I would guess."

"Approximately how many times have you worked with her?"

"I would say twenty or thirty times."

"Did you work with her on *Charlie's Angels,* Mr. Harrison?"

"Yes, sir."

"How often have you stunt-doubled for a leading man?" Grey asked.

"That would be very difficult to say," he replied. "At least fifty . . . maybe seventy-five times over the years."

"Have you ever been called upon to double for a female leading actress?"

"Yes, I have," he replied.

And nearly every other stuntman in Hollywood had too. It was a very common practice in those days, as it is today. And it always goes only one way: stuntwomen are almost never called upon to double for a man.

Harrison had been on hand at the *Charlie's Angels* production meeting in Vail, Colorado, in 1978 when the producers decided not to allow Julie to double for Kathleen Nolan, a guest star on the show, and to have a stuntman double for her instead.

"Did there arise in Vail a difference of opinion about whether Julie Johnson was going to operate a snowmobile during the filming of stunt work there?" Grey asked.

"Objection!" Koska asserted. "Irrelevant. Calling for a conclusion."

"Overruled," the judge said. "You can answer."

"I recall something about that, but I don't recall the specific incident."

"Weren't you present at a meeting that evening in Mr. Ed Lasko's hotel room where that subject was discussed?" Grey asked.

"Yes, sir," Harrison said, suddenly remembering.

"For everyone's benefit here, who was Ed Lasko?"

"The producer," Harrison answered.

"Who else attended the meeting in Mr. Lasko's room that evening?"

"Elaine Rich, Lasko's assistant, and Ronnie Rondell."

"And yourself?"

"Yes, sir."

"And Julie Johnson?"

"I don't recall. I don't believe Julie was there," Harrison said, incorrectly.

"Let me see if I might be able to refresh your recollection, Mr. Harrison. Didn't Mrs. Rich call Julie on the telephone and ask her to come and join that meeting?"

"Objection," Koska said. "Hearsay."

"Overruled," the judge said. "You can answer."

"If she did, I do not remember it, sir."

"Did you discuss at that meeting whether or not Julie Johnson was going to be permitted to drive the snowmobile and jump it through the air?"

"I don't recall," Harrison said, although that is what was discussed at the meeting.

"Was Julie Johnson eventually replaced with a male substitute to drive the snowmobile?" Grey asked.

"I was told that occurred. Yes."

And it did. And it was the most humiliating moment of Julie's career and direct evidence of the kind of gender discrimination stuntwomen face every day.

Grey then turned to the question of drug abuse on two of Aaron Spelling's biggest hits.

"Besides *Charlie's Angels*," Grey asked, "did you work with Julie Johnson on *Fantasy Island?*"

"I do not recall working with her on *Fantasy Island*," Harrison replied. "I may have, but I don't recall."

In fact, he'd worked with Julie—and allegedly offered her cocaine—on both shows.

"Roy Harrison offered me cocaine twice," Julie later recalled. "Once in the van on *Charlie's Angels* and once on *Fantasy Island*." She turned him down both times.

"Did you work on *Charlie's Angels* during the period 1978 through 1980?" Grey asked.

"Yes, sir," Harrison replied.

"During that same period, did you ever encounter any drug—or alcohol-related problems that had a negative impact upon your ability to safely work in the stunt field?"

"No, sir," he said.

"During the same period, Mr. Harrison, whether you were at the *Charlie's Angels* set or working on *Fantasy Island*, did you ever use cocaine during the workday?"

"Absolutely not," he answered.

"Did you ever offer cocaine to any other person during the regular workday at or near a production lot during that period of time?"

"Absolutely not."

"Did you ever offer any illegal drugs to Julie Johnson while she was the stunt coordinator on *Charlie's Angels*?"

"Absolutely not."

"I have no other questions," Grey said and returned to his seat at the plaintiff's table.

Koska rose from the defendant's table and began his cross-examination.

"Mr. Harrison, while you worked on *Charlie's Angels* from 1978 to 1980, was there in effect any policy with regards to safety?"

"Yes, sir," he replied. "There was always safety first."

"What about with regard to drug use on the set?" Koska asked. "Was there a policy involving that?"

"Yes, sir. It was not allowed on the set at any time."

"Did you ever work on a show entitled *Diary of a Teenage Hitchhiker*?" Koska asked.

"Yes, sir," Harrison answered.

"Now, we had some testimony on Friday from Ms. Jeannie Coulter," Koska said. "Did you ever travel in a van, at some point on that show going from location to location, and offer drugs to Ms. Coulter?"

"No, sir," he said.

"Did you ever, at any time after Ms. Johnson left the *Angels* series, tell any stunt coordinator not to hire her?" Koska asked.

"No, sir."

"Did anyone ever tell you not to hire Ms. Johnson after she left the *Angels* series?"

"No."

"I believe that's all the questions I have, Your Honor."

The judge looked at Grey to see if he wanted to ask any more questions on redirect.

"No further questions, Your Honor," Grey said.

"All right, you may step down, Mr. Harrison," the judge said.

Harrison left the witness stand and winked at Julie as he left the courtroom. It would be up to the jury to decide who was telling the truth. It wouldn't be a hard call.

Chapter 36

Monty Mason Goes to Jail

Monty Mason had saved himself—but not for long.

On November 22, 1988, he was hauled before a federal grand jury and questioned about the class action cases he'd been handling down in San Diego. A short while later, he was arrested and charged with racketeering, mail fraud, and making false declarations to a grand jury. Monty and eleven other Southern California lawyers were accused of taking part in a massive scheme to defraud insurance companies by drawing out complex civil cases and bilking insurers out of millions of dollars in billable hours and expenses.

Monty went on trial and was convicted in June of 1991. On September 23, he was sentenced to forty-six months in federal prison and fined $25,000. Following his conviction, he was suspended from the California State Bar. His twenty-three-year law career was over.

Free on bond pending his appeal, Monty worked as a secretary and took voice lessons in the hope of putting his distinctive baritone to use as a voice-over artist on TV commercials. He never told Julie he was sorry for abandoning her, but he did the next best thing. On May 10, 1992, while his own case was still pending appeal, he signed a declaration, swearing under penalty of perjury, that he'd resigned as her attorney on the eve of her trial on orders from the Mafia.

A front-page story about it ran in the *Hollywood Reporter* under a banner headline that read: "Lawyer Feared 'Mafia' Hit."

"She asked me to write the declaration. I felt I owed it to her," he said, choking back tears, in an emotional hour-long interview for this book. "I would be held up to ridicule for the balance of my life anyway. I figured if it helped Julie, then that's fine."

Monty's own case was submitted to the Ninth Circuit Court of Appeals on November 3, 1993, which seven months later affirmed Monty's conviction. He was then loaded into a prison bus and driven out into the California desert to Boron Federal Prison.

Granted, Boron was a minimum-security prison, but it was no country club. There were no high walls, no barbed wire, and no guard towers, but it didn't need any. Located on the western edge of the Mojave Desert, it was surrounded by miles and miles of nothing but miles of nothing. There was no escape because there was nowhere to escape to.

"It was one of the bleakest places on earth," Monty recalls.

Monty spent three and a half years there, turning sixty in prison. It was not a happy birthday.

Julie was one of the few people who stayed in touch with him while he was in jail. She hadn't forgiven him, but she didn't abandon him either. They corresponded occasionally, and in his letters, he played down the hardship of prison life.

"Actually, prison is no big deal," he wrote to her on January 6, 1998. "You make a little nest in your corner of the concrete and weather the sameness. Only very occasionally is there drama. It happens. But for me, adjusting was quite easy."

He was even able to joke about it.

"Can you imagine a place where you work a seven-hour day and pay no taxes?" he wrote. "A place where you cook no meals, do no shopping, avoid freeway traffic, and have every Runyonesque character at your immediate disposal for entertainment?"

As many do, he'd grown philosophical in jail.

"As far as something good coming from all this," he told Julie, "of that I am increasingly sure. True, nothing material remains except for perhaps adding 'ex-con' to my résumé. But the hurt is gone. In its place is a certain adventuresomeness—albeit enforced. I'm old, toothless and decrepit, and forced to face new horizons. It's like a great weight has been inadvertently taken from me—a weight that was compelling me to walk the expected, the acceptable, and the routine. None of these are mine now, although I spent my life desperately seeking them. I'm now in a position not to care, and that is like becoming the wind that I strove so hard to shut out."

He didn't apologize for sabotaging her case, but he signed the letter: "Your very good friend, Monty."

The prison was closed in 2000—five years after Monty's release. It burned down ten years later.

Monty, who now lives with his stepmother in Santa Barbara, maintains his innocence to this day.

Chapter 37

The Last Days of Bobby Bass

No one, of course, could have known it the day that Julie and Jeannie Coulter were nearly killed out at Indian Dunes, but tragedy was waiting in the wings for many of the *Charlie's Angels* stunt performers on location there that day.

In horrifying succession, one of them would be killed in a terrifying skydiving accident, two of them would be involved in an ill-conceived movie stunt that would leave one of them paralyzed for life, one of them would get the terrible news that his son had been killed in a fiery helicopter crash while shooting a TV show not far from this very same location, and one of them would commit suicide just six months after being questioned by police in one of Hollywood's most famous unsolved murders.

Veteran stuntman Howard Curtis, who had been riding in the front seat next to Bobby Bass when Julie and Jeannie bailed out of the car that day, would be the first to die.

Ten years earlier, Curtis had been involved in one of the most memorable movie stunts of all time. The film was *Butch Cassidy and the Sundance Kid*, and when the title characters, played by Paul Newman and Robert Redford, jumped off a cliff into a raging river below, it was Curtis, doubling for Newman, and stuntman Mickey Gilbert, doubling for Redford, who made the actual jump.

A skilled stunt pilot, Curtis had nearly been killed in 1961 during production of *Ripcord*, a short-live TV show about two guys who operate a skydiving service. Two planes filming a scene for the show crashed in midair and spiraled to the ground in flames. Curtis and the pilot and crew of the other plane all managed to parachute to safety.

Ironically, Curtis would be killed in a parachuting accident on September 2, 1979—just eight months after witnessing Julie and Jeannie Coulter nearly getting killed. He died a hero during a skydiving exhibition at Lake Elsinore, California, while trying to save an amateur skydiver who'd gotten tangled up in his own chute. When Curtis soared over to try and untangle him, the man panicked, grabbed hold of Curtis, and wouldn't let go. Both men fell to their deaths.

Stuntwoman Heidi von Beltz was out at Indian Dunes the day her fiancée, Bobby Bass, almost killed Julie and Jeannie Coulter; and three years later, he nearly killed

Heidi too while coordinating stunts on *Cannonball Run*. High on coke yet again, he put her into a stunt car without any seat belts; and when the car crashed, she was thrown into the windshield and left a quadriplegic.

Tragedy would also find Ronnie Rondell. Six years later, and not far from where Julie and Jeannie were nearly killed, his twenty-two-year-old son, Reid Rondell, who'd followed his father into the family business, would be killed in a fiery helicopter crash while filming a stunt for the TV series *Airwolf*. He, too, had been high on cocaine.

Bobby Bass would also die tragically—by his own hand. But not before his name had come up in two of the most famous unsolved murder cases in Hollywood history. And there are some today who think he may have had a hand in both.

In 1994, Warner Bros. Television had completed a two-hour pilot for a TV show called *Frogmen*, in which O. J. Simpson starred as the leader of a team of Navy SEALS. In one scene, O. J. is shown holding a knife to a woman's throat.

Bobby Bass, it turns out, was the weapons consultant hired on the show to train O. J. in the fine art of slitting a woman's throat.

A few months later, O. J. was arrested and charged with slashing the throat of his estranged wife, Nicole Brown Simpson, and then stabbing her friend, Ron Goldman, to death.

Frogmen never aired. After O. J.'s arrest, NBC wisely decided to cancel it. In the course of the murder investigation, the Los Angeles district attorney's office examined the completed film, the outtakes, the production reports and scripts to see if there were any clues there that might help them solve the murders.

O. J., of course, was eventually acquitted of the murders, which technically, to this day, have never been solved. And despite all the evidence pointing to O. J. as the killer, there are some in the tight-knit stunt community who believe that Bobby Bass may have a hand in the killings. Bass, the theory goes, was not only a former Green Beret and weapons expert, but also an undercover CIA operative highly trained in the art of killing people at close quarters.

The trial that followed marked the first time that Bass's name would come up in connection with a sensational murder case, but it wouldn't be the last. In 2001, his name would surface again in the investigation of the murder of Bonnie Lee Bakley, the wife of actor Robert Blake, who had been shot to death while sitting in a car outside Vitello's Restaurant in Studio City. And there are those think he may have had a hand in that murder as well.

During Blake's trial, it would be revealed that he tried to get Bass and three other stuntmen to murder his wife. The revelations made headlines across the country and sent shockwaves through the stunt community.

It unfolded like this: Ten days after Bonnie's murder, stuntman Gary "Whiz Kid" McLarty walked into the North Hollywood police station and told detectives that Blake had offered him $10,000 to kill her. Two days later, police got a tip that Blake had offered money to another stuntman to murder his wife. His name was Ron "Duffy" Hambleton. At first, Duffy refused to talk to the cops, telling them that he feared he'd be "a dead duck for being a snitch." He later sang like a bird. He eventually told the police that seven weeks before Bonnie had been killed, Blake drove him through the alley behind Vitello's and pointed out places he could hide before ambushing her. He said that Blake wanted her dead because he hated her but couldn't divorce her because he feared that Bonnie, who'd been married nine times before, would get custody of their daughter. Blake told Hambleton he feared if that happened, his child would "wind up a porn star."

A third stuntman, Roy "Snuffy" Harrison, told police that he'd served as the middleman in the murder plot. Harrison, who'd worked with Blake in the 1970s on his hit TV show *Baretta*, testified that he'd arranged for McLarty and Hambleton to meet with Blake at Du-Par's restaurant in Studio City to discuss the job.

Why Blake allegedly reached out to four different stuntmen to kill his wife remains a mystery. Maybe they'd been coke buddies; maybe he figured that some stuntmen would do just about anything for money. Whatever Blake's reason, it said as much about certain stuntmen as it did about him.

"These were the kind of people I had to deal with," Julie recalls with a sigh. "For years, I felt like I was in the crosshairs."

During the subsequent trial, McLarty's testimony about Blake's search for someone to kill his wife would be damning, but he was not the most credible of witnesses. McLarty's estranged wife testified that he used cocaine for the majority of their thirty-year marriage; and his son testified that his father was paranoid, delusional, and constantly under the influence of cocaine.

This was not the first time that McLarty's testimony in a sensational trial would be called into question. In November of 1986, he spent three days on the witness stand in the trial of director John Landis and four others accused of manslaughter in connection with the deaths of actor Vic Morrow and two children who were killed in 1982 when a helicopter crashed on top of them during the making of *Twilight Zone: The Movie*.

McLarty was the stunt coordinator on that film and was in the helicopter when it crashed. If his wife and son's testimony during the later Blake trial was any indication, he was probably high on coke the night of the *Twilight Zone* disaster as well.

At that trial, McLarty initially testified that the doomed stunt that took the lives of Morrow and the children out at Indian Dunes had been carefully planned and rehearsed. Under intense cross-examination, however, he acknowledged that there had been no rehearsal at all.

Fortunately for him, he was never asked if he was on coke the night of the crash.

Bobby Bass, meanwhile, would never get the chance to testify at the Robert Blake murder trial. Shortly after the murder, he told police in a sworn affidavit that although Blake had contacted him, he declined to meet with the actor. A few months later, Bobby Bass would be dead too.

On November 7, 2001—six months after Bonnie was murdered—Bobby's wife Norma kissed him on the cheek and left their modest home on Dalton Avenue in the South Bay town of Torrance, California, to do some shopping. Bobby seemed fine, although he was not well. A year earlier, he'd been diagnosed with Parkinson's disease and had been in declining health ever since.

Bobby and Norma, who was Bo Derek's mother, had been together for twenty years—ever since he dumped Heidi von Beltz after she was paralyzed on *Cannonball Run*.

After Norma drove away, Bobby, wearing multicolored pajama bottoms, white socks, and a T-shirt, walked into his den and looked around the cluttered room, which was filled with a lifetime of memories. There were awards and trophies from his days as a champion martial artist, mementos and medals from his days as a Green Beret, and photos and plaques from his career as a top Hollywood stuntman. There was nothing, however, to commemorate his years of service to the CIA. They don't give out plaques or trophies for that.

Bobby went to his desk and took a Glock 17 semiautomatic pistol from a drawer. He placed the extended barrel against his right temple and pulled the trigger. He was dead before he hit the ground.

Norma returned home an hour later and found her husband lying in a pool of blood in the den, the gun under his right thigh, a single spent cartridge on the floor beside the body. She rushed to his side, but could see that he was already dead. She called 911 and paramedics arrived twenty minutes later, but there was nothing they could do.

In their official report, responding officers wrote that "Norma Bass said her husband was a very 'macho' type person who was depressed because he could not come to grips with depending on someone else to help him care for himself. His health had been declining ever since he was diagnosed with Parkinson's disease. He spent most nights up and about the house because he was not able to sleep. He had episodes of anxiety and was very restless. He never spoke of suicide and she had no idea that he might do something like this."

He was sixty-five years old, and he left no note.

Besides the entrance and exit wounds to his head, an autopsy report found "several tiny metal particle fragments" in Bobby's chest, abdomen, and back. The medical examiner didn't remove them or speculate about their origin, but in all likelihood, they were bullet or shrapnel fragments from his work with the military and the CIA.

The medical examiner found no alcohol in Bass's bloodstream. A test for cocaine was not conducted.

Bobby's suicide deeply saddened the stunt community. He was well-liked by all and loved by many. In the end, Julie forgave him for ruining her career, and Heidi von Beltz forgave him for ruining everything.

Chapter 38

Betrayal

For Julie, the darkest day of the trial—and one of the darkest days of her life—came when Jeannie Epper took the witness stand to testify against her.

Julie had expected Bobby Bass and Roy Harrison to lie. They could have gone to jail if they told the truth. And there was no way that Aaron Spelling was going to tell the truth. But she and Jeannie Epper had been friends, colleagues, and sisters in a man's world. They'd worked together many times and they'd co-founded the Society of Professional Stuntwomen. But now she was being called as a defense witness to denounce her; to smear her; to destroy her.

Julie sat at the plaintiff's table with her head bowed as Epper took the witness stand; she couldn't bear to look at her. Betrayal is the worst thing in the world.

"How could she do this to me?" Julie thought, but the answer was sitting right in front of her. Not everyone in the good old boys' network is a boy—some are the daughters of good old boys. Jeannie was part of a storied stunt dynasty—the daughter of legendary stuntman Johnny Epper, who'd doubled for Gary Cooper, Henry Fonda, Errol Flynn and Ronald Reagan, and her brothers were famous stuntmen, too.

Blood, it's been said, is thicker than water, but in the Hollywood stunt community, blood is thicker than everything.

Under questioning by Richard Grey, Epper toed the party line. She swore she'd never, ever, seen anyone doing drugs on the set of *Charlie's Angels,* and that she'd never, ever told Julie that she—and every other member of the Society of Professional Stuntwomen—would be blacklisted if Julie didn't drop her lawsuit.

"Julie actually formed the Society of Professional Stuntwomen," Epper testified. "She came to me and asked me if I would be interested in getting involved with her. We met several times and I agreed to help her."

"Do you recall in April of 1982," Grey asked, "a meeting of the group at the home of Jeannie Coulter at which there was a controversy between yourself and Julie Johnson?"

As Jeannie Coulter had sworn in her deposition, Epper had walked into her dining room and delivered a message to Julie and the five other stuntwomen assembled there. "I've got something to say," Epper told the women. "Julie, I've been sent here to tell you that if you don't stop making waves and drop this lawsuit, none of us are going to work in this business." And on that day, Julie's blacklisting had begun.

Koska, of course, didn't want the jury to hear any more about that.

"Objection!" he cried. "Irrelevant! Immaterial! Cumulative! Hearsay!"

"Sustained," the judge ruled.

"Did you ever tell the members of that group in April of 1982 that they should have nothing more to do with Julie Johnson if they wanted to continue working?" Grey asked.

"I did not," Epper said before Koska could object.

"Objection!" he hollered. "Hearsay! Cumulative! No foundation!"

"Sustained," the judge said again.

"Did you ever observe anyone with a cocaine problem on the set of *Charlie's Angels* when you worked there from 1978 to '80?" Grey asked.

"Objection!" Koska bellowed. "Hearsay! Vague and ambiguous!"

"Sustained," the judge agreed.

"During this time," Grey asked, "did you ever see anybody working on the set in a condition where they were impaired so that they couldn't work safely?"

"Same objection," Koska said.

"Overruled," the judge said, to Koska's surprise.

"No. I did not," she answered. The code of silence was in full force now.

"Did you ever see anybody use cocaine on *Charlie's Angels?*" Grey asked.

"Objection!" Koska said. "Vague and ambiguous! Irrelevant! Hearsay!"

"Sustained," ruled the judge, who had now become the enforcer of the code of silence.

When Epper stepped down from the witness stand, Julie didn't look up; it took every ounce of Julie's strength to keep from crying, but she held back the tears until the jury left the courtroom. No doubt, they'd all seen the pained expression on her face as her friend testified against her. And surely, any juror who'd ever been betrayed by a friend would know who was telling the truth.

Chapter 39

Julie Johnson Takes the Stand

It was only six or seven short steps from the plaintiff's table to the witness box, but it had taken seven long years for Julie to get there. And now, after all those years, she was finally going to get to tell her story.

Wearing a beige business suit and a pained expression, Julie raised her right hand and took the oath. She was nervous at first, but remembering what her lawyer had told her in the hallway calmed her down. "All you have to do is tell the truth," he said.

Richard Grey began his questioning by asking about her early life.

William Koska, sitting at the defense table, sniffled throughout her entire testimony. He'd come down with the flu and could barely speak above a hoarse whisper.

"Miss Johnson, when were you born?" Grey asked.

"September 1940," she answered. She was 46 years old.

"Did you grow up here in Southern California?"

"Yes," she said. "In Fullerton."

"As you were growing up, did you have any special aptitudes or interests?"

"Yes," she said. "Because my father was a coach and my grandfather is in the Baseball Hall of Fame, my interests were always sports."

"And what is your occupation, Miss Johnson?"

"I'm a stuntwoman and stunt coordinator," she answered—at least she had been until she'd been blacklisted for bringing this lawsuit.

Grey then walked Julie through her early career, going over the many films and TV shows she'd worked on, and the more than 60 well-known actresses she'd doubled for, including Ava Gardner, Farrah Fawcett, Doris Day, Kim Bassinger, Jessica Walter, Carol Burnett, Stephanie Powers, Susan St. James and Julie Harris, just to name a few.

Summarizing her stunt experience, Julie told the jury: "I've performed almost every conceivable stunt in the business. I've worked with the best in the business and learned from them. And I've worked with the worst in the business, and learned from them, too."

Grey then asked her a series of questions about the nuts and bolts of the stunt business.

To be a good stunt person, she explained, "You have to be a good athlete. You have to have exceptional timing and coordination. You have to be healthy, and be able to take direction. And you need a working knowledge of how to work in front of a camera."

"Can you tell us how someone goes about establishing a good reputation as a stunt player?" Grey asked.

"Well, you're only as good as your last job," she answered. "So by doing a good job, you're remembered, and you get called back"—if you're not blacklisted, that is.

"Were there any special techniques that one could use to maximize the possibility of getting work?" Grey asked.

"Well, besides waiting for the phone to ring," she laughed, "you make contact with people."

"Can you tell us what a stunt coordinator is?" Grey asked.

"A stunt coordinator," she said, "is like a ramrod. The stunt coordinator is a management job; they design and manage the stunts. They are responsible for safety, and for hiring the proper people for the job. It covers a very wide spectrum."

"And how many shows have you coordinated?"

"I coordinated 28 episodes of *Charlie's Angels*," she said, "and before that I was a co-coordinator on the show. Prior to that, I coordinated a fight sequence between Carol Burnett and Geraldine Page on *Pete 'n' Tillie*. I also coordinated a couple of fights for Ida Lupino on *Women in Chains*, and prior to that, any time I worked with a director by myself, I coordinated that piece of action."

"Would that have been true on *Play Misty for Me*?" Grey asked. "Did you coordinate the fight scene at the end of the movie when Clint Eastwood knocks Jessica Walter through a plate glass window, over a railing and off a cliff?"

"Yes, sir," she said. "I assisted Mr. Eastwood in the choreography of that scene."

"You mentioned choreography," Grey said. "That's normally a dance term. How does it apply here?"

"Well, choreography is very much like coordinating a stunt scene," she said. "We work things out in slow motion before the scene is filmed. We work it out step-by-step, piece-by-piece."

"Were there any unique problems on that film?" Grey asked.

"Well, one of the unique problems was that if I overshot the railing, I really would have fallen down the cliff," she said.

Grey then asked her if she recalled the first Spelling-Goldberg show she worked on.

"I believe it was on *The Mod Squad*," she said—a show about three hip crime fighters.

"How long did you work on *Charlie's Angels?*"

"I started there in 1976," she answered, "and continued to double on the show every season through 1980."

"How many episodes of *Charlie's Angels* did you appear in?" Grey asked.

"In excess of 80 shows," she answered, or about three-quarters of the show's 110 episodes.

"And how many of the show's episodes did you coordinate?" Grey asked.

"I coordinated 28 shows myself," she said, "and I assisted on another 10 or 12."

Grey then asked her how she got her first job coordinating *Charlie's Angels*.

"Dick Ziker recommended me for the job," she said.

Ronnie Rondell had been the show's coordinator, but he was leaving to oversee the stunts on all of Spelling's shows. Ziker, who'd coordinated the pilot and most of the first season, thought Julie would make a great stunt coordinator, and told Ronnie to give her a chance. Ronnie thought so too, so he let her co-coordinate a dozen shows.

"How did that work?" Grey asked

"Well, Ronnie would often set up a piece of action, and then he'd be called away, and I'd be there to finish it for him."

Grey then asked her about her salary when she first became a coordinator.

"$842 a week," she said. "The Screen Actors Guild's weekly scale."

That wasn't bad pay in 1978, but it represented a pay cut for Julie, because as a stunt double, she could earn two or three times that by working two or three different shows a week. But as a stunt coordinator, which was essentially a fulltime job, she was committed to working only for *Charlie's Angels*.

"Did you have a chance to negotiate for something different before your second season as a stunt coordinator?" Grey asked.

"Yes, sir."

"What were you trying to obtain in that negotiation?" he asked.

"A raise," she answered, "and to earn residuals whether I was on camera or not."

Residuals are the lifeblood of any actor. For a long-running show that goes into re-runs—and then into syndication—an actor can receive many-times more in residuals than his or her initial payment. But because stunt coordinators aren't generally seen on camera, as stunt doubles are, they often don't get residuals—or have to negotiate for them. On *Charlie's Angels,* all the male coordinators before Julie had negotiated deals for residuals, and that's what Julie wanted too.

"And did you have discussions with anyone at Spelling-Goldberg about receiving residuals whether you appeared on camera or not when you stunt coordinated in the second season?" Grey asked.

"Yes," she said. "I spoke with Ronnie Rondell. The first time was a week before he left. He told me he'd be leaving and that I would be coordinating. I explained the situation to him about the raise and the residuals."

"And what did he say?" Grey asked.

"He said he didn't know if he could get that for me, but that he'd try. He told me to meet him the next day at the production office, and that he would be seeing Norm Henry that morning, and that he'd come back and tell me if I was to get that deal."

Norm Henry was the show's production manager, and if he gave the okay, she'd get residuals for shows she coordinated—even for those she didn't appear in on-screen.

"Was there anything else you told Mr. Rondell?" Grey asked.

"Yes," she said. "I explained to him that if I couldn't get that deal, I really didn't want to stay on as coordinator because I was losing too much money and I would rather just do stunts and be free to go out on other jobs."

"Besides the residuals, how much additional money were you asking for?"

"I asked for parity," she said—meaning parity with the men who'd preceded her on the job. "But Ronnie told me, 'Well, maybe I can get you $1,000 instead of $842." But that was still below what the men had been paid.

The next day, Julie told the jury, "Ronnie went into Norm Henry's office and told me to wait outside until he came back." An hour later, Rondell emerged from Norm's office and gave Julie a big smile.

"Did I get my deal?" she asked Ronnie. "And residuals?"

"And then he went like this," she showed the jury, pressing her thumb to her forefinger, "and he winked and gave me the a-okay sign."

Grey looked at the jury for a moment, and then addressed claims made by some of the defense witnesses that Julie wasn't a very good coordinator.

"In the course of your entire career," he asked, "has any actress ever asked you to leave or discontinue working for them as a stunt double?"

"No," Julie answered truthfully.

"Miss Johnson, did any actress on *Charlie's Angels* ever ask you to discontinue working with them as a stunt coordinator?"

"No, sir."

"Miss Johnson, do you believe that you posses the qualifications to do good or excellent work as a stunt coordinator?" he asked.

"Yes, sir."

"And why is that?"

"My expertise and my years in the industry dictate that," she replied. "My time in the bucket, so to speak . . . of working with the very best and learning from them. I believe that gives me my qualifications."

"Miss Johnson, in your years of experience, would you say that performing stunts is a hazardous profession?"

"Yes," she said. "It can be very hazardous."

"And what are some of the more dangerous stunts you have performed?"

"This is the most dangerous stunt I have ever performed," she answered, and nearly everyone in the courtroom laughed, even the normally stone-faced judge.

"I am sure," the judge said to Julie, still chuckling, "that we here would think that the work you do is more dangerous."

"Outside of this courtroom," Grey asked, joining in on the fun, "what were some of the most hazardous stunts that you've performed?"

"There are many horror stories I could tell," she said. "We would be here all day."

No one was laughing anymore.

"Just a few examples then," Grey said, coaxing her along.

Julie recounted a few of her more harrowing experiences: Getting kicked in the head by a horse on *Little Big Man;* the near-fatal motorcycle crash on *Mannix,* and nearly getting killed while suspended upside down from a hot-air balloon on *Nickelodeon* when two of the cables snapped. Then she told how she'd nearly been crushed to death in a crowd scene on *Raging Bull* as director Martin Scorsese looked on in horror.

"I got trampled on pretty good," she recalled of her work on the movie, considered by many to be the best boxing film ever made.

Filmed at the Olympic Auditorium in Los Angeles in 1979—just a few months after Bobby Bass nearly killed her—Julie had been hired on *Raging Bull* to portray a woman who falls to the floor and is trampled to death when an angry crowd goes on a rampage at a boxing match.

The call had come in from Teddy O'Toole's during hiatus—a break in filming on *Charlie's Angels*. Teddy told her to bring lots of padding—knee pads, back pads, elbow pads—everything she had. It was going to be that kind of job.

When Julie got to the auditorium, she got into her pads and costume, and then the famed director explained the shot to the stunt and camera teams.

"This is where you fall and this is where you get trampled," Scorsese told Julie, pointing to a spot on the floor next to the boxing ring.

The camera would be at ground-level, filming Julie as she's knocked to the floor, then move in for a close-up as dozens of men step on and stumble over her in the ensuing stampede. Scorsese told the stuntmen involved—some 30 or 40 of them—to make it look real, but not *too* real. No one, he told them, was to stomp on her head.

Finally, with everyone in place, Scorsese yelled "Action!" from a safe perch in the ring directly above Julie and the camera.

The scene starts when an angry fan throws a chair into the ring. A stampede for the doors begins, and then we see Julie knocked to the floor, her face contorted in agony as one heavy-footed man after another tramples on her.

After a minute or so, Scorsese had gotten what he wanted. "Cut!" he yelled through a bullhorn. "Cut!"

But the place was going crazy. People were yelling and throwing chairs and nobody could hear him calling for them to stop. One of the stuntmen tripped and fell on top of Julie, and then another fell on top of him. The shoot had quickly gotten out of hand.

"Cut!" Scorsese yelled as loud as he could. "Cut! Cut! Cut!"

Finally, one of the stuntmen heard him and spread out his arms, bracing himself and holding back more stuntmen from falling on top of Julie. Somebody whistled and Scorsese continued yelling and waving his arms for everyone to stop. Finally, the auditorium grew quite. One stuntman, then another, got up off her. Julie was dazed and bruised, but she was all right.

"Everything okay?" Scorsese asked her as two stuntmen helped her to her feet.

"I'm fine," she said, her legs a bit wobbly. "I'm good."

It was another close call that could have gotten her seriously injured—or worse.

"I was really being trampled," Julie told the jury. "The director was screaming 'Cut! Cut!' but they couldn't hear him because everyone else was screaming. It seemed to take forever for them to cut."

"Thank you, Miss Johnson," her lawyer said.

Then, with the judge's permission, Grey turned the lights down in the courtroom and played a video of some Julie's stunt scenes from *Charlie's Angels*. After each scene, Grey would stop the videotape, turn up the lights, and ask Julie to describe the preparation that went into each stunt. Then he'd turn down the lights and restart the tape. This went on for nearly an hour. First up was Julie, doubling for Cheryl Ladd, racing down a hill in a golf cart and jumping out just before it turned over; then Julie doubling for Shelly Hack, jumping out of a speeding boat; then Julie, doubling for Kate Jackson, leaping from a balcony into the back of a truck; then, the one that Grey had secretly been building up to, a fight scene in a woman's football team locker room.

"Stop it right there," Grey told his assistant, who stopped the tape and turned the lights back up in the courtroom. "What was your involvement in the scene we just saw?"

"I was doubling Jaclyn Smith," she said, "in a fight sequence with Heidi von Beltz."

The judge had already ruled that he would not allow any testimony on the *Cannonball Run* accident that had left von Beltz a quadriplegic, but Grey was going to take another shot at it anyway.

"Heidi von Beltz was your opponent in that fight?" Grey asked.

"Yes," Julie replied.

"Do you know how she got that job?" Grey asked, knowing that she got it through her fiancé, Bobby Bass.

"Objection!" Koska wheezed, finally stirring from his flu-induced stupor. "Irrelevant! Speculation!"

"Sustained," the judge ruled.

"Do you know whether Heidi von Beltz had any significant experience as a stunt player when you and she did this scene?" Grey asked, knowing that she had not.

"Objection!" Koska said, struggling to his feet. "Irrelevant! Immaterial! Hearsay!"

"Sustained."

"Do you know whether Heidi von Beltz, shortly after that scene was filmed, suffered any serious injury because of her lack of experience in the stunt field?" Grey asked.

"Objection! Irrelevant! Hearsay! Speculation!" Koska coughed. He was really worked up now.

"Sustained," the judge sighed.

"Do you know whether Heidi von Beltz had any close relationship with Bobby Bass?" Grey asked.

"Objection!" Koska said. "Evidence Code Section 352"—the section of the California Evidence Code that allows a judge to exclude testimony if it would create an undue prejudice in the mind of the jury.

"Sustained on all grounds," the judge said in a stern tone. "I don't think you should go any further with this, Mr. Grey."

"All right, thank you, Your Honor," Grey said, having given the jury as many of the details of Heidi's tragic story as he possibly could without ever getting an answer from any of his questions.

It was time to move on; it was time to talk about drugs.

"Did you ever run into any drug-related problems that caused you significant concern about safety on the set of a Spelling-Goldberg production?" he asked.

"Yes, sir," she answered.

It first happened in 1978 on a location shoot for *Fantasy Island* at the Los Angeles County Arboretum in Arcadia, a beautiful botanical garden located a dozen miles northeast of downtown L.A. It had been a cold and windy October day, and the gardens were lush and spectacularly green from the recent rains.

Julie was doubling one of the guest stars that morning and trying to stay warm between takes. At noon, everyone broke for lunch. Julie grabbed a sandwich off the catering truck and saw Roy Harrison, the show's stunt coordinator, sitting in his van. She decided to join him.

"Tell us exactly what you observed during the lunch hour that caused you concern about drugs on the job," Grey said.

"He had a van there," Julie answered, "and the side door was open. We were just talking, and he offered me some cocaine. I turned it down."

"Would you describe the substance that Mr. Harrison offered you that day?"

"It was some white powder in a little bitty vial," she said.

"How did he offer it to you?" Grey asked. "Describe what he did or said."

"We just were talking, and all of a sudden this vial appears. He offered me some, and I said, 'No, thank you.' Then he turned away from me and sniffed from the vial."

"And what did you do after that?"

"I just turned away," she said. "I mean, I have never been in the presence of someone that used that."

Grey then asked Julie about the next time 'Snuffy' offered her coke.

"Was there another incident on or near the *Charlie's Angels* set that caused you additional concern about drug-related safety problems?" he asked.

"Yes," she said. "There was another time in January of 1980," she said.

"And where did this second incident occur?"

"I was doubling for Farrah Fawcett on the stage directly in front of the main entrance of 20th-Century Fox. After lunch, I went outside and Snuffy was standing by his van."

"What was he doing there that day?" Grey asked.

"I believe he was just visiting," Julie said. "And I saw him and I needed to talk to him about his work call the next day. So I went over and talked to him."

"And when you did that, did you see anything that caused you concern?"

"Objection!" Koska sniffled, rising weakly from his chair. "Irrelevant! May we approach, Your Honor?"

"Come up, all of you," the judge said, waving them forward.

The lawyers and the court reporter approached the bench and huddled around the judge out of earshot of the jury.

"Your Honor," Koska whispered, "by the witness' own testimony, Mr. Harrison was not working and was not even on the set. He was just visiting. And what he does at that point in time is irrelevant to what happens on *Charlie's Angels*."

"It does seem to be remote," the judge concurred.

"Your Honor," Grey argued, "if I might theorize a bit, here is a lady who, the year before, was involved in an accident and complained to Mr. Rondell about cocaine. Mr. Rondell, by his testimony, said he looked into the matter by going to Mr. Harrison and to Mr. Bass. When each of them told Mr. Rondell 'No'—that they didn't know anything about cocaine being used on the set—Mr. Rondell dropped it. Then Mr. Harrison appears on the set and again offers cocaine to Julie Johnson. I think we are in a position to argue that they were trying to involve her in cocaine use, and when she didn't do that, she was let go, and had she gone along with it, she would still be there."

And that was the case in a nutshell. If Julie had been a Cocaine Cowgirl, the Cocaine Cowboys would have let her keep her job.

It was another key moment in the trial—the third piece of the 'cocaine triangle' at the heart of the case. The jury had heard Julie's testimony that Roy Harrison had offered her coke on location for *Fantasy Island* in 1978, and that he'd been the first person Ronnie Rondell interviewed when he investigated Julie's complaint that

Bobby Bass had been high on coke when he fractured her neck in January 1979. But would the judge allow the jury to hear that Harrison had offered her coke again on *Charlie's Angels* in January 1980?

"I don't want to get into an indictment of the entire film industry," the judge whispered to the lawyers, "but I'll overrule the objection. You may proceed."

Grey breathed another sigh of relief, and everyone returned to their places so that Grey could resume his questioning.

"Would you tell us what you saw and heard that day in January 1980 when you ran into with Mr. Harrison on the Fox lot where *Charlie's Angels* was filming?" he asked.

"Well, he was standing by his van and the side door was open," Julie recalled, "and I just went over to talk to him about his availability to work on the show. While we were talking, he offered a little vial to me, and I said, 'No, thank you.' Then he leaned into the van and put the vial to his nose and sniffed real hard. I said, 'I'll check with you later' and walked away."

It was just like two years earlier when he'd allegedly offered her coke out of his van on the set of *Fantasy Island*—it was a different set and a different vial, but it was the same van.

"Miss Johnson," Grey asked, "prior to these events, were you concerned about drugs and safety on the set?"

"Yes," she replied. "Beginning in 1977, I became heavily involved at the Screen Actors Guild with the situation of drugs on the set. The stuntwomen had gotten together and we were talking about the incidents we'd seen. So yes, I was very, very concerned."

At SAG, Julie had been named co-chair of the Stuntwomen's Sub-Committee, which in 1982 released a survey on drug use in the stunt community. More than half of the 41 stuntwomen who responded said they'd witnessed "drug dealing" on the set; more than half said they'd "worked with someone under the influence of drugs," and more than half said they'd been "offered drugs" on the set. One-out-of-six said they'd lost a job because they'd refused drugs that had been offered to them, and nearly one-in-four said they believed that the use of drugs was the "cause of most accidents" on film and TV shoots.

The survey made front-page headlines in the local papers.

Grey then turned to the coke-fueled incident that nearly cost Julie and Jeannie Coulter their lives out at Indian Dunes.

"In January of 1979," he asked, "did you suffer an injury in a stunt that required you to jump from a moving vehicle?" he asked.

"Yes, I did," she answered.

"Do you remember clearly what happened during filming that day?" he asked.

"Yes, sir. I do."

The jury had heard testimony about the accident before—from Jeannie Coulter, Roy Harrison and Ronnie Rondell. They'd also heard second-hand accounts of

Bobby Bass' cocaine use that day, but this would be the first time they'd hear an eye-witness account of it.

"Let's start at the beginning," Grey said, and walked Julie through events of that day.

They'd been shooting *Charlie's Angels* on a dirt airstrip in Valencia. Julie was doubling that day for Farrah Fawcett, Jeannie was doubling Cheryl Ladd, and Bobby Bass was driving. It was supposed to be a piece of cake. The car would come racing down the airstrip; Bobby would slow down when they hit their mark, and the girls would jump from the backseat, tumble, and then bounce to their feet. But of course, it didn't go that way.

Julie got the first hint that something was wrong during rehearsals.

"First," Grey began, "how many times did you rehearse it that day?"

"Four times," Julie answered.

"How long did it take to complete the four rehearsals, from start to finish?" he asked.

"20 . . . 25 . . . 35 minutes at the most," she answered. "We were just making the runs to check the speed."

"On the first run-through," he asked, "what were you doing?"

"I told Bobby, 'It's too fast. Slow it down. Slow it down.'"

"And on the second run-through?"

"When I got the door open, I asked Bobby what speed we were doing," she answered.

"And what did he say?"

"He said, '15 and coming down.'"

After the second rehearsal she asked Jeannie if she felt comfortable with the speed of the car. "Well," Jeannie told her, "as long as it doesn't exceed 10 miles an hour."

"What happened on the third run-through?" Grey asked.

"We told Bobby to start out at 15 miles an hour and then drop back to 10."

"And what did Mr. Bass say in response to that request?" Grey asked.

"He didn't respond," she said. "It was just understood that he would do that."

"Why was it necessary to run through that stunt a fourth time?" Grey asked.

"We wanted to make sure that he got it down to 10 miles an hour," she replied.

"And after the fourth rehearsal," Grey asked, "were you satisfied?"

"Yes, sir."

"What happened after the fourth and final rehearsal was over?" he asked.

"We needed a break," she said, "so we went back to the honeywagon. Jeannie's wig needed some scooching or something. She needed some help with it. So we took a break and got some water."

Bobby parked next to the honeywagon, she testified, "and the guys jumped out. I stayed in the car. I didn't have to do anything; I was ready. Jeannie got out to go fix her hair, and a friend of mine—another stuntwoman on the show—came over and we sat in the car and talked while I waited."

Ten minutes later, Julie and the other stuntwoman were still talking when the walkie-talkie, which had been left unattended on the front seat, began squawking. It was Ronnie Rondell, and he wanted to know where the hell everybody was.

"So I looked around to see if they were coming back," Julie said, "and I was going to get out of the car and go get them."

Just then, she saw Jeannie emerge from the hair and makeup trailer—her wig fastened tightly to her head—and Bobby Bass and Howard Curtis coming out of the honeywagon.

Just then, Julie said, "a guy passed by saying 'Bobby got the last of the coke this morning! God damn it!'"

"Did you hear that?" the stuntwoman asked Julie in a whisper, her eyes wide open in surprise.

"Yeah. Something about coke," Julie replied, not knowing for sure what it meant.

"A flash went through my mind," Julie told the jury. "I knew that Coca-Cola was always on the set, but I couldn't understand why it was all gone so early in the morning."

Her friend had to explain it to her. "Bass got the last of the cocaine this morning," she whispered to Julie.

"At that moment," Julie testified, "they all jumped in the car and the walkie-talkie was going, giving us instructions to start the scene. Then we just went on and did the stunt."

"You didn't have time to think about the remark when you started filming the sequence?" Grey asked.

"No," Julie answered.

For Koska, this had gone on long enough. "Objection!" he sniffled. "Hearsay!"

And he was right. With few exceptions, courts do not allow hearsay to be admitted as evidence. And what Julie heard someone say that day—that Bobby had gotten the last of the coke, was clearly hearsay—information gathered by one person from another concerning events to which the first person had no direct experience. And even though it was true in this case, it was still hearsay. Indeed, it was the very definition of hearsay.

So unless Grey could come up with something quick, Julie's testimony about having overheard someone say that "Bobby got the last of the coke" would be ruled inadmissible—or worse. Koska was now going to ask for a mistrial. And for Julie, that would be a disaster. She was broke and it might take months—maybe even years—to get the case back on calendar.

"May counsel approach the bench with the reporter?" Koska asked.

"All right," the judge said, and the lawyers and the court reporter huddled around the judge again and spoke in quiet voices the jury couldn't hear.

"Two points, Your Honor," Koska coughed. "First, I move to strike all the testimony pertaining to this alleged statement by an unknown person walking by the vehicle. It is a clear violation of the hearsay rule. Second, even if the court chooses to strike that testimony, I believe that it has created an unduly prejudicial atmosphere on the jury, and one that I am not going to be able to cure no matter what happens."

There it was. The whole case would hinge on what Grey said next.

"Mr. Grey?" the judge said, looking down his nose at Julie's attorney.

"Your Honor," Grey gulped, "a statement is not hearsay when it is offered to prove that the hearer of that language acted in conformity with it."

Boom! Grey had hit upon one of the few exceptions to the hearsay rule that might be relevant to this case. There was no dispute that Julie had reported her suspicions about Bobby's drug use to Ronnie Rondell, so it would make no sense not to allow her to testify about *why* she had been suspicious in the first place. But would the judge see it that way?

Judge Savitch thought about Grey's argument for a moment. "That's right," he finally said. "The action that was justified was the act of complaining about the drugs to Mr. Rondell. The argument is persuasive, so I'm going to deny the motion to strike."

Then the judge turned to Koska.

"I have voiced my intention that this claim of drugs not transcend *Charlie's Angels*, and not go into an indictment of the industry," the judge said. "I don't think that has been done here. We are going to hear further testimony, and at some point I may want to reconsider, but in my view, this is a proper and relevant area. Therefore, the motion for a mistrial is denied."

Grey breathed yet another big sigh of relief. Neither Julie nor the jury had any idea that he'd just won a major victory, but Grey winked at her as he returned from the bench.

"With the court's permission," he said, "I'd like to show the jury Exhibit No. 5."

"Granted," the judge said, and once again the lights went down and the TV monitor in front of the jury box blinked to life.

The jury had seen this scene before; during Jeannie Coulter's and Ronnie Rondell's testimony. But Grey wanted them to see a station wagon racing down a dirt airstrip, and then, as the car approaches the camera, the right rear passenger's door swinging open, and a few seconds later, a woman falling out of the car onto the road in a cloud of dust. The camera didn't even capture Julie doing the same thing on the other side of the car. The camera angle was completely wrong, just as Julie had said it would be.

When the tape ended, the lights came back up and Grey resumed his questioning.

"Miss Johnson," he said, "tell us what happened just before this scene was shot."

Julie then re-told the now-familiar story of the accident: the car getting up to speed, Julie and Jeannie expecting Bobby so slow down when he got to their mark; Howard Curtis telling them to jump; the heavy car doors knocking them backwards; the two stuntwomen falling into heaps on the dirt runway.

Of course, it differed significantly from Bobby Bass' version of the story.

"When we got to the airstrip, we were going full speed," Julie said. "I was getting prepared. I cracked the door open and tried to get my feet in position to get out of the car."

Grey asked her if she talked to anyone in the car as it raced down the airstrip.

"No, sir," she said. "We were waiting for our cue."

"Did you have any concerns about the speed before you jumped?"

"Yes. That we were going too fast."

"Did you expect the car to slow down?"

"I was waiting for him to back off the speed," Julie answered.

"Did the car ever back off its speed as you prepared to exit the car?" Grey asked.

"Yes, it backed off a little," Julie said, "and that was a cue that we were getting into the position to go."

"During the filming," Grey asked, "were you controlling the speed of that car?"

"No, sir."

"Were you telling Mr. Bass, 'Faster' or 'slower'?"

"No, sir," she answered. "I only did that in rehearsal."

"Did you talk to Mr. Bass at all while you were traveling down the airstrip road?"

"No, sir."

"Were you waiting for a cue from someone else?"

"Yes, sir," she said. "From Howard Curtis, who was in the front seat next to Bobby."

"Did that eventually happen?"

"Yes, sir," she said. "He got the cue on the walkie-talkie. He gave us a cue, but he gave us a false go—like a half-go—and then a go, and it messed our timing up."

Grey asked her how much time elapsed between the false go and the go.

"Just seconds," she said. "Maybe one second."

"Who exited the car first—you or Miss Coulter?"

"Jeannie Coulter," Julie answered. "I felt her start to go at the false go—on the half-go—and at that point, not wanting to ruin the shot, I got into position to go, too."

"Did the fact that Miss Coulter had exited the vehicle on the false start influence your decision whether or not to jump?" Grey asked.

"Yes," she said. "It influenced me to go ahead, because by that time, I was getting the full-go. I mean, it's split-second timing. That's all I can say."

Grey then asked if she ever considered calling off the stunt.

"I was concerned about the speed," she said, "and I was within a split second of calling it off, but then I got the clear cue to go, and when we get a cue to go, we go."

"At the instant you exited the vehicle, what happened?" Grey asked.

"The car sped up," she answered, "and the door came back on me."

"Are you saying that the car started going faster again as you were trying to get out?" Grey asked, so the jury could hear the question and answer twice.

"Yes, sir."

"And you are certain that the door came back on you?"

"Yes, sir."

"And what was the effect of the door hitting you?"

"It spun me round," she said. "When I was coming out, the weight of the door pitched me back and my foot got hung up for a second."

"Do you remember what happened immediately after that?" Grey asked.

"I remember saying, 'Oh, shit!' all the way out the door."

Juror No. 2 laughed, but stopped immediately when the judge shot her a stern glance.

"Do you remember what happened next?" Grey continued.

"As I exited the car, I remember that I was concerned about my foot getting caught under the car's rear wheel," she answered. "From then on, I don't remember anything."

"You don't remember hitting the ground?" Grey asked.

"Yes," she said. "I remember the actual contact with the ground. I remember seeing a very bright yellow light."

Grey asked her if she felt or saw anything else when she hit the ground.

"The back of my head felt numb," she answered.

"What is the next thing you remember?" Grey asked.

"I remember trying to get up, and I remember my mouth was full of dirt," she said. "I was lying face down in the dirt."

And she was going into convulsions. Ronnie Rondell, the first on the scene, threw himself on top of her to keep her still to prevent further injury. But Julie didn't know what was happening. All she knew was that she couldn't get up and that there was a great weight on her back.

"That's when I thought, 'Oh, God, I broke my back! I can't move!'"

"How did you finally get to your feet?" Grey asked.

"I believe Ronnie helped me up," she said. "I remember hearing voices. I don't remember focusing too good, but I remember seeing Farrah."

"Was she up close to you at that point?" Grey asked.

"Yes. She was talking to me . . . concerned."

"Was anybody assisting you?"

"Yes," she said. "They brought over a director's chair for me to sit in for a minute to regain my composure. And people were talking to me. They were asking me questions, and somebody was looking in my eyes."

"What did they ask you?"

"They asked me what day it was, and how old I was, and when my birthday was," she said. "They were trying to find out how coherent I was."

"Did you observe what happened to Jeannie Coulter after the jump?"

"No," Julie said. "I had no idea where she was."

Jeannie, it turns out, had gotten up from the dirt airstrip and was wandering around in a daze. Cheryl Ladd, who'd been watching the scene from the sidelines, rushed over to her to keep her from getting hit by the chase car.

The injured women were then loaded into the back of a station wagon and taken to the Henry Mayo Hospital in Valencia. On the way, Julie told Jeannie what she'd heard about Bobby Bass getting the last of the coke. Waiting in the emergency room to have their X-rays taken, they talked about what had happened, and realized that Bobby had sped up when he was supposed to have slowed down. Julie had a big lump on the back of her head, and the doctors determined that they'd both suffered concussions, and that Julie had sustained a hairline fracture in her neck. They both felt lucky to be alive.

"When you were through at the hospital," Grey asked, "were you brought right back to the location?"

"Yes, we were," Julie answered.

Julie then recounted how, upon their return, they stood in line for lunch and had that bizarre encounter with Bobby Bass.

"We got in line . . . there were maybe five or six people in front of us."

"And did you encounter Mr. Bass in that line?" Grey asked.

"Yes, we did," she said.

"Was there anybody with Mr. Bass in line that day?"

"I remember Heidi von Beltz," Julie answered.

"Anyone else?"

"I don't remember if Howard Curtis was there or not," she said. "He might have been because they usually ate together."

"What happened after you got in line behind Mr. Bass?" Grey asked.

"I was going to go over to him, but he turned and looked at us, and the look on his face was such that it frightened me for a second. So I decided not to go talk to him."

Grey then asked her to describe, as best she could, the look on Bass' face.

"It looked like he had the worst hangover of his life," she said. "He looked glazed."

"Did you make eye contact with him at that moment?" Grey asked.

"Yes, sir."

"Did he say anything to you at that moment?" he asked, his voice growing louder with each question.

"No, sir. He just looked away."

"Did you say anything to him?" he asked, almost shouting the question to let the jury know that this was a key moment in the trial—a moment that would call Bass' credibility as a witness into question.

"I was afraid of the look in his eyes," she answered, "so I didn't say anything."

"Did he come over and say anything to you?" Grey asked, pounding the plaintiff's table for emphasis, knowing that Bass hadn't, and that he'd testified that he had.

Grey's theatrics were too much for the judge. "You don't have to pound the table, Mr. Grey, nor raise your voice," he said. "Just ask the question, please."

"Did Mr. Bass come to you at any time that day and ask you how you were doing?" Grey asked in a normal voice.

"No, sir," Julie answered.

"Did he join you and sit with you while you were eating lunch?"

"No, sir."

Grey shuffled some papers on the plaintiff's table, letting the jury think for a moment about these two contrasting accounts of the same event.

"How long had you known Bobby Bass before that particular day?" Grey asked.

"I knew him through meetings and on sets for possibly ten years," Julie answered.

"Were you in a friendly, close working relationship with him as fellow stunt persons?"

"Yes," she said. "We were all friendly."

"You didn't have a grudge against one another at that time, did you?"

"No, sir," she answered. And it was true. She'd always liked Bobby. Everyone did. He was a teddy bear—at least he was when he wasn't coked up.

"You never had any serious controversy with Mr. Bass before, had you?" Grey asked.

"No, sir," she said, and that was true, too. There was no reason for her to say any of these things about Bobby, other than that they were true.

Grey was almost done with Bass now. There was just one more incident on the day of the accident that he wanted to explore with Julie that showed that there was definitely something wrong with Bobby Bass that day.

After the strange encounter in the lunch line, there was just one more stunt to do that day. Bass was supposed to spin the car they'd all been riding in and slide it safely under the wing of a waiting airplane. Julie and Jeannie, picking up from the spot where they'd jumped, would chase the car and stop the bad guys from getting away. For any good stuntman, spinning a car on dirt is an easy job. But Bobby couldn't do it. He tried it again and again and again, but just couldn't get the station wagon to spin.

"Did you see Bobby Bass at work later on that afternoon?" Grey asked.

"Yes, sir," she said. "Jeannie and I observed him attempting to throw a 180 degree slide under the wing of the airplane."

"What do you mean 'attempting' to do a 180 under the wing?" Grey asked.

"Well, he tried to get it sideways and he couldn't. And so he backed the car up and he tried it again. He tried it three or four times."

"Did he ever do it?" Grey asked.

"Not while I was there," Julie said.

On Bobby's fourth attempt, one of the car's wheels came off, and after it was repaired, Ronnie Rondell had to come in and do the stunt.

Grey stopped his questioning and looked at the clock on the wall. It was 4:30.

"This might be a good time to recess," he told the judge.

"All right," the judge said. "We're going to adjourn until tomorrow morning at 9 o'clock. Ladies and gentlemen, thank you."

It was almost over now. After a three-week trial, Julie had just one more day on the witness stand. Then the lawyers would make their closing arguments, the judge would give his final instructions, and the case would be handed to the jury.

But the drama wasn't over yet.

Chapter 40

Damages

The next morning, after the jurors were seated, Judge Savitch dropped a bombshell. He'd already told the lawyers, and now he was going to tell the jury.

"Good morning," he said to the seven men and five women sitting in the jury box. "Let me first make these statements to you about the case, and then we'll talk about where we are at this point. On Aug. 19, 1987, plaintiff Julie Ann Johnson testified that during the filming of a *Charlie's Angels* episode, she and a fellow stuntwoman were sitting in a vehicle from which Miss Johnson was to perform a stunt, when they both overheard an unnamed passerby state that the driver of the vehicle, Bobby Bass, just got the last of the coke.

"Plaintiff further testified that immediately upon hearing the foregoing statement, the stuntwoman turned to plaintiff and exclaimed, 'Did you hear what was just said?' And after the plaintiff responded affirmatively, the stuntwoman further stated, 'Bobby Bass just got the last of the cocaine.'"

Of course, all the jurors remembered that; many had written it down in their notebooks.

"Such statements," the judge continued, "were not offered to prove the truth of these statements, but rather, that the plaintiff was aware of drug use on the set and the resultant danger."

The judge could see by the looks on several of the jurors' faces that they didn't understand what he was getting at.

"I see some quizzical looks," he said, "so let me repeat it so that you'll understand it."

He then repeated what he'd just said, although many of the jurors still weren't sure what he meant—which was that they were supposed to consider what Julie had overheard as it may have affected her state of mind, but not as evidence that Bobby Bass had actually taken cocaine that day.

"Let me further state," the judge continued, "that on Aug. 14, 1987, the witness Jeannie Coulter testified that she saw Roy Harrison and Ron Rondell sniff cocaine while in a van en route to locations on the set of *The Hitchhiker*."

And of course, the jurors remembered that, too. It was one of the most vivid images of the trial.

"The court now instructs you to disregard this testimony," the judge stated, "and it is stricken from the record."

"What?" several jurors thought. Wasn't drug use on the set at the very heart of the case? Hadn't Julie been fired in retaliation for complaining about drugs and safety?

This turn of events was very perplexing to the jury, but from a legal standpoint, it really didn't matter if Bobby Bass or Roy Harrison or Ronnie Rondell were coke-heads. To find in Julie's favor, all the jury had to decide was that she'd been terminated because she complained about drugs and safety. Retaliation was the key, not drug use.

Still, the judge's ruling left many of the jurors scratching their heads.

"All right," the judge said, calling the court to order. "Let's proceed."

"May Miss Johnson resume the stand, Your Honor?" Grey asked.

"Yes," the judge said.

Julie took the witness stand and smiled bravely at the jury. She was just as confused as many of them were.

Grey, though he looked like a mild-mannered professor, was really a pit bull of an attorney. But now his job was to elicit sympathy from the jury by showing them the damages Julie had suffered, both emotionally and financially, because of her unjust termination. And she'd suffered a lot. In fact, she was so broke that she didn't have enough money in her purse that day to buy lunch at the courthouse cafeteria.

"Has the termination caused you feelings of sadness or depression?" he asked her.

"Of course," she said.

"Can you describe that for us, please, as you have experienced it?"

"Well, sadness and depression really pretty much go hand in hand," she said. "The depression is strong. It's the sadness of not being able to be what I could be."

"Do you cry very often when you think about the termination and what has happened to you since that time?" he asked.

"Not as much as maybe I . . . I . . . I did in the beginning," she said, stammering a bit and holding back tears at just the thought of those terrible days. "I'm . . . I sometimes feel that I'm numb to the point where I just don't feel. Sometimes I wish I could cry."

"Before the termination, Julie, did you have a basic set of goals that you would try to accomplish in your life?" Grey asked. It was the first time during the entire trial that he'd referred to her only by her first name. He didn't want the jury to think of her as Miss Johnson anymore. Now he wanted them to think of her as Julie.

"Of course," she said.

"What were those goals?" he asked.

"To become . . ."

"Objection!" Koska coughed. He was still suffering from the flu. "Irrelevant! Immaterial!"

"Overruled," the judge said. "You may answer."

". . . to become one of the best stuntwomen and stunt coordinators in the business," she finished saying.

"Up to the time you were terminated," Grey continued, "how did you feel about your ability to fulfill that goal?"

"I felt I was accomplishing it," she said, "when I had the opportunity to work for Mr. Aaron Spelling."

"Have your goals changed in any way after the termination?"

"The goals have diminished," she said, "but I still hold on to that hope."

"Julie, in your life, to what degree of importance was your work?" Grey asked.

"I believe that your ability to make a living is just as important as one's health and one's family," she said earnestly.

"Have you felt any emotional impact as a result of your inability to obtain work within your profession on any kind of a regular basis since the termination?" he asked.

"Yes," she said. "My ability to function constructively has diminished."

"What differences have you noticed in your professional reputation since your termination?" Grey asked.

"Objection!" Koska wheezed. "Hearsay! Speculation!"

"Overruled," the judge said.

"I have increasingly become isolated," she answered. "I spent my entire adult life in the motion picture industry, and I don't work anymore, so needless to say, I'm having problems with my identity. My reputation seems to no longer exist because if people associate with me they won't work."

"Move to strike the latter portion," Koska coughed.

"That part—'people associated with me won't work'—is stricken," the judge ruled. "The jury is to disregard that."

Grey had to approach her blacklisting from a different angle.

"Have you been shunned by people within the industry with whom you were formerly closely associated since your termination?" he asked.

"Object to the form of the question as leading and suggestive," Koska said.

"Overruled."

"Yes, sir," Julie answered.

"Has all this made it more difficult for you to secure employment similar to what you had before the termination?" he asked.

"Yes, sir."

"Julie, have you gone through all of your savings?" Grey asked.

"Yes, sir," she said.

"Irrelevant!" Koska said, his voice nearly shot. "Immaterial!"

"Well, I'm going to strike the answer," the judge said. "It is not an element of damage."

It was an odd ruling. She was flat broke as a direct result of being unjustly terminated and blacklisted, but the judge didn't think that was an element of the damages she'd suffered.

Grey would try a more direct approach.

"How much money do you have in your purse today, Julie?" he asked.

"Objection! Irrelevant! Hearsay! Immaterial!"

"Sustained," the judge ruled, even though it wasn't irrelevant, hearsay or immaterial.

"Have you had the means to pay for any lunches in the courthouse or other places since this trial began?" Grey persisted.

Koska objected before Julie could tell the jury that she didn't.

"Irrelevant!" he coughed. "Evidence Code Section 352."

Evidence Code Section 352 again—undue prejudice and all that.

"Sustained," the judge ruled.

"Julie," Grey continued, "in the five years before you were terminated, and according to the tax records that are in evidence, what was your average annual income attributable to stunt work?"

"In excess of $50,000," she answered. "$68,000 at its highest."

That's about $190,000 in today's money.

"And how often were you working in those same five years?"

"On average, nine months out of the year," she said.

"And how many days have you worked so far this year in the stunt field?" he asked.

"I haven't had a day's work since 1986," she said.

"Have you ever worked again for Spelling-Goldberg Productions?"

"No, sir," she said.

"Have you worked again on any other show where Aaron Spelling was a principal?"

"No, sir."

"Did you buy a house for your mother in 1979?" Grey asked.

"Yes," she answered. "I purchased a little fixer-upper for her that was close to me."

"Did you lose the house after you were terminated?" Grey asked.

"Objection!" Koska said, rising weakly from his chair.

"I'm going to have to grant the motion to strike," the judge said. "The jury is to disregard this question."

"Is your mother presently living with you?"

"Yes, sir," she said.

"When did that first begin?" Grey asked.

"When I lost the house in 1983," she answered.

"Move to strike the answer as non-responsive to the question asked," Koska said.

"The answer is stricken," the judge ruled.

"Since 1983," Grey asked, "have you and your mother shared expenses and worked together to live together as economically as possible?"

"Immaterial," Koska wheezed.

"Sustained."

But Grey kept trying. He wanted the jury to know that his client, who had once been one of the highest paid stuntwomen in the business, now had to live with her mother to make ends meet.

"From 1983 on," Grey asked, pressing ahead, "have you provided any portion of your mother's support out of your own limited income?"

"Objection! Irrelevant to the issues in this case!"

"Sustained," the judge ruled.

"Julie, what are you doing to make any money to support yourself?" Grey asked.

"The residuals that have been coming in from prior shows have been a help, and I'm an equipment manager for a band," she said. "I take care of their equipment and set it up on the weekends, which gives me pin money."

"And what does that job entail?" Grey asked.

"I load speakers and sound equipment in and out of a truck on Fridays, Saturdays and Sundays," she said. "I put the equipment on the stage, I set it up. I hook up all the cables. I make sure that the band has something to drink. I do errands for them."

"Is there an informal job title for the work that you just described?" Grey asked.

"Yes, sir," she said. "It's called a 'roadie.'"

"Could you tell us more about that work?"

"I do it because it keeps my weekends busy," she said, "and I do it because it's physical work—heavy work—and it still gives me a feeling of having a stage presence and to be able to feel useful. I do it for that."

"You do that on Fridays and Saturdays regularly?" he asked.

"I have for the last four or five years," she answered.

"And how much money do you make on a weekend for that type of work?" he asked.

"$10 a night."

Grey paused for a moment to let the jury think about that; about what it does to a person who goes from being one of the highest paid women in her profession, to being a $10-a-night roadie.

"Before your termination," Grey asked, switching gears again, "had you at any time before ever been involved in a grievance or controversy arising out of your work?"

The answer was 'no,' but she didn't get a chance to reply.

"Objection!" Koska said. "Irrelevant. Immaterial. No foundation."

"Sustained," the judge said.

"What has been the emotional impact upon you after becoming involved in this grievance, and in this lawsuit?"

"Objection," Koska said wearily. "Immaterial. Leading and suggestive. Hearsay."

"Seems to me it has been asked and answered, too," the judge said.

Grey decided to ask the same question a different way.

"Have you experienced any emotional problems that you attribute to feeling unwanted?"

"Yes," she said. "I miss my peers. I miss looking forward to going to work every day."

"After the termination, have you experienced any sense of disappointment?"

"Objection!" Koska interjected before she could respond—but the jury already knew the answer.

"Sustained," the judge ruled.

"Have you ever felt that you were expendable, Julie?" Grey asked.

"Object to the form of the question as argumentative and leading," Koska argued.

"Sustained," said the judge, but once again the jury already knew what her answer would be.

"Julie, do you still live in your own home?" Grey asked.

"Yes, sir."

"Any problems about paying for that?" he asked.

"Yes, sir," she said. "My property taxes haven't been paid for three years."

"Have you required any outside assistance in order to pay the mortgage?" Grey asked.

"Sometimes I've gone to the Motion Picture Relief Fund, and they've assisted me."

"Julie, have you kept a tally of the number of days you've worked since being terminated by Spelling-Goldberg?"

"Yes, sir."

"How many days' work, all together, have you had in the past seven years in your field of stunt work?"

"23 days," she said, and all the jurors wrote the number down in their notebooks.

"Have you ever worked again as a stunt coordinator?"

No, sir.

"Is that because you decided that you don't want to do that kind of work?"

"No, sir," she said, almost coming to tears. "It's because of this lawsuit."

"Move to strike as non-responsive," Koska said, rising from his chair.

"All right," the judge said. "It is stricken. The answer is stricken."

But the jury, seeing the anguish in her face, knew that it was true.

"Julie," Grey asked pointedly, "do you contend that you've been deliberately prevented from working again in the stunt field since you were terminated by Spelling-Goldberg Productions?"

"Objection!" Koska yelped, still on his feet. "Calls for a legal conclusion!"

"Overruled," the judge said. "You can answer it."

"Yes, sir," she said firmly.

"I have no further questions," Grey said. He took a long look at the jury and then sat down next to Julie, who placed a hand on his hand and mouthed the words "Thank you."

Chapter 41

We, the Jury

Waiting for the jury to return with a verdict was agony.

The lawyers had spent all day Thursday, August 27, making their final arguments, and then the judge read the jury his instructions. By then, it was late in the day, so he excused the jurors until Monday morning. It would be three torturous days until the jury even began its deliberations.

Julie spent the weekend at home with her mother, puttering around the house, trying to keep her mind off the long legal ordeal she'd just been through. But it was impossible. She went over the events again and again in her mind: the terrible lies that had been told about her and the truth that she'd tried to tell, but had been prevented from doing so, on so many occasions, by Koska's constant and unrelenting objections.

Monday morning finally arrived, and Julie got up early and drove downtown to the courthouse. Richard Grey was already in the courtroom when she arrived.

Court was called into session at nine o'clock sharp, and the jurors—seven men and five women—retired to the jury room to begin their deliberations.

Julie and her attorney would stay close by until the jury returned with a verdict. Mostly, they hung out in the cafeteria up on the ninth floor, eating lunch—Julie always brought hers in a brown paper bag—or sipping coffee and reading the paper among the endless parade of lawyers, jurors, plaintiffs, defendants, and court personnel who did the same while waiting for their cases to resume. Occasionally, she'd stroll around out on the balcony, where smokers, oblivious to the spectacular views of downtown Los Angeles all around them, nervously puffed on cigarettes.

She never saw Koska up there. He always ate lunch at one of the fancy restaurants nearby, which was just fine with Julie. She didn't care if she ever saw him again.

Monday came and went without a verdict and Tuesday too.

"Is it good that they're taking so long?" Julie asked her lawyer.

"Depends," Grey said, noncommittally. "Sometimes it's good, sometimes it's bad."

On Wednesday afternoon, Julie was up on the ninth floor balcony, looking down at the beautiful fountain in the courtyard far below, when Richard Grey sidled up beside her.

"They've reached a verdict," he said.

"Really?" Julie said, her expression a mix of excitement and worry. "Okay," she sighed. "Let's go."

They took the elevator down to the second floor and went into the courtroom. Koska was already there, sitting at the defense table.

The jury filed into the courtroom at 3:40 p.m. and took their seats. Julie looked closely at their faces to see if she could discern anything and thought she caught a smile from Juror No. 11, a middle-aged Hispanic woman.

"Would you please hand the verdict to the clerk?" the judge asked the jury's foreman.

The clerk took the verdict forms and gave them to the judge, who looked at them, scowled disapprovingly, and handed them back to the clerk.

"Please read the verdict," the judge said.

"We, the jury in the above entitled action," the clerk read, "find for the plaintiff, Julie Ann Johnson, and against the defendants, Spelling-Goldberg Productions . . ."

Julie looked at her lawyer, her eyes wide with excitement and relief.

". . . and assess and award to the plaintiff compensatory damages," the clerk continued reading, "in the total amount of $111,000 . . ."

She'd won! After all these years, she'd won!

". . . plus residuals for all episodes, fourth and fifth seasons . . . ," the clerk continued.

"Oh my god!" Julie thought. The residuals she'd fought so hard for—which all the male stunt coordinators got, but which Spelling refused to pay her even after it was agreed that she'd get them for the shows she coordinated.

"We further find," the clerk continued, "that plaintiff is entitled to punitive damages in the sum of $1 million."

One million dollars? Did he say one million dollars? If she could have, Julie would have gotten up and hugged each one of the jurors personally. Instead, she remained seated and thanked God.

"All right," the judge said and turned to Koska. "Do you wish to have the jury polled?"

"Yes, Your Honor," Koska said. It looked like the air had been let out of his fancy suit.

"All right," the judge said. "Poll the jury, please."

The clerk then called each juror by name and asked them if this was their verdict. All twelve answered yes. It was unanimous.

Then the judge addressed the jury for the last time.

"Ladies and gentlemen of the jury," he said, "that completes your duties on this case. This court wishes to thank you for your attention and the sacrifice of your time for this important public service. I know how attentive you were and how seriously you have taken this case, and this court appreciates it. You are now discharged. Thank you very, very much."

And just like that, it was over.

The jurors went back to the jury room to collect their books and bags and then filed out into the hallway, where Koska and Grey waited to question them, as often happens at the end of trials. Both lawyers wanted to know what they'd done right and what they'd done wrong in the courtroom, but more important for Koska, he wanted to find out if there had been any jury misconduct that he could hang an appeal on.

Terry Ziegler, Juror No. 6, told Koska, "During the course of our deliberations, we found that Ms. Johnson had an implied oral contract and that the defendant violated her rights when she was terminated. All of the jurors decided that Ms. Johnson's termination had been wrongful."

The evidence of malice to support the punitive damages award, Ziegler said, was based on the fact that Julie had "repeatedly complained of unsafe work conditions and possible drug use in the work environment and no corrective action was ever taken." The jury, he said, also determined that California public law provides that "an individual cannot be terminated for complaining about safety conditions in the workplace."

This was not at all what Koska wanted to hear.

Jose Perez, Juror No. 12, told Julie's lawyer, "In order to reach this punitive damage verdict, we had to find malice on the part of Spelling-Goldberg. We felt that their failure to heed many warnings about the lack of safe conditions on the set did, in fact, show that Ms. Johnson had been the victim of malice. Specifically, we found that Spelling-Goldberg had consciously disregarded her safety and the safety of others and terminated her employment because she complained about those unsafe conditions."

This was exactly what Grey wanted to hear—that the jury got it and came to the correct verdict based entirely on the law and the judge's instructions.

John Langholff, the jury foreman, told Koska, "We, the jury, found that the number of times that the production company provided Ms. Johnson with defective cars warranted a finding of deliberate disregard for safety."

Interviewed for this book twenty-five years later, Langholff, a retired tradesman now living in Arizona, said that Julie's credibility was the key to the case.

"We paid attention to what she said, and it all made sense," he said. "Listening to the evidence, we came to the conclusion that they did wrong to this woman, that there had been no grounds for termination, and that she had been subjected to quite a bit of harassment. We also felt that she probably had been blacklisted. I'm sure there is no 'official' blacklist, but I'm also sure that word gets around."

He was certainly right about that.

When they'd begun their deliberations, Langholff recalled many years later, "The first thing I said to everybody was, 'Do we feel that there is merit to the case?' And we decided that there was. Then we deliberated as to the validity of the alleged injustices directed toward her, and we all agreed that the evidence supported that she had been treated badly. Then we had to decide what her financial future would have been if this had not happened to her—what her earnings would have been, and that's how we came up with the number to remunerate her."

And although this didn't affect the jury's decision, he said that Koska's demeanor and attire in the courtroom sure didn't help his case.

"Some of us felt that he was way over the top," Langholff laughed. "He's a fancy-Dan lawyer who wore a new suit every day, or so it would seem. It was just a bit too much, like who are you trying to impress, the jury or your bosses? It certainly didn't impress the jury."

Marcia Graves, Juror No. 9, told Grey, "In deciding to award punitive damages, we were telling Spelling-Goldberg that they should not maliciously terminate employees who complain about unsafe working conditions. But we limited our verdict to $1 million to indicate that while we felt that they were wrong, we were not trying to bury them."

Another excellent comment, Grey thought, and a clear indication that the jury was seeking justice, not revenge.

All the other jurors' comments were in this same vein—all, that is, but one.

Carolyn Tanzola, Juror No. 10, had a completely different take on how the jury came to its verdict.

"There was never a decision made as to what malicious conduct might be," she told Koska in the hallway that day, "and I voted for punitive damages based solely on my emotional reaction to drugs and, specifically, cocaine. The majority of the jurors became so emotional during deliberations that rather than discuss the evidence, they were quick to find that there had been 'malice,' merely so that they could find a large award for punitive damages."

This was just what Koska wanted to hear—a juror saying that she'd based her vote entirely on her "emotional reaction" to stricken testimony about cocaine abuse. Even better, she was saying that most of the other jurors didn't even want to discuss the evidence, but merely wanted to slap Spelling-Goldberg with large punitive damages.

Julie and her attorney had no idea that one of the jurors had gone rogue and was telling Koska all this. Standing in the hallway after all the jurors left, Julie hugged her lawyer and kissed him on the cheek.

"I love you," she told him. "You were the only one who believed in me."

They said their good-byes, and Julie headed home through the downtown rush-hour traffic. It was stop-and-go all the way, but she didn't mind. She turned on the radio, and to her surprise, KFWB broadcast a news flash about her case and the million-dollar verdict she'd just won. It would be in all the local papers the next day.

The trial was finally over, and now she'd finally have some money. Doing the math in her head on the long drive home, she figured she'd come away with more than $660,000 – $1,111,000 minus the 40% that would go to her attorney. It would be enough to save her house from the bank and then some. She hadn't done it for the money of course. A simple explanation and an apology from Aaron Spelling would have sufficed. But now, after all these years without work, the money would sure come in handy.

Or so she thought.

CHAPTER 42

A Reversal of Fortune

Julie's victory was short-lived.

Spelling's lawyers, claiming that the verdict was the result of a "runaway jury," quickly filed a motion for a judgment notwithstanding the verdict, asking the judge to toss it out. The judge agreed and summarily cut the award by more than half—from $1.1 million to $440,000.

In his ruling, handed down two months after the trial ended, Judge Savitch determined that the jury had made improper inferences regarding illegal drug use on the set of *Charlie's Angels*, which he said caused the jurors to become "emotionally inflamed."

In fact, the show had been awash with cocaine, and there was ample testimony to support such a finding. But the judge had instructed the jury to disregard most of that testimony, so the jury's mistake, if it can be called that, was in not disregarding the truth.

Judge Savitch also noted that the jury had improperly inferred that Aaron Spelling had *blacklisted* Julie, even though that was true too. The judge determined that no direct evidence had been introduced at the trial to show that other production companies had refused to hire her after she'd been branded a troublemaker. But in fact, all the evidence—including the fact that she'd only worked twenty-three days in the seven years since being terminated—indicated that she had, indeed, been blacklisted.

Unfortunately, Judge Savitch did not understand how Hollywood works.

In Hollywood, blacklisting is not a notice they post on a bulletin board or an announcement they make over a loudspeaker. It's more like a cold or the flu—it spreads silently.

Blacklisting is not something that one person—or even one company—can do on its own. It takes the tacit approval of the entire town to blacklist someone. And in the stunt community, once the stunt coordinators, who do all the hiring and who are virtually all men, decide that someone is a troublemaker and a whistle-blower—that person doesn't work anymore. And that's especially true if that someone happens to be a woman.

It's all based on fear.

Aaron Spelling could only blackball Julie from working on his shows—which he did. She never worked on any of his many shows again. But Hollywood is based on relationships, and anyone who hired Julie after she'd been blackballed by Spelling risked any relationship they had, or hoped to have, with one of the most powerful and vindictive men in town.

Julie's attorney maintains to this day that the jury, and not the judge, got it right, and that the judge caved under pressure.

"The jury decides questions of fact, and the judge decides questions of law," Grey stated over lunch one afternoon. "The judge has tremendous power over the jury. The judge can declare a mistrial, instruct the jury to do certain things or to not do certain things, to accept evidence or to ignore certain evidence. We had a fairly good judge, all things being equal. It's just that he relented to pressure from the other side. He was indecisive. If the judge's job is to make tough decisions, and the person doing that job is indecisive, you've got a problem."

Spelling's lawyers, however, didn't even want to pay Julie the $440,000 that Judge Savitch thought was fair. They didn't want to pay her anything. Any kind of payment might encourage others to sue. Spelling didn't want to pay Julie a dime because somewhere down the line, it might mean he'd have to pay a nickel to someone else he'd cheated.

And then along came *Foley*.

A year after Julie's trial ended, the California Supreme Court handed down a landmark wrongful termination case called *Foley v. Interactive Data Corp*. In their wisdom, the state Supreme Court justices rewrote California law—retroactively—as to when a wrongful termination case can be brought.

Julie had filed her case within the three-year statute of limitations that was then in effect. But in *Foley*, the court ruled that all wrongful termination cases had to be brought within one year and then applied that ruling to every wrongful termination case still in the legal pipeline—including Julie's.

Spelling's attorneys jumped at this, filing an appeal with the Second District Court of Appeal, asking that the jury verdict be reversed.

"The thing that really messed Julie up—and a lot of people—was a decision that came down called the *Foley* decision," Grey recalled glumly. "Everybody was waiting for the *Foley* decision, because it would define exactly what a wrongful termination case was, what the elements of it are, what the statute of limitations is, all this stuff that was uncertain. And the California Supreme Court came down with a decision that gave the definitional criteria, but they also reduced the statute of limitations, which as long as I could remember had always been three years. And they reduced it down to a one-year statute of limitations. Fine. That's okay. But they did something much worse. They made the ruling retroactive—to cover all cases that were still pending in the California courts. And Julie's case, although it had been filed within the proper statute when it was three years, hadn't been filed within one year. So her case got wiped out. I'd never seen anything like it in my whole career."

Julie appealed, but guided by the *Foley* decision, the California Court of Appeal held that Julie hadn't filed her case within the new one-year statute of limitations and reversed the jury's verdict. The appellate court also found that while there was "circumstantial evidence of blacklisting" in Julie's case, it found no "direct evidence" that she'd been blacklisted.

So after all these years of fighting Hollywood and fighting the courts, she would get nothing.

"Imagine that—going from $1.1 million down to zero," Grey said, shaking his head.

Julie appealed to the United States Supreme Court on the grounds that the *Foley* decision had denied her due process and on the grounds that the appellate court had set the bar impossibly high to prove blacklisting.

"How can any litigant prevail in any court if only confessions—'direct evidence'—will prove their case?" she asked the High Court.

The U.S. Supreme Court, however, declined—without comment—to review her case.

Her day in court—which had turned into a decade-long legal nightmare—was now over.

Chapter 43

Lily

One day in the spring of 1990, Julie got a postcard in the mail from the Screen Actors Guild announcing a seminar for actresses who want to become directors. A postcard rarely changes someone's life, but this one certainly changed hers.

Julie didn't want to become a director, but she'd written a brief synopsis for a screenplay about her life and her ordeals behind the camera and in front of a jury. Maybe she could get someone at the seminar to read it.

It was going to be held in three weeks at SAG's headquarters on Hollywood Boulevard, formerly the site of the Hollywood Congregational Church—which was only appropriate, because right now, more than anything, Julie needed a miracle.

She penciled the date into her empty calendar, folded the postcard, and propped it up on her makeup table, which she rarely used anymore. Then she went back to bed. She'd fallen into another funk. She felt hopeless and helpless and didn't want to talk to anyone.

Every day, though, she'd see the card sitting there by the mirror, silently urging her to get out of the house. And every time she saw it, she'd think, "Just go! You've got to make yourself get out! Just go!"

Still, something held her back. She dreaded being around people, talking to them and listening to them.

"I'd totally lost my ability to relate to people," Julie sighs. "I'd just lost it. I was just silent."

Finally, the day of the meeting arrived. It was a Saturday, and as had become her custom, she slept in late, then lay in bed for another hour, going back and forth about whether to go to the meeting or not.

"Okay," she thought. "I'll go."

She got out of bed, showered, dressed, and put her face on. Then she got her purse and headed for the door. Stepping outside, she found it terribly bright, like God was shining a spotlight on her. She turned to lock the front door, but hesitated.

"No," she thought, "I'm not going."

She went back inside and headed to her bedroom to change clothes. Passing her makeup table, she saw the postcard, beckoning her to go, and turned around and went back outside. This time she locked the front door behind her. She walked to her car, opened the door, and got inside, but changed her mind again. She got out, slammed the car door, and headed back up the porch. At the front door, she found the house key on the ring, but something held back her hand. She could not put the key into the lock. So she went back to her car, got in, started it up, and backed out of the driveway.

"Something was forcing me to go to that meeting," she recalls with a laugh. "So I went."

Once again, a hidden hand was directing her; once again, she was being "placed."

She drove over Laurel Canyon into the city and then headed east on Hollywood Boulevard, arriving at SAG's headquarters, which, with its red-tiled roof and double steeples, still looked very much like a church. It was beautiful.

Julie went inside, found the room where the meeting was being held, and took a seat in the very back row. The meeting was about to start; Julie had been one of the last to arrive. Up front, two women were sitting in director's chairs on stage, and another was standing at the lectern. She was a striking sixty-five-year-old actress turned director who looked so familiar, but Julie just couldn't quite place her name.

"Hello. My name is Lilyan Chauvin," she told the audience in a lovely French accent. "Welcome."

"Aha!" Julie thought. "That's who she is!" Julie remembered her now. They'd worked on the two-hour pilot of *McMillan & Wife* back in 1971. Lilyan played the sister of a murdered antiques dealer, and Julie double for the show's costar, Susan Saint James. They'd never met; they hadn't even been on the set at the same time, but their work was featured in the show's very first episode.

Julie had seen her hundreds of times on TV—most recently on *The Young and the Restless* and *Falcon's Crest*, and over the years, they'd worked on many of the same shows from *Mannix* and *Mission Impossible* to *The Magician, Fantasy Island*, and *The Man from U.N.C.L.E.*—but never on the same episodes.

"Welcome to the possibility of becoming directors," Chauvin told the women gathered there that afternoon. "The three of us up here were lucky enough to make the transition from in front of the camera to behind the camera. Let me introduce, on my right, Nancy Malone, and on my left, Judy Chaikin."

Each received a warm round of applause and then took a turn at the dais to talk about their battles against Hollywood's glass ceiling.

Chauvin had been a leader in that battle for years. As vice president of Women in Film—and a longtime member of the Women's Steering Committee of the Directors Guild of America—she'd worked tirelessly to empower and promote women in the entertainment industry.

Malone was a familiar face to everyone in the audience. She'd appeared as a guest star on numerous TV shows, including *The Rockford Files*, *The Twilight Zone*, *Bonanza*, and *The Fugitive*. In 1976, she became the first female vice president of television at 20th Century Fox and, in 1981, made the transition to the directing, working on such shows as *Dynasty* and *Hotel*.

Chaikin, meanwhile, had started out as an actress and stand-up comedienne and then moved into writing, directing, and producing documentaries, including the Emmy-nominated *Legacy of the Hollywood Blacklist* for PBS.

All three described their own battles in the industry, and each concluded by saying that they couldn't have made it on their own—that a mentor had made all the difference.

Julie, however, didn't need a mentor. She needed a producer—someone to take an interest in her synopsis and turn it into a movie.

After their presentations, the three speakers answered questions and then met in small groups with members of the audience. Julie wanted to leave, to go home and crawl back into bed. But something pushed her forward. Somehow she knew that this was where she was supposed to be that day.

Nancy Malone was shaking hands with someone and moving toward the door. Julie saw her chance and stepped forward.

"Hello, Ms. Malone," she said. "I'm a stuntwoman. I coordinated *Charlie's Angels* and was fired for complaining about drugs and safety on the set. I have a controversial synopsis for a screenplay, and I wonder if you'd take a look at it."

Malone looked at her blankly and then blew her off.

"I'm sorry," she said. "I don't have time. I'm on my way to Europe, and I don't know how long I'll be gone."

Julie thanked her and then joined a small group of women standing around Chaikin. When the crowd thinned, Julie stepped forward and made the same pitch.

"I'm sorry," Chaikin said. "I've already done something controversial, and I don't want to do it again."

Julie thanked her politely and then joined several women talking to Lilyan Chauvin. Lilyan answered each of their questions in her beautiful French accent, and then Julie was left standing alone with her.

"Hello, Ms. Chauvin," Julie said, extending her hand.

Lilyan took her hand and shook it warmly. It was the first hand Julie had shaken in nine months.

"I'm a stuntwoman," Julie told her, "and I have a synopsis of a true story about when I was a stuntwoman and stunt coordinator on *Charlie's Angels*, and I was wondering if you'd be interested in looking at it."

Lilyan looked at her for a moment. "Yes, I'd be interested," she replied. "Can you call me in a month? I'll have more time then."

Lilyan gave Julie her card, and Julie said she'd call her in a month.

"Thank you," Julie said, shaking Lilyan's hand again. "Thank you. Thank you so much."

Lilyan smiled. She'd never seen a more grateful person.

Julie left and drove back to the Valley. As soon as she got home, she went straight into the kitchen, took the calendar off the wall, counted off thirty days, and wrote "LILYAN" in block letters on the date.

The trip into Hollywood that day snapped Julie out of her funk. She called Doug, a handyman she'd employed for odd jobs around the house—back when she had money—and asked him if she could work for him.

"Sure," he said. "Ever lay bricks?"

"No," Julie said, "but I'm a fast learner."

The next morning she was helping Doug unload bricks from the back of his truck and pushing them in a wheelbarrow to the worksite, where he was laying bricks for a backyard patio. It was hard work, but Julie was strong, and it felt good to be back in the world. And at the end of the day, he paid her $30.

Over the next few weeks, she helped Doug on other jobs—yard work, clearing brush, and laying more bricks. And at the end of each day, he'd pay her $30. And every evening when she got home, she'd check off another day on the calendar.

On day 30, Julie called the number on the card that Lilyan had given her. Lilyan answered on the third ring.

"Hello, Ms. Chauvin?" Julie said. "This is Julie Johnson. I'm the stuntwoman you met last month at the Screen Actors Guild. I told you about a synopsis I'd written, and you said to give you a call."

"Oh, yes," Lilyan said. "I remember. Why don't you come over tomorrow morning? Would eleven o'clock be all right?"

"Yes!" Julie said. "Eleven's fine."

Lilyan gave her directions to her house in the hills of Studio City, and Julie carefully wrote them down.

"Thank you, Ms. Chauvin," Julie said. "I'll see you at eleven."

"See you then," Lilyan said. "And please call me Lily."

"Okay, Lily," Julie said. "See you then."

The next day, Julie drove up the winding, tree-lined street to Lily's house, parked in front, and walked up the steep driveway to the front door. There was no hesitating now. Standing on the front porch, Julie rang the doorbell, which set off two of Lily's four dogs, who barked every time the bell rang. Lily answered the door in a light summer dress.

"Hello, Julie. Come in." She had the most welcoming smile.

Julie stepped inside and, right away, caught a whiff of something not quite right. There were two cats in the living room and two more hiding somewhere in the house that had to be constantly separated to keep them from fighting. But it wasn't a cat smell. It was something else.

"Does one of your dogs have an ear infection?" Julie asked.

It was an odd question, but it was spot-on.

"How in the world did you know that?" Lily asked, truly amazed.

Julie tapped her nose. "I got a whiff of it," she laughed. "I've had dogs too, and that's the smell of an ear infection."

Lily laughed and showed Julie the medicine she had to put in one of the dog's ears every day to fight the infection. No one else had ever noticed the smell—or had the nerve to mention it.

Right away, Lily took a liking to the brave stuntwoman standing in her kitchen. Lily's father had been a Resistance fighter in France during the war, and she kept a box full of the letters he wrote while imprisoned by the Nazis. So there was nothing she admired more than bravery.

Lily showed Julie around the house, and then they sat down at a table in the living room to talk. Julie had brought her synopsis and her résumé, and Lily looked them over.

"Oh my god, all this work!" Lily said, scanning Julie's film and TV credits. Then, seeing that Julie had worked as a stunt double on *Whatever Happened to Aunt Alice*, she said, "You worked on *Aunt Alice*? I sang the lead song on that."

"Really?" Julie said. "I doubled for Ruth Gordon and Geraldine Page. Ms. Gordon was wonderful. She wanted me to meet her husband, Garson Kanin, the famous writer. She kept saying, 'I want you to meet my husband. I want to introduce you to him.'"

They both laughed and talked about the many shows they'd both worked on. Then Lily read Julie's three-page synopsis.

"Is this all true?" Lily asked when she'd finished reading.

"Yes, ma'am," Julie replied.

"My god!" Lily gasped.

They talked for a while about the synopsis and about Julie's vision of turning it into a movie. Finally, Lily said, "Well, let me think about it and we'll meet again."

Julie couldn't have been more pleased. This great woman was interested in her story!

Lily took Julie out back to see the pool, which was lovely, but the backyard was an overgrown mess. Julie looked around and then screwed her courage up one more time.

"Do you need any help around here?" she asked. "I need a job and I'm looking for work and I could really make this look nice."

Looking around, Lily realized the place needed a lot of work. "Well, yes," she said. "I could use some help around here. Why don't we talk about it next week?"

"Great," Julie said. "I'll call you next week."

A week later, Julie gave Lily a call, and they talked about Julie helping out around the house.

"What would you charge?" Lily asked.

"I don't really have a price," Julie said, so she suggested $5 an hour. It's what Doug the handyman had been paying her.

"Okay," Lily said. "When do you want to start?"

"Well, anytime," Julie said. "I'm ready."

It was a Thursday, so Lily said, "Why don't you start Monday?"

"Okay," Julie said. "How many days?"

"As many days as you want," Lily replied.

They were both early risers, so they agreed that Julie would start Monday morning at eight o'clock and work six hours a day, five days a week.

Julie had been one of the highest paid stuntwomen in Hollywood. She'd earned $68,000 as a stuntwoman in 1980, which is equivalent to nearly $190,000 in today's money. Now, ten years later, she'd be working as a housekeeper and gardener for $30 a day, $150 a week, $600 a month, $7,200 a year. Even so, she was delighted and grateful to have the work.

Monday morning at eight, Julie rang Lily's doorbell, which started the dogs barking, and then she went to work. Her first chore each day was to scoop up all the dog poop on the cement backyard and hose everything down where they'd peed. Then she'd clean out the cat boxes, mop the floors, vacuum the carpets, wash the dishes, and straighten up the living room. Then it was time for the yard work.

The front and back yards were a jungle. There was no lawn, but plenty of overgrown flowerbeds and untamed landscaping. She'd rake and hoe and gather up big piles of debris, then stuff it all into large trash bags and drag it down the driveway to the trashcans. It was hard work, but Lily always made her a nice lunch—soup and a sandwich, usually—and at the end of the day, Julie would scoop up the dog poop again, hose everything down, and then change the cat boxes before going home.

That had been her routine every day for the first two weeks. But in the third week, Julie would take on a grave new responsibility.

"Will you drive me somewhere?" Lily asked her one day.

"Sure," Julie said. "Where do you want to go?"

"I'll tell you in the car," Lily answered mysteriously.

They got into Lily's car and headed down the hill.

"So where we going?" Julie asked when they got to Ventura Boulevard.

"Turn left," Lily said. "There's a place over on Riverside Drive that makes special bras."

"Special bras?" Julie asked.

"Prosthetic bras," Lily said. "I had breast cancer. They removed my left breast three years ago."

"Oh, jeez," Julie said, worry spreading across her face.

They drove along in silence for a few blocks, and then Julie spoke up. "I hope you've kept up with the other breast."

Silence.

"Lily," Julie said sternly, "when was the last time you had the other one checked?"

More silence.

"I'm waiting," Julie said, as a mother would to a petulant child.

"Well," Lily stammered, "it's been a couple of years. My doctor retired. He left his business to somebody else."

"So who have you seen since then?" Julie asked.

"A guy in Santa Monica," Lily answered sheepishly.

"Well, I work for you," Julie said firmly. "You should have the other one checked. You make the appointment, and I'll take you."

"Okay," Lily said.

That afternoon when they returned from the bra store, Lily made the appointment; and a few days later, Julie took her to the doctor's office, which was across the street from St. John's Hospital on Santa Monica Boulevard.

Lily went in to see the doctor, and twenty minutes later, Julie looked up from an old *National Geographic* magazine to see Lily hunched over in the doorway, her head down, the very picture of despair.

"Uh-oh," Julie thought, tossing aside the magazine and rushing to Lily's side before she could collapse.

"He felt a lump," Lily said as Julie steadied her. "I have to go across the street for a mammogram."

Holding Lily by the arm the whole way, Julie guided her down the hall, into the elevator, out the front door, and across the street to St. John's. Lily's doctor had called ahead, and a technician was waiting there to give her the mammogram.

They left that day not knowing the results.

The doctor called the next day with the news. The results were not good. The mammogram turned up a lump in her right breast the size of a smashed pea. And so began the eighteen-year odyssey of Julie being Lily's right hand and caregiver.

It's funny how things work out sometimes—not funny ha-ha, but funny strange, and sometimes, funny wonderful. Julie had started out looking for someone to save her life, and she ended up saving someone else's.

The doctor gave Lily two choices.

"Do you want a lumpectomy or a mastectomy?" he asked.

It was a hard choice.

She'd already had one mastectomy, and it had been very painful, both physically and emotionally.

"Well, let's do the lumpectomy," she told the doctor, hoping he could remove the tumor without having to remove the breast.

"So I took her back down to St. John's for that," Julie recalls with a sigh, "and I waited there while they did the surgery. After a while, the doctor came out and said, 'Well, there's good news and bad news.'"

"Tell me the good news first," Julie told him.

"We got it all," he said. "But the bad news is that we found two microscopic cells in the lymph nodes."

It was very bad news indeed. It meant that the cancer had begun to spread.

"I'm going to get you with an oncologist," he told Lily.

And so that was the next trip—to see the oncologist to figure out what to do next.

The oncologist gave her another choice: radical chemotherapy, whose side effects include hair loss and terrible flulike sickness, or a pill called Tamoxifen, which taken once a day, can slow or stop the growth of cancer cells present in the body.

"I'll try the Tamoxifen," Lily told the oncologist.

It was the wrong choice.

"She didn't want to lose her hair," Julie recalled, shaking her head. "God, if she'd just taken the radical chemo up front right away, gotten it over with, and lost her hair—so what? But she was working on a couple of series, and she was a regular on *The Young and the Restless*. She was just constantly working, and she didn't want to lose her hair. So she decided on the Tamoxifen."

Everything was fine at first, and life returned to normal. Lily, who was one of Hollywood's most respected acting coaches, continued seeing her students and didn't miss a day's work on *The Young and the Restless*. And Julie settled back into her routine. Monday through Friday, she'd scoop up the dog poop and change the cat boxes, then straighten up the house, do the yard work, and run errands until 3:00 p.m., when it was time to go home and take care of her mother.

Julie made sure that Lily took her Tamoxifen every day, and every three months she'd drive her down to the hospital in Santa Monica for blood work and scans.

"For the first two years, everything was clear, looking good," Julie recalls.

But in 1992, a scan turned up cancer cells in her liver. Now she didn't have a choice.

"I'll start chemo now—right now," Lily decided.

Once a week for the next several years, Julie drove Lily back to St. John's for the chemotherapy—an intravenous drip in the arm.

"We wore a path down there," Julie sighed. "I could drive it in my sleep."

The chemo worked for a while, although she lost her hair—twice—and lost some weight. But it never made her sick, as chemo often does.

"She took her medicine like a trooper," Julie said.

After a while, though, the chemo stopped working too. She'd become immune to it.

Then one night, Julie was watching TV at home with her mom when she saw a news item about clinical trials that were being held for a new drug called Xeloda—a pill to treat breast cancer that's come back after treatment with other medications failed.

Julie wrote the name down on a slip of paper and gave it to Lily the next day.

"The next time we go to the hospital," Julie told her, "ask the doctor about this pill and see if you can get on it."

"Yes, it's in trials," the doctor told Lily the next time Julie took her to St. John's. "I'll see if I can get you the pill." And he did, and it worked—for a while. But there were some nasty side effects at first.

"We had to find the right dosage," Julie recalled. "She had to start with a high dosage, and she got blisters—horrible blisters—in her mouth. Then we started cutting the pill back to what she could tolerate. So she was on that a good year or two, and it was working. And then it stopped working."

Tumors started forming in her liver, so the doctors opened her up and did cryosurgery on the liver—freezing the tumors. After the cryosurgery, however, Lily contracted an infection between the lungs and the liver; so they had to open her up again, go back in, remove the infection, and sew her back up.

"The cryosurgery helped extend her life," Julie said, "because the tumors were getting pretty big. So they froze them and they disappeared, but there were still smaller ones, and there were still cancer cells going through her system. So she was never off some type of treatment during all those years. She'd go back on the drip with another kind of chemo and then more surgeries."

But all during this time, Lily was still working, still teaching. She still had students coming to the house for classes or private coaching. And when students had auditions, they'd bring their scripts to her and she'd get them ready. And if they couldn't come to the house, she'd help them over the phone.

"She had people from Canada who'd call her and fax the script to her," Julie laughed. "She'd read it and talk to them and coach them on the phone. So she was just always busy, and I think that helped her too. Her students really helped keep her alive."

Julie was busy too. She wasn't taking care of just one dying woman; she was taking care of two.

Julie had bought a little fixer-upper house in the Valley in 1979 when she was still work on *Charlie's Angels* and moved her mom into it. Julie worked on it tirelessly until 1983, when the bank took it. She'd been unemployed for three years and couldn't make the mortgage payments. So her mom moved in with her.

In 1996, her mother suffered a series of ministrokes called TIAs—transient ischemic attacks—and the onset of dementia.

"When she had an attack," Julie recalled, "she'd get dizzy, and if I was with her, I'd catch her before she'd fall. She fell a couple of times, and I'd have to get her back up."

It was reminiscent of the time when Julie was five years old and her mother, drunk in the alley after drinking too much gin, had slumped to the ground against a neighbor's garage door, and little Julie had somehow managed to get her to her feet. But Virginia was sober now and had been for more than thirty years now—ever since returning from South America and taking a job as a nurse's aide at St. Jude's Hospital in Fullerton.

Three decades of sobriety had been Virginia's greatest gift to her daughter, but her dementia signaled that the end of her life was near.

"She started hallucinating," Julie recalled sadly.

Almost every day now, Virginia would pass by Julie's door and ask the same questions.

"Did Stan say when he'd be back?" she'd ask.

"No," Julie'd reply.

"Well, what time did he leave?"

"I don't know what time he left," Julie would tell her.

"Well, I was wondering when he was coming home."

Julie didn't have the heart to tell her that Stan had been dead for years.

With the last of her savings gone, Julie had refinanced her house twice—essentially taking out $50,000 in loans against its equity—to cover her and her mom's living expenses. But that money was gone in a couple of years, and then she was living on nothing but her residuals, which weren't enough to pay all the bills.

"The bank is going to take my house," she told Lily one day. "Do you want my house?"

Lily owned two rental properties in the Valley and another in Park City, Utah, and was a very astute businesswoman.

"Sure," she said and worked out a generous deal. Julie would quitclaim her house to Lily, who would then make the $1,000-a-month mortgage payments. Julie and her mom would continue to live in the house, and in exchange, Julie would work for Lily gratis.

"We worked things out that way," Julie recalled thankfully.

Julie's financial situation had stabilized, but her mother's dementia was getting worse and worse. Then, one late afternoon in the winter of 1997, it became unmanageable.

It was getting dark, and Virginia wanted to go outside. She was too unsteady on her feet to go very far without falling, so Julie said she'd go with her.

"No!" her mother said. She wanted to go alone.

Julie couldn't let her go out alone, but the more Julie said no, the more aggravated Virginia became. Finally, she started screaming at her daughter.

"If you don't let me out, I'm gonna take this chair and throw it throw the window!" she yelled.

Julie tried to calm her.

"Maybe we should talk to the doctor," she said in a reassuring voice.

"Fine!" Virginia pouted. "Call him."

Julie called the doctor and told him what had happened, and he asked her to bring her mother to the Encino Hospital.

"The doc wants me to take you to the hospital," Julie told her mother.

"Fine," Virginia said, although she was still very agitated.

Julie got her into the car and drove her to the hospital. The doctor was already there when they arrived. Right away, Virginia wanted to go back home.

"Why am I here?" she kept asking. "I want to go home. I don't want to be here."

As one of the nurses tried to calm Virginia down, the doctor took Julie aside and told her he'd like to keep her mother there for a full evaluation. They'd keep her there in the psych ward for seventeen days, he said, and Julie wouldn't be able to see her for a week.

Julie looked at her mother arguing with the nurse and knew that this is what had to be done. She filled out the admission forms and kissed her mother good-bye.

"I'll see you in a few days," Julie told her. As she left, she could hear her mother pleading to go home. It broke Julie's heart.

After the first week, Julie visited her mom in the hospital every day, but her mom was still confused.

"I don't understand," she'd tell Julie. "Why am I here?"

"It's for an evaluation, Mom."

"I don't believe you," she'd say.

When the seventeen days were up, the doctor told Julie that her mom should be under constant care and suggested a facility where she could be looked after.

Julie checked it out, but it was a horrible place, and it smelled bad.

"The patients there were just out of their minds," she recalled. "I just couldn't do that to her."

So Julie found a place on her own—the Studio City Rehabilitation Center. It was clean and quiet, and the staff was friendly and patient.

Julie was nearly broke, but thankfully, Virginia's Social Security and Medicare would cover the costs. Julie couldn't possibly afford the around-the-clock care that would be required to keep her mother at home, so this was the best option—the only option.

Julie went to see her mom there every day for the next three years. She'd work at Lily's from eight to three, then head down the hill and spend three or four hours with her mother. And every day it was the same routine. She'd change her diaper, clean her up, and put her back into bed. Then Julie would go to the laundry closet and take out some clean towels and washcloths, unfold them, and lay them on her mom's bed.

"Look here, Mom," she'd say. "There's some towels to fold."

Virginia couldn't crochet anymore, but she loved folding the towels and washcloths.

"She'd fold them absolutely perfectly," Julie recalled wistfully, "and then I'd take them back and put them in the laundry closet."

Julie fed her dinner every night and then would take her out for a stroll in the wheelchair. Virginia would nod and say hello to everyone they encountered, but as the end approached, she lost her ability to speak and then her ability to chew and swallow.

In the last days, they took her to St. Joseph's Hospital in Burbank and put a feeding tube into her stomach. Virginia was still strong enough to pull it out, though, so every time she did they'd have to put it back in.

Julie had been running errands for Lily one day in June, and when she returned, Lily greeted her with a very worried look on her face.

"Uh-oh," Julie thought.

"The hospital just called," Lily said gravely. "You'd better call them."

Julie called and was put through to the nurses' station.

"It's not good," a nurse told her. "You better come right over. She probably only has three or four hours left."

Julie raced to the hospital and, when she got there, found that her mother was in a coma. Julie sat by her bed as the nurses came and went, checking her vital signs and scribbling notes on her patient chart.

"I put her hand on top of my head and rubbed her hand so she would know I was there," Julie recalled.

About four hours later, one of the nurses called the doctor in.

"You have to make a decision," he told Julie. "I can bring her back, but . . ."

"But what?" Julie asked, tears rolling down her cheeks.

"But she'll be in a vegetative state," he finished.

"No," Julie said. Virginia had been miserable for years. If he could bring her back for a few more minutes of happiness, Julie would have said yes, but not for a few more hours or days of misery and suffering.

"No," she said again, wiping away the tears. "Let her go."

The doctor and nurses left, and Julie kept crying and rubbing her mother's hand.

"It's okay," Julie whispered to her mom. "You can go now."

A few minutes later, Virginia took her last breath. She died on June 13, 2000, just three days short of her ninety-third birthday. She was buried a few days later at Rose Hills Cemetery in Whittier, next to her mother and brother, and one day, Julie will be buried there too. Julie's nephew, Sam Hodson, a pastor, presided over the gravesite service, which was attended by only a handful of relatives. Virginia had outlived her two husbands and all of her friends.

Lily, a woman of boundless compassion, knew how Julie felt. Ten years earlier, her own mother—her beloved Ta Ta—had suffered a stroke while visiting Lily, and Julie was the first person she called.

"She was visiting from Laguna," Julie recalled. "I was at my house in Van Nuys, and Lily called. She was very upset."

"Can you come get me?" Lily asked. "The paramedics are here to take Ta Ta."

"I'll be right there," Julie told her.

Ta Ta had lapsed into a coma and died four days later without ever regaining consciousness. So when Julie's mom died, Lily was there for her too. She cried and mourned with Julie and comforted her at the funeral.

"Lily was profusely sorry," Julie said, fighting back tears.

The death of a mother is always hard, but the end of suffering can make it easier to bear. And Virginia had suffered terribly in the last three years.

"It was bittersweet," Julie recalled of her mother's death, and she could still cry about it twelve years later. "She had been in so much pain, but now the suffering was finally over."

Sometimes, though, death is not the worst part. Sometimes, the worst part is being left alone. But worse than that is being left alone twice.

Lily would live another eight years, growing weaker and weaker with each passing year. She was always undergoing some kind of chemotherapy, so not long after Virginia died, Julie moved into Lily's spare bedroom and put the house in Van Nuys up for sale. Real estate was booming in those days, and Julie got a good price for it. After paying off the bank, she was left with a cool $128,000. Julie told the real estate agent to make out two checks—one for $88,000 and another for $40,000.

Back home, she found Lily in the sunroom and handed her the check for $88,000, which had been made out to Lilyan Chauvin.

"What's this!" Lily said, dropping the check as if it were on fire.

"That's the money you put into the house," Julie told her. "That's what you invested."

"You're kidding," Lily said.

"No. This is your money," Julie said, picking the check up off the floor and handing it to Lily again.

"Well, I don't believe this," Lily said. "I never expected to see this."

"Well, Lily, this is the money you paid," Julie said. "You should probably get back even more in interest."

"No, no. I just don't understand why you're giving me this."

"Because it's your money, Lily!"

They argued about it a little more—like two old friends wanting to pay the check at a restaurant—and finally Lily relented.

"Well, okay," she said and handed the check back to Julie. "Here, go build your room in the back and fix the pool. Take this money and do the backyard the way you want it."

They'd been talking for some time about building a little cottage in the backyard where Julie could live, which would mean shortening the pool by about three feet.

"Wait a minute," Julie said. "Are you sure?"

"Yes. You have to have a place to live. Just do it."

"So I said okay," Julie recalled. "It cost $80,000 to do the pool and the little cottage. There was nothing there before but two old lean-to shacks—horrible-looking, broken-down things that Lily used to throw furniture in."

And when the little cottage was completed, Julie moved out of the spare bedroom and into a place of her own. And right outside her front door was one of the most beautiful deep-blue pools in the world.

"Lily would get in there every single day in the summer," Julie recalled with a laugh. "She had a little inner tube and she did her little laps, and that helped her. I had these steps built so that she could get in and out of the pool, and I got her a wetsuit top, because her shoulders would get cold. When the weather was nice, she'd spend forty-five minutes in the pool every day."

On warm evenings, they'd sit by the pool and talk and laugh. And sometimes they laughed a lot.

During her trial, Julie's lawyer had asked her about her sense of humor. It was an odd question with a purpose—to give the jury a glimpse of the emotional damage she'd suffered since being wrongfully terminated. "I *had* a good sense of humor," she answered before Koska could object—"had" being the operative word.

For years afterward, nothing seemed very funny to her, but now, despite everything—despite her mother's death and Lily's illness—her sense of humor was returning. She could laugh now because she was healing. She could laugh now because she had a friend. She could laugh now because she wasn't alone. Julie's nephew, Sam Hodson, described it best: "Lily became that older sister that Julie never had."

Yes, she'd lost her job; and worse yet, she'd lost her career. But she'd found a kindred spirit. And in all her years of taking care of Lily, she'd found something else—she'd found her purpose. They'd come from different worlds—Julie growing up with an alcoholic mother in sunny Southern California, and Lily coming of age in Nazi-occupied France—but here they were, sitting by the pool in a lovely garden, laughing about the twists of fate that had brought them to this place.

Julie felt blessed. She knew she'd been "placed."

"We use to laugh that our fathers in heaven must have met and said, 'I think your daughter should meet my daughter,'" Julie recalls with a laugh. "That's how we always said we met. And believe me, she met her match when she met me. Lily was tough, being a director and all, but there were times when I would stop her in her tracks and make her listen . . . and vice versa."

When Julie would get all riled up about something, Lily would tell her, in that colorful way she had of putting things, to let it go.

"Drop the bone!" she'd say.

And Julie would say, "I'll drop the bone when I find one with more meat on it!"

Then Lily would throw her hands up, and they'd have a big laugh about that too.

Between trips to the doctor, Lily kept working. She had featured roles in several films, including Steven Spielberg's *Catch Me If You Can* and the Coen Brothers' *The Man Who Wasn't There*. And there was lots of TV work too. Between trips to the chemotherapist, she guest starred on *Alias*, *ER*, *CSI*, and *Malcolm in the Middle*.

"Every time I took her for an audition, she'd get the part," Julie laughs. "Big parts, small parts—she didn't care. She just wanted to work."

And of course, there were her students.

"The house was always a bustling place, either with her classes or with her private coaching," Julie recalled. She'd been one of the most sought-after acting coaches in town, and over the years, her students included Raquel Welch, Linda Gray, Suzanne Somers, Kevin Nealon, and soap star Kin Shriner, among many others. She'd also taught French to many American movie stars, including Richard Gere and Lauren Hutton for their roles in *American Gigolo*.

Lily's students not only kept her alive but also gave meaning to her life.

And she changed their lives as well.

When actor Scott Roberts first arrived in Hollywood, someone told him, "You're new in town? There's one person you should see—Lilyan Chauvin."

For her students, she was not just a mother hen, she was Mother Hollywood. For those new to the business, she wouldn't just prepare them for their first auditions, she'd *take* them to their first auditions. She wouldn't just tell them to get head shots, she'd take them to get them. She wouldn't just recommend an agent, she'd get them one.

And when students came to her house for lessons, Lily always greeted them the same way, at her front door with a kiss on each cheek. And when she was not feeling well from the chemo, she'd tell them she had the flu. No one but Julie and Lily's dear friend, actress Jacqueline Bisset, knew how sick she was.

"My life would have been very different had I not known Lily," said one of her students. "It was she who opened my young eyes and made me challenge myself to be the best that I could be and to chart unknown avenues with fortitude."

"Next to my parents," said another, "Lily was my greatest influence. She taught us how to breathe life into our characters—to become detectives, seeing beyond the obvious, to show humanity, to be self-aware, to appreciate nature, to be kind and thoughtful to all, and never say 'I can't.'"

"We encounter many people on our life's journey," said another student. "Some encounters can last years and yet produce no effect. But a few are so significant that they touch all the way down to our core and affect who we are. I feel blessed to have been affected this way by Lily."

"Lily once told me that her life was made whole by the knowledge she passed on to others," recalled Katia Louise, her friend and former student. "She said, 'If you can pass one bit of knowledge onto another living soul, your life will not have been in vain. Knowledge is the key to life.'"

And the knowledge that Lily passed on to her students wasn't just about acting. She inspired them to love one another and to stop each day and notice the simple wonders of the natural world all around—a hummingbird at the window or a flower in the garden.

"You didn't go over there just to be coached by Lily," recalled *Dallas* star Linda Gray. "You were coached in life. She was an angel, but she was a very tough angel. She was my mentor, my friend, and sometimes, my mother superior. She was always there for me. I just adored her."

"Lily was the quintessential role model in many ways," said Katia Louise. "She persevered through challenges of cancer and chemotherapy for many years without most people suspecting that she was the slightest bit ill. A family member told me, 'We did not know that Lily was ill and we were very surprised by the news. She never spoke of it.'"

And Lily was able to pull it off because Julie was always there for her.

"Julie was there by her side for years as her assistant and helped make it possible for Lily to lead so many of us to believe that she was just as healthy and vibrant as she appeared," Katia said. "Julie was the invisible glue holding everything together."

It was getting increasingly more difficult, however, to hold Lily together. Her heart had been weakened by all the chemotherapy, and now the cancer had gotten into her lungs. A short walk of a few steps would leave her out of breath.

Lily spent more and more time in bed—either in her bedroom or in the bed Julie had set up in the sunroom, where Lily could look out at her lovely garden.

"I'd put birdseed out and the birds would come," Julie said. "Lily liked that. And there was a little squirrel that I taught to come and take a peanut from my hand. Lily would go out and feed him, and he would jump up and sit on her lap. She'd hold a peanut between her teeth, and the little squirrel would take it right out of her mouth! She just loved that. She called the squirrel Mommy Sweetie, and she even wrote a little story about it."

But even that ended sadly. One day, Julie was working in the garden and found the little squirrel near death. It had been badly mauled—probably by a coyote.

Julie wrapped it up in a towel and rushed it to the vet, but it was too far gone. The vet had to put it down.

Julie didn't have the heart to tell Lily that Mommy Sweetie had died.

Lily's last performance was in 2007 on ABC's hit series *Ugly Betty*, playing a hundred-year-old *curandera*—a Mexican fortune-teller—who finds Betty's lost earring and the missing branch of Betty's family tree.

Julie drove her to the Paramount Pictures studio in Hollywood, where the show was shooting, helping her with her lines while keeping an eye on the traffic. At the studio gate, the guard directed them to the soundstage, and Julie steadied her as she walked in with the help of a cane. Inside, Lily was reunited with an old friend, Rita Moreno, who was also guest-starring on the show. They hadn't seen each other in years.

"They hugged and talked," Julie remembered. "It was just lovely."

Julie hovered in the wings while Lily filmed her scene. It was nice for both of them to be back on a soundstage. Everything went well. Lily nailed her lines, and afterward, she thanked everyone and said good-bye to Rita.

By the time Julie got her home, Lily was exhausted. Julie put her to bed and brought her a little supper.

Lily's acting career was over now, but she still saw a few of her students.

"After *Ugly Betty*, a few students would come to the house," Julie recalled. "She stopped her regular class, and then she finally stopped seeing her students altogether."

Then came the first collapse.

Julie was fixing dinner one evening when Lily hobbled into the kitchen.

"I don't want to eat," she said weakly.

"You have to eat something," Julie pleaded.

"I just want to go to bed," Lily said.

Julie helped her down the hall to her bedroom, and then Lily collapsed on the bed.

"Lily! Lily!" Julie called to her.

Lily's eyes rolled up into her head, and she babbled something. She was delirious and incoherent. Julie frantically called 911, and paramedics arrived in minutes. They took her vital signs, brought in a gurney, and wheeled her out to the ambulance.

"What hospital are you taking her to?" Julie asked one of the paramedics, panic rising in her voice.

"St. Joseph's in Burbank," he answered.

"Okay," she said. "I'll follow you there."

Julie rushed back inside, got her keys and coat, and chased the ambulance to the hospital. Lily was already in a room in the emergency ward when Julie got there. She was feeling a little better and smiled wanly when Julie came in. Julie sat by her bed, held her hand, and told her she was going to be okay. Doctors and nurses came and went; and after a while, one of the doctors told Julie that she should go home, that they'd be keeping Lily there for a few days to do some tests and to make sure she was stabile.

They sent Lily home four days later, but it was too soon.

Julie had put a hospital bed in the sunroom and hired two twelve-hour nurses to help care for Lily. Lily bonded with the nurses, and naturally, they fell in love with her too.

"She was laughing right up to the end," Julie said, tears welling in her eyes.

A few days after Lily came home, Julie and the nurses were helping her to the bathroom one morning when she collapsed in the hallway. They caught her before she could fall and sat her down gently.

"Lily!" Julie cried out. "We've got you! You're going to be okay!"

She was delirious again and unresponsive. Once again, Julie dialed 911, and once again they came and took Lily to St. Joseph's. This time they kept her for six weeks.

Julie visited her every day, twice a day, at lunch and dinnertime, spending four or five hours at her side. The doctors and nurses were great, and the hospital's chaplain, Margaret Burdge, was so kind. She prayed for Lily and Julie every day, and they prayed for her too. To this day, the chaplain remembers Lily—and Julie—fondly.

"Lily was a patient in our hospital when I met her," Burdge recalled. "My first concern, of course, was for Lily's quality of life, her dignity, and her sense of meaning and purpose and hope. But she was pretty self-contained and so well-supported by Julie and her dear friend, Jacqueline Bisset, that my attention soon went to supporting Julie. Julie was a single-mindedly faithful, conscientious, protective friend and caregiver. And over time, Julie taught me about Lilyan Chauvin—the great actor, director, teacher, and Julie's soul sister. Julie so wanted Lily to live, but that began to look less and less likely, and Julie struggled, and I tried to help her through this really, really difficult time."

"In time," she said, "I also came to know Lily with a quality of intimacy that can be the unique privilege of a hospital chaplain. My discovery was a woman of deep beauty, intelligence, and wisdom—wonderfully introspective and curious, honest, earthy, and forgiving. Her humor was delightful, her devotion to her students inspiring. She approached death with great dignity, and in addition to everything she has left to the wide world, Lilyan Chauvin left our little hospital a better place. Lily's life was, and is, and always will be, a blessing."

Lily came home in June of 2008; there was nothing more the hospital could do.

Those last days were hard, but they were also filled with moments of grace: Lily, resting in the sunroom, looking out at the garden she loved so much, marveling, one last time, at the wonders of the natural world—the birds in the trees, the clouds passing by, the flowers bending to the sun. Mommy Sweetie, the little squirrel, was gone now; but there were other squirrels, although none quite like her. And soon, Lily would be gone too. And of course, there would be other actresses and other teachers, although none quite like her.

Julie was asleep in her cottage by the pool early one morning when one of the nurses knocked at her door. Julie looked at the clock. It was six thirty.

"Lily doesn't look so good," the nurse told her.

Julie threw on some clothes and rushed to Lily's side. Lily looked terrible. She was damp and clammy and unresponsive.

"This is it," she thought. There would be no more ambulances. No more doctors. No more hospitals.

Julie called the one person she knew Lily would have wanted her to call—Lily's dear friend, Jacqueline Bisset. They'd met forty years ago on the set of *The Mephisto Waltz* at 20th Century Fox and had been best friends ever since.

"If you want to see Lily," Julie told her, "I think you should come as quick as you can. Things are not good."

Bisset, widely regarded as one of the most beautiful actresses of her era—or of any era—was getting ready to leave for France, where she would be shooting a movie.

"I'll be right there," she said in her lovely British accent.

It took Jackie twenty minutes to drive from her home in Benedict Canyon to Lily's place in the hills of Studio City. When she got there, Lily was unconscious. It looked like she might be too late.

Julie ushered her to a little stool beside Lily's bed. Jackie took Lily's hand and held it gently in hers. But she wasn't coming to. Then, one of the nurses came in, leaned over Lily, and said in a loud voice, "Lily! Wake up! Jacqueline's here!"

Miraculously, Lily's eyelids fluttered open for the last time. Julie, overjoyed that these two old friends could say their final good-byes, wept silently at the foot of the bed.

Lily couldn't speak, but her eyes sparkled dimly at the sight of her dear friend. Jackie stroked her hand and told her that she was going to France to shoot a movie, but wanted to see her before she left. Lily nodded; she understood. Then she made a sign with her hand, like eating with a spoon from a bowl.

"You want your breakfast?" Julie asked, amazed that Lily was hungry and could still communicate. Lily nodded.

"Good! I'll go get you your little breakfast," Julie said and hurried off to the kitchen to make her a bowl of oatmeal and strawberries, with a little milk poured on top. It was Lily's favorite breakfast, and it would be her last.

Julie brought it to her on a tray, and to everyone's amazement, Lily ate it without any help. "My god! That's great!" Julie said after Lily had finished.

Jackie held Lily's hand and talked to her a little while longer. Then it was time to go.

"I have to go now," Jackie said. "I have to catch a plane. Good-bye, my dear."

Lily nodded and smiled weakly; she understood. Jackie kissed her on both cheeks, and then Julie walked her out to her car.

"I'll be in touch," Jackie told her and gave her a big hug. "Call me if you need me."

Julie thanked her and said she would. She waved good-bye as Jackie drove away and then went back into the house. Walking into the sunroom, she knew right away. Lily's eyes were closed. She'd slipped into a coma. She would not be waking up again, ever.

It took three more days for Lily to die, and Julie never left her side. Julie didn't eat; she didn't sleep; she held her hand for three straight days. Has there ever been a truer friend?

"I kept hold of her the whole time," Julie cried. "Just like with Mom."

A hospice nurse came late one night and showed Julie how use a little eyedropper to put morphine on Lily's gums when her breathing became labored.

Finally, Lily's breathing became slower and slower.

"It's okay," Julie told her, tears rolling down her cheeks. "You can go. You can go now."

And as if on cue, Lily took her last breath.

It was almost dark outside. Julie laid her head on Lily's hands and cried for a long time. Then, slowly, she got up. Her back and legs ached. She hadn't walked in three days, except to go the short distance to the bathroom. Now she walked all around the house, pacing back and forth, trying to compose herself. When she stopped crying, she called the mortuary.

"We can come pick her up right now, if you like," the funeral home director said.

"No," Julie said. "It's dark outside. I can't send her out in the dead of night. Can you come tomorrow morning?"

"Yes," he said, "Of course."

The nurse bathed Lily's body and pulled the covers up to her chest. She loved Lily too, and she and Julie hugged and cried. When the nurse left, Julie went into Lily's room and spent a long time with her there, crying. She found Lily's favorite hat—a baseball cap with the letters *DGA* on it—and gently placed it on her head.

"Just be peaceful," she told Lily. "The struggle's over. You're on your way."

Julie kissed her on the cheeks.

"I'll be back," she whispered and went to her cottage and showered.

The shower felt good, like hot tears running down her body, until there were no more tears to shed. After drying off, Julie fell into bed and slept for the first time in days. She awoke at six thirty the next morning, dressed, and went down the steps to the house to spend a little more time with Lily before they came to take her body away.

"I felt her shoulders," Julie recalled, "and she was still warm . . . so warm. And she looked so peaceful. She was at peace for the first time in eighteen years—after eighteen years of battling cancer."

Julie arranged for a memorial service to be held at the Directors Guild of America, which Lily considered her home away from home. Held in the DGA's main theater, it was attended by more than two hundred of Lily's friends and former students. And with the haunting harp accompaniment, for Lily's spirit, it must have seemed like heaven away from heaven.

Speaker after speaker spoke of how Lily's love of life, her love of nature, her love of acting, and her love of teaching had changed their lives.

Lily's old friend, Jacqueline Bisset, perhaps said it best.

"How does one say good-bye to a friend—a very good and faithful friend?" she asked in her loving tribute. "Lilyan was a person I could trust. She was a sane and principled human being who loved acting and teaching. It gave her energy. She loved her students, and she took amazing pride from their ventures. For me, she was sometimes an ironic mirror. She would listen with an inner smile, trying not to judge all my life's adventures—and she knew plenty. She worried about me. But for these last few years, I worried about her."

Bisset then told those attending the memorial service that she wanted to thank someone very dear to Lilyan.

"I'd like to thank Julie Johnson," she said, "who's been her dear friend and her constant companion. Julie's been unbelievable, taking care, looking after the paperwork, looking after the house, looking after the comings and goings, and looking after Lilyan's need to be productive. She wrote several scripts, even after she wasn't well, and she had a rough time too. I call Lilyan a warrior—really a warrior. I mean, nobody I know in my life fought as hard and took the moment as it came. And she didn't complain. She . . . she was really heroic, and such a role model for her students in many ways and such a role model for me personally."

"I'd like to read you something that Julie wrote," Bisset said in her closing remarks. "Julie has obviously been absolutely side-swiped by this. And Lilyan's nature, being a collector—a saver of things—not letting anybody throw anything away—has left Julie with an enormous task that she has been very gentle with—she didn't push when she probably wanted to clear things out. And now she is faced with the enormous task of missing a friend—a dear, dear, dear friend. Julie Johnson wrote this cry from the heart. It's a prayer."

Bisset then gave Julie's prayer a dramatic reading that brought the audience to tears.

> Oh, Lord. The sound of my breaking heart is deafening.
> My spirit is shattered, my soul left empty.
> My eyes can only see through tears.
> This is not a quiet journey you have sent me on, without my friend Lily.
> How do I pray? And what do I pray for?
> All seems gone. Strength and courage—they have no meaning anymore.
> Heaven on earth is a distant memory.
> I have felt alone before.
> But not like this.
> This is beyond words—beyond "alone."
> To rise above this depth of sadness seems impossible without my friend Lily.
> Memories will just never be enough.
> Oh, Lord, I ask you for some light to see.

It's been four years now since Lily died, and Julie has been given that light to see.

Back in their early days together, when Julie would fume about the injustice of having had her career taken away—and of the $1.1 million jury award that had been denied her—Lily would laugh and tell her, "Don't worry about that $1.1 million. I think you'll get it back."

"I had no idea she was talking about the properties," Julie said, shaking her head.

She had no idea then that Lily was planning to leave her entire estate to her—the house and cottage on the hill in Studio City, the two rental properties in the Valley, and the apartment in Park City.

Today, living in the house whose floors she mopped so many times when Lily first hired her as her housekeeper, Julie is happy, healthy, and financially secure. She thinks of Lily every day, and like Lily, every day she tries to make the world a better place. She has been blessed. She has been "placed."

And in the end, who could ask for anything more?

Lilyan Chauvin, Actress, Director, Writer, Drama Coach

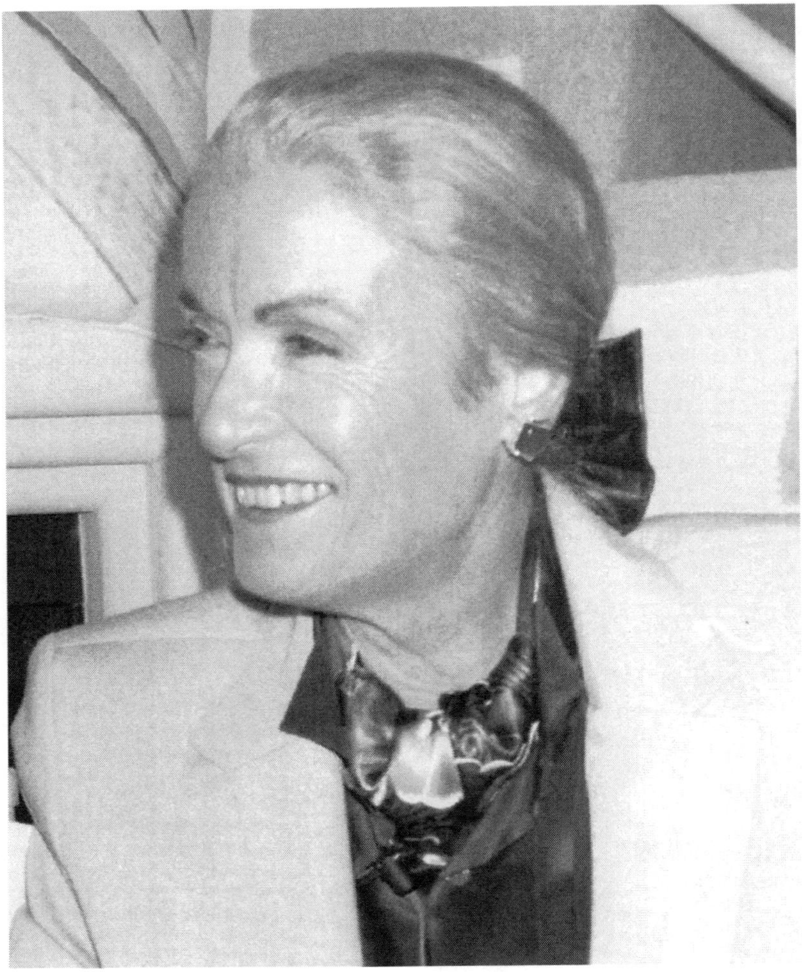

JULIE JOHNSON

In Her Own Words

David Robb and I wrote this book to show how difficult it is, especially for women, to break into the stunt business and how easy it is to be broken by it.

It's a dangerous business. Women have gotten killed on the job, and many others have been seriously injured—some of them permanently. I know three stuntwomen who have committed suicide. Many others' lives have been destroyed by drugs and alcohol.

And yet, being a stuntwoman is the most exciting job in the most exciting industry in the world. Unfortunately, the stunt business is also the most sexist in Hollywood—an industry rife with male chauvinism.

I spent most of my working life hanging from helicopters and hot-air balloons, running on high catwalks, jumping across rooftops, falling down stairs, crashing through windows, turning over cars, being hit by trucks, and fleeing from fires and floods. I got concussions and fractured my neck, cracked my ribs, tore muscles and tendons, and I still have a dent in my head from being kicked in the head by a horse on *Little Big Man*. But the most dangerous thing I ever did was to complain about unsafe working conditions and about the drug abuse problem that made a dangerous job all the more hazardous. Blowing the whistle cost me my career and livelihood. Drug users almost cost me my life.

Discrimination is subtle and not always clear-cut. The old boys' network is constantly lurking in the wings, in every position of the industry.

Women are still vastly underrepresented in Hollywood—not just in stunts, but in all creative positions. It's hard for anyone trying to break into the business, but for women, it's even harder. You are judged more harshly, and you have to be twice as good as a man in your selected field. The longer the women in this industry remain silent, the more oppressed they will be.

I realize that there are women all over the world whose lives are much tougher than ours could ever be. But pain is pain. Oppression is oppression. Not being able to be all that you can be is hell. If you don't want us to care, don't teach us to feel.

The answer to nearly all the wrongs in the world is to put a woman in charge. Try it, you might like it.

It's a privilege of the highest order to work in this business. My advice to young women entering the stunt business today is simple:

- Be humble.
- Be proud.
- Be thankful.
- Be useful.
- Learn the craft, and never, ever be late for your job.
- Stay away from abusing drugs and alcohol to be popular or trouble will surely follow.
- Never surrender your honor and integrity.
- Project an image of strength and courage.
- Just remember, as my friend Eve Brent told me when I was starting out, "You don't have to go to bed with any of them." Consequences can be deadly.
- Don't be a slob, hang your wardrobe back up like you found it.
- Be safe and look out for the safety of others.
- And above all, you have a duty and a responsibility to yourselves and to those whose shoulders you stand upon, to protect, preserve, and enhance the power we have acquired for you. Use it with dignity and grace and wisely pass it on. You will evolve into the next generation of stuntwomen, stronger and more educated than mine; and when you become stuntwomen with purpose, and have no fear of speaking up, you will have arrived.
- Or as my as my father use to say, "Just use good common sense, let self-control and your conscience be your guide."
- And remember: for inequality to prevail, all that good men and women have to do is nothing.

I always believed that if I took a grievance to my superiors, there would be an appropriate and considered response. I now know, however, that my commitment was shared by few others. It behooves all producers to speak in person to a stunt person if there is an issue.

I figured that being labeled a troublemaker was a reasonable price to pay to make some changes. This led me into the world of the unknown, blacklisting, personal harassment, and intimidation. Few people are prepared to handle retaliation, but I chose to take a stand and take any punishment they handed out. Sadly, except for a few brave souls, my friends and peers slowly disappeared. Life, as I had known it, was gone. If I had done cocaine with the "right people," I'd still be working or dead.

I dug my own grave, but I did what I had to do. They can blacklist me, but they can't kill my spirit . . . ever.

While waiting in a doctor's office, I saw this written in a magazine:

I am hurt, but I am not slain.
I will lie down and bleed for a while.
Then I will rise to fight again.
(St. Barton's Ode)

These few words helped me get through some of the toughest times of my life.

A friend once asked me, "What's it like to feel blacklisted?"

I told her, "It feels like you're being led to slaughter, like you're being thrown into solitary confinement, like everyone is armed against you, to hurt you, to deny you, that you have been cast out."

And yet, I hope and pray that my solitude will somehow bear fruit in the hearts of the very people who destroyed me. My father taught me to be brave and to stand up for what's right. So I wear my blacklisting like a badge of honor.

To quote Eleanor Roosevelt, "Everyone has the right to life, liberty, and the security of person."

This is 2012 . . . where is *our* security of person? Without it, life and liberty are hopeless dreams, and hopeless dreams are not conducive to building better-educated and stronger stuntwomen.

As long as management is false to their obligations, we are rendered unproductive.

What a waste of important talent. To me, this is unspeakably sad.

To the stuntmen, I say, say what you will about me. Call me what you wish, but whether you like it or not, you are my brothers, and you taught me well. I have no ill will, just concern. But next time, just think with clearer minds before you decide to destroy someone.

To all the producers, directors, actresses, and crewmembers who applauded my work over the many years, I applaud you for your gracious help, your unmatched stamina in your chosen fields. You all inspired me. Thank you for letting me be me.

And a heartfelt thank-you to Jeannie Coulter, Leslie Hoffman, Irene Lamothe, and Jade David for not abandoning me. We share something in common—blacklisting. I would also like to thank David Robb, Kathleen Nolan, and posthumously, Norma Connolly.

Lest we forget, all those in our industry who died, those who were injured beyond repair, all for the sake of the passion for their work . . . lest we forget.

Eddie, if you're out there, "Time Remembered."

Mom and Dad, thank you for my life.

Lily, you are always in my thoughts and prayers and tears.

And finally, with this book, I lay down my sword. But if I have to, I'll pick it up again.

Julie Ann Johnson

Postscript

The infamous Hollywood Blacklist of the 1940s and '50 lasted for thirteen years. Julie's has lasted much longer and is still going on today. A few courageous stunt coordinators have given her a few jobs in the last ten years. In *Spider Man 2*, that's Julie in a scarf and long coat flying up the side of a skyscraper and holding onto the ledge for dear life. But essentially, her career was over.

Her battle against Hollywood's glass ceiling, however, didn't go unrecognized. In 2010, she was honored by the Diamond in the Raw Foundation with its Helen Gibson Legendary Stuntwoman Award, which was given "in recognition of her fearless and outstanding achievements in the entertainment industry."

The award is named after a pioneering stuntwoman from the silent movie era.

One day there may be an award named after Julie.

Printed in Great Britain
by Amazon